D1124395

Madrid

Spain

KNOPF
CITY GUIDES

THIS IS A BORZOI BOOK PUBLISHED BY ALFRED A. KNOPF, INC

ISBN 0-375-70257-1

Library of Congress number 97-80569

First published May 1998
Revised and updated Feb. 1999

Originally published in France by Nouveaux Loisirs, a subsidiary of Gallimard, Paris 1997, and in Italy by Touring Editore, Srl., Milano 1997.

SERIES EDITORS
EDITORIAL MANAGER: Seymourina Cruse
MADRID EDITION: Vincent de Lapomarède, Caroline Cuny and David Beytelmann
GRAPHICS
Élizabeth Cohat, Yann Le Duc
LAYOUT: Olivier Lauga, Yann Le Duc
MINI-MAPS, AIRPORT MAPS: Kristoff Chemineau
MADRID MAPS: Édigraphie
STREET MAPS: Touring Club Italiano
PRODUCTION
Catherine Bourrabier

Translated by Laura Ward

Edited and typeset by Book Creation Services, London

English edition revised by First Edition Translations Ltd, Cambridge, UK

Printed in Italy by Editoriale Lloyd

Authors

MADRID

Things you need to know: Pilar Careaga (1)

Author of travel guides on CD-Rom, Pilar Careaga spent her teenage years guiding visitors around the Prado museum.

Where to stay and where to eat: Victor de la Serna (2)

Victor de la Serna has written about food for the Spanish newspapers *El País*, *Diario 16* and *El Mundo*. He was the Spanish correspondent for the London magazine *Decanter* and a columnist for the Spanish *Sibarita* magazine. He is now joint editor of the daily *El Mundo*.

After dark: Jaime Iglesias (3)

Jaime Iglesias trained as a lawyer and journalist and is now a publicity director. He has been among Madrid's night-owls for many years.

What to see: Mariano Navarro (4)

Consultant to the Spanish TV program *Trazos e Imágenes*, exhibition curator, editor of books for bibliophiles and writer of supplements on Velázquez, Goya and Gauguin for *El País Semanal*, Mariano Navarro is currently arranging Madrid's latest exhibitions of 20th-century art.

Further afield: Consuelo Álvarez de Miranda (5)

Art historian and expert on Baroque architecture, Consuelo Álvarez de Miranda has taught in various schools, edited the six-volume *Historia del arte hispánico* (1976–1980) and was joint author of the guide *Madrid práctico – Todo Madrid* (1995).

Where to shop: Paloma Sarasúa (6)

Author, journalist and sociologist, Paloma Sarasúa has just published *Trabaja, mujer, trabaja* for Acento Editorial, an essay on women's work in modern-day society. She was also joint author of the guide *Madrid práctico – Todo Madrid* (1993).

Things you need to know ➡6

Where to stay ➡16

Where to eat ➡34

After dark ➡66

What to see ➡88

Further afield ➡110

Where to shop ➡124

Maps ➡146

Symbols

- ☎ telephone
- ➠ fax
- ● price or price range
- opening hours
- credit cards accepted
- credit cards not accepted
- toll-free number
- @ e-mail/website address
- ★ tips and recommendations

Access

- subway stations
- bus (or tram)
- private parking
- parking attendant
- no facilities for the disabled
- train
- car
- boat

Hotels

- telephone in room
- fax in room on request
- minibar
- television in room
- air-conditioned rooms
- 24-hour room service
- caretaker
- babysitting
- meeting room(s)
- no pets
- breakfast
- open for tea/coffee
- restaurant
- live music
- disco
- garden, patio or terrace
- gym, fitness club
- swimming pool, sauna

Restaurants

- vegetarian food
- view
- formal dress required
- smoking area
- bar

Museums and galleries

- on-site store(s)
- guided tours
- café

Stores

- branches, outlets

The Insider's Guide is made up of **8 sectio**
each indicated by a different color.

Things you need t
know (mauve)
Where to stay (blu
Where to eat (red)
After dark (pink)
What to see (greer
Further afield (or
Where to shop (ye
Finding your
way (purple)
Where to
M Goya Modern Spanisl
9–11.30pm; closed Aug. 1
Practical information
is given for
each particular
establishment:
opening times,
prices, ways of
paying, different
services available

How to use this guide

In the area
Located north of Retiro Park, this
developed into an upmarket shop
Where to stay ➥ 24
Where to shop ➥
138 ➥ 140 ➥ 144

The section **"In the area"** refers you (➥ 00) to other establishments that are covered in a different section of the guide but found in the same area of the city.

Serrano/Velázquez **D** DI - **F** AI

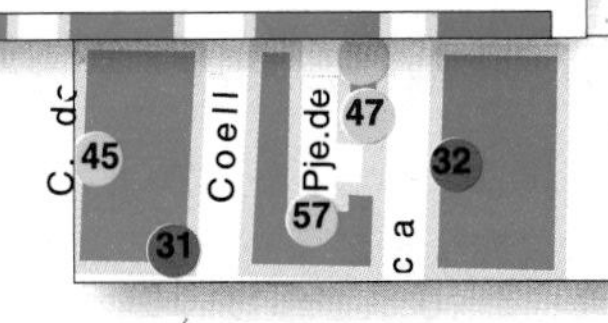

The small map shows all the establishments mentioned and others described elsewhere but found "in the area", by the color of the section.

The name of the district is given above the map. A grid reference (**A** B-C 2) enables you to find it in the section on Maps at the end of the book.

Not forgetting
■ **La Trainera (32)** Lagasca 60,
A rustic tasca serving up excellent sea

The section "Not forgetting" lists other useful addresses in the same area.

"Bargain!"
This star marks good value hotels and restaurants.

The opening page to each section contains an index ordered alphabetically (Getting there), by subject or by district (After dark) as well as useful addresses and advice.

The section "Things you need to know" covers information on getting to Madrid and day-to-day life in the city.

Theme pages introduce a selection of establishments on a given topic.

The "Maps" section of this guide contains 9 street plans of Madrid followed by a detailed index.

Getting there

Pets

To bring a dog or cat into Spain, you need a rabies vaccination certificate and certification, issued within the previous three months, to show that the animal is in good health.

Electric current

In line with the rest of Europe (except the United Kingdom) the voltage is 220, using two-pin plugs.

Average temperatures

Summer temperatures range from 12°C to 39°C (53°F to 102°F); winter temperatures are between -8°C and 17°C (18°F and 63°F).

46 Things you need to Know

Passports

EU nationals can stay in Spain for up to six months if they have a national identity card, and for an indefinite period if they have a valid passport. US and Canadian tourists visiting Spain for up to three months do not currently require a visa. Others should enquire about visa requirements before departure.

Health

EU nationals are covered for urgent medical treatment and should take form E111 with them ➡ 15. Non-EU nationals are not covered and are therefore advised to take out adequate medical insurance before departure.

Driving

Motorists should carry a national or international driver's license and a green card issued by their insurers.

INDEX

Basic facts

Madrid's only international airport, Madrid-Barajas, lies about 10 miles to the east of the city. Internal flights with Iberia (Spain's national airline) or Aviaco also operate from this airport, forming a network with Spain's major cities, other European capitals (such as London, Paris, Geneva and

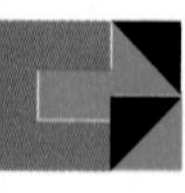

Getting there

Information

☎ *91 305 83 43 or 91 305 83 44*

Left luggage
In the arrivals area of the international terminal.

Tourist office
☎ *91 305 86 56*
🕒 *Mon.–Fri. 8am–8pm; Sat. 9am–1pm*
In the arrivals area of the international terminal.

Lost property
☎ *91 393 61 19*
🕒 *Mon.–Fri. 8am–3pm; Sat. 8am–2pm*
Opposite the left luggage.

Police
The office is located near the Iberia desk in the departures area of the international terminal.

Telephones

Payphones take coins or cards. The cards are on sale in the kiosks or from dispensers in the international arrivals and domestic departures areas (taking 1000 peseta and 2000 peseta notes).

Currency exchange

Automatic cash dispensers are located in both domestic and international terminals.

Argentaria
☎ *91 305 55 51*
Two offices are open from 6am to 11pm and two open 24 hours (inside the terminals). Exchange rates are slightly higher than in the city.

Airlines

American Airlines
☎ Madrid
91 597 20 68
☎ UK
0345 789789
☎ US
800-433-7300

Aviaco
Domestic flights
☎ *91 305 86 85*

British Airways
☎ Madrid
91 431 75 75
☎ UK
0345 222111
☎ US
800-247-9297

Iberia
☎ Madrid
91 240 05 00
☎ UK
0345 222111
☎ US 212-644-8839

TWA
☎ Madrid
91 310 30 94
☎ UK
0171-439 0707
☎ US
800-892-4141

Getting into the city

Buses
☎ 91 431 61 92
Yellow buses run between the airport and Plaza de Colón (the terminus is under the Jardines del Descubrimiento). The journey takes about 30 minutes when traffic flows freely. Buses also stop at Canillejas, Avenida de América, María de Molina and Velázquez.
🕒 *First bus at 4.45am, second at 5.45am, then every 15 minutes from 5.45am to 7am,*

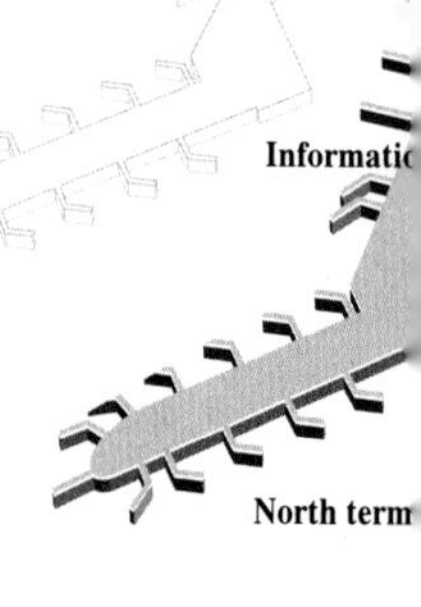

Brussels), and with major cities in North America.

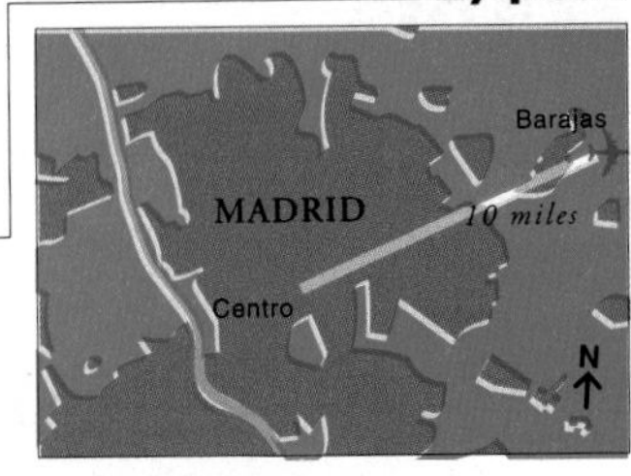

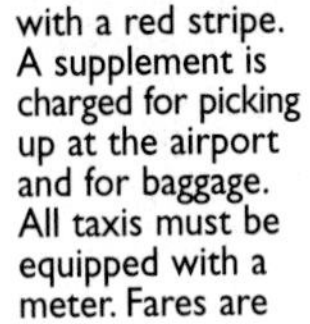

then every 10 minutes from 7am until 10pm, and every 30 minutes from 10pm until 1.30am. ● *One-way fare: 370 Ptas.*

Taxis
Outside the airport. Official taxis are white with a red stripe. A supplement is charged for picking up at the airport and for baggage. All taxis must be equipped with a meter. Fares are usually shown on a list on one of the rear windows. The fare to Plaza de Colón is about 2000 Ptas, including baggage supplement.

Airport hotels

Barajas
Avenida Logroño 305, 28042
☎ *91 747 77 00*
➠ *91 747 87 17*
24-hour transport.

Sofitel
Campo de las Naciones, 28042
☎ *91 721 00 70*
➠ *91 721 05 15*
Courtesy bus.

Car rental

Hertz
☎ *91 393 72 86*

Avis
☎ *91 393 72 22*

Eurodollar Atesa
☎ *91 393 72 32*

Europcar
☎ *91 393 72 89*

adrid / Barajas Airport | **Madrid**

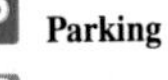 Parking

 Bus
 Taxis / Car rental

Basic facts

RENFE, Spain's national rail company, runs standard and high-speed trains. There are two overnight services from Paris to Madrid. Arriving by car can be straightforward, but roads in the city are congested and parking can be difficult.

Getting there

Trains

Information for all train services and all stations can be obtained from a centralized telephone bureau, open 24 hours:

RENFE
(Red Nacional de Ferrocarriles Españoles)
☎ *91 328 90 20*
Ask about special deals on fares.

AVE
Alta Velocidad Española (Spain's own high-speed train).

Estación de Chamartín
Agustín de Foxá, 28036
Ⓜ *Chamartín*
Trains for Europe, Spain and Madrid suburbs
Situated in the north of the city, Chamartín links Madrid with most of Spain and with other countries throughout Europe. The *cercanías*, or local network, can be the quickest way to travel within the city, and links up with the subway system. An underground train connects Chamartín and Atocha Stations, with stops at Nuevos Ministerios and Recoletos-Colón. To reach the rest of the city take the subway (the station for this is in the main-line station), taxi or bus (found outside the main-line station).

Estación de Atocha
Plaza Emperador Carlos V, 28012
Ⓜ *Atocha Trains for Portugal, southern Spain and Madrid suburbs*
Opened in 1851, Atocha is Madrid's oldest station but is also now its most modern. It consists of two stations: Atocha-Mediodía (for regular trains) and Puerta de Atocha (for the high-speed AVE). Both connect with the subway. Atocha boasts one of the world's most beautiful waiting rooms ➡ 98 and a restaurant, Samarkand overlooking tropical greenhouses. Buses and taxis depart from Plaza Carlos V.

Principle Pío
(or Norte)
Paseo de la Florida, 28008
Ⓜ *Principe Pío*
Suburban services.

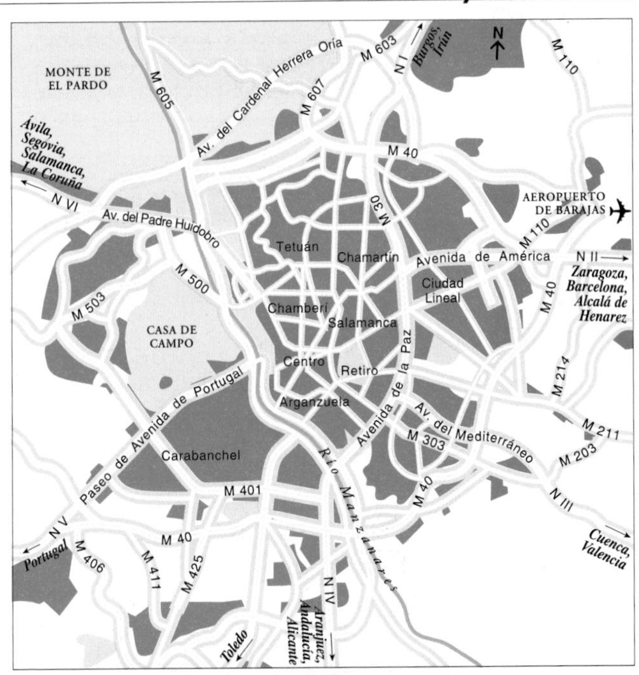

Cars

Madrid is located at the hub of six main roads radiating across Spain. Distances from the capital are measured from the center of Puerta del Sol. Two ring roads – the M-30 and M-40 – encircle the city and are less congested than the main thoroughfares of central Madrid. The N-I (Hendaya) enters the city from the north via Plaza de Castilla. The N-II (Figueras) comes from the northeast and joins the Barajas freeway and Avenida de América.

Traffic information

900 123 505
91 742 12 13
24-hour service

Gasoline

A liter of premium costs around 120 Ptas. Most gas stations sell premium (*super*) unleaded (*sin plomo*) and diesel (*gasoleo*).

Safety

Deposit your luggage in the hotel at once on arrival; don't leave it in the car.

Long-distance buses

Cheap but not very fast.

Estacion Sur de Autobuses
Méndez Álvaro, corner of Calle Retamar, 28043
Méndez Álvaro
91 468 42 00

This is the bus station for arrivals and departures of Euroline (international) company buses and Spanish domestic services. For detailed information, the monthly *Guia de Horarios*, which is available from most news-stands, lists all bus routes and times (it has information about train and airline times as well). Tickets for long journeys should be bought in advance from the bus station. Bus services are much reduced on Sundays. When planning a trip, watch out on timetables for the words *diario* (daily) and *domingos y festivos* (Sundays and holidays). The word *laborables* means "workdays and Saturday".

Basic facts

Bonometro and *bonobus* tickets (each allowing ten journeys) work out cheaper than buying one-way subway or bus tickets for each trip. Licensed taxis are white with a red stripe on the side.

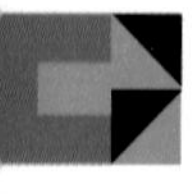

Getting around

Subway

☎ *91 552 59 09*

The Madrid subway is Europe's third-oldest subway system after London and Paris. *El Metropolitano* was opened in 1919 by King Alfonso XIII. It has 129 stations (now mostly air conditioned), carries over a million passengers every day and is the quickest way to get around town.

Tickets

One-way ticket 130 Ptas for any journey. The pink and white *Metrobus diez viajes* entitles you to ten trips for 670 Ptas. Subway tickets can be bought at subway stations, *estancos* (tobacconists), EMT (*Empresa Municipal de Transportes*) information offices, and news-stands. These tickets can also be used on the buses.

Timetables

The subway runs daily from 6am to 1.30am.

Rush hours: 7–9.30am; 1.30–2.30pm.

Taking the subway

There are ten subway lines, each with its own number and color code. The *circular* line (no. 6, gray) runs around the city, while the rest run from north to south, or from east to west. Pick up a free color map (*plano del metro*) of the subway system from any station. They are easy to read even if you have no Spanish.

Buses

The heavy city-center traffic is slow going, but the bus is still a practical way of getting along the main thorough-fares, such as the Paseo de la Castellana. Buses are air-conditioned in summer.

Tickets

Fares are the same as the subway. The ten-trip ticket (*Metrobus*) is a long cardboard strip which is punched every time you take the bus. These tickets cannot be bought on the bus. They are available from special sales points; *estancos* (tobacconists), EMT information offices and news-stands. One-way tickets can be bought on the bus.

Timetables

Buses run from 6am to midnight. Between midnight and 2am night buses run every 30 minutes from the Puerta del Sol. Between 2am and 5am they run hourly.

Waiting for the bus

Bus-stops can be recognized by a blue sign showing the number of the bus route, with the main stops listed underneath. Spaniards wait in line for the bus.

Biobus

A unique Madrid experience – some EMT buses run on vegetable-based fuel (a mixture of diesel and sunflower oil). There are plans to extend the same fuel to private cars.

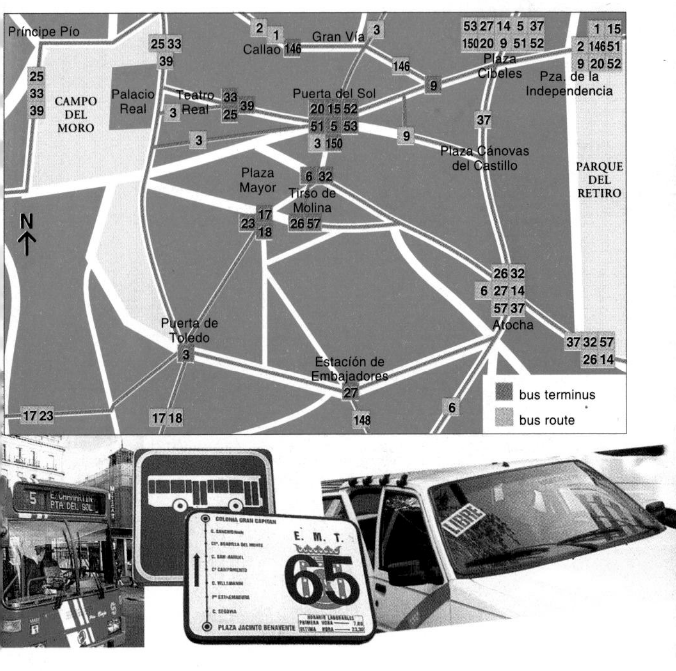

Taxis

Radioteléfono
☎ *91 547 82 00*
Radio-taxi
☎ *91 447 51 80; 91 447 32 32*
Tele-taxi
☎ *91 371 21 31*

Taking a cab

Taxis are usually white, but some are black with a red or green diagonal stripe on the side. They can be found at stands near hotels or major tourist attractions, or they can be hailed in the street. A green sign on the windshield shows that a cab is free. A red notice shows which way the driver is heading if they are about to go off duty. The driver will only accept passengers bound for the same destination. At night, when the subway is closed and there are only night buses, taxis become thin on the ground.

Fares

Supplements are charged at night, on Sundays and public holidays, and for picking up at stations, the airport, stadiums and bullrings. Tips (normally about ten per cent) are appreciated but they are not expected. All fees should be clearly posted in the taxi. If, when you reach your destination, you feel you have been overcharged, ask for an official receipt (a white form bearing the city coat-of-arms and perforated with a license number) and send to city hall: *Área de Circulacíon y Transportes, Plaza de la Villa 4, 28005.*

Cars

Parking

Few hotels have private parking lots. Take advantage of those that do by leaving the car there except for excursions out of the city, and getting around by taxi or public transportation. The symbol **P** identifies Madrid's numerous municipal parking lots (Plaza de Colón, Plaza de España y Princesa, Plaza Mayor, Plaza de Santo Domingo, Plaza de las Cortes, Plaza de Santa Ana, Sevilla, Auditorio Nacional and Orense). Madrid is regulated by ORA (*Operación de Regulación del Aparcamiento*), which limits parking Mon.–Fri. 9am–8pm; Sat. 9am–2pm. Parking permits can be obtained from *estancos*. To save parking fees when renting a car for a day trip or a longer tour, arrange for it delivered to the hotel on the day of departure.

Car rental

Atesa
☎ *91 559 78 26*
Avis
☎ *91 348 03 48*
Europcar
☎ *91 555 99 31*
Hertz
☎ *91 101 001*
Rentalauto
☎ *91 441 36 02*

Breakdown services

Grúas ADA
☎ *91 519 33 00*
Radio-Grúa
☎ *91 508 42 42*
Real Automovil Club (RACE)
☎ *91 593 33 33*

Basic facts

Madrid has plenty of automatic cash machines and places to change money, but many Madrid banks are not open in the afternoons. Stores are generally open until late, but many close for an hour or more at lunchtime. A 24-hour news-stand is located in the Puerta del Sol (2)

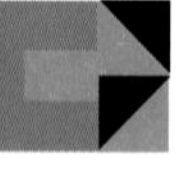

Getting by

Money

Currency exchange
232 Ptas = £1,
140 Ptas = $1
(October 1998)
Most banks exchange cash, traveler's checks and Eurocheques.
⌚ Mon.–Fri. 8am–2pm; some banks are open until 4.45pm; some branches are open on Sat. 9am–noon.
Currency can be exchanged in travel agencies, hotels, department stores and 24 hours a day at the airports ➡ 8.

Tipping
Tip at your discretion in bars and taxis. 50 Ptas to 100 Ptas in modest restaurants, and 5 to 10 % of the bill in upmarket ones. 25 Ptas for restroom attendants and cinema attendants. 100 Ptas per person for ushers in theaters and concert halls.

Media

Spanish press
Principal dailies: *El Mundo; ABC La Vanguardia; El País.*
Weekly supplements: *Blanco y Negro; La Revista; El País Semanal.*

Radio
RNE (state radio, 5 stations)
SER (commercial station, part of the *El País* and *Canal +* group)
COPE (station operated by the Catholic Church)
Onda 0 (belongs to a group of charities)

Television
Public broadcasting channels: *TVE I* and *La 2.*
Commercial channels: *Canal +* (subscription), *Antena 3 Televisión* and *TV 5.*
Local channel: *TELE Madrid*

Telephone

Area codes
The former area code 91 must now be dialed for all numbers in Madrid, either from inside the city or outside.
National inquiries ☎ 003
International inquiries ☎ 025

Public telephones
Payphones take coins or phonecards.
Phonecards are available on sale at tobacconists (*estancos*), news-stands, post offices and *7 Eleven* stores.

Tariffs
In hotels charges are often higher.
In public payphones a 50% reduction is given on calls made Mon.–Fri., 10pm–8am; Sat. from 3pm.

***Telefónica* (3)**
Gran Vía 30, 28012
⌚ 9am–midnight

International phonecards
Calls from hotels are often higher than standard rates.
Worldtalk
900 97 44 08
● *2000 Ptas*
In bureaux de change Chequepoint (Puerta del Sol).
Mainly international calls.

Mail

Letters can be mailed from large hotels.
Post offices are identified by the word *correos* above the door.
Mail boxes have the same word and are yellow.
Postage stamps (*sellos*) can also be bought at tobacco stores.

Main post office (4)
Palacio de Comunicaciones, Plaza de Cibeles, 28014
☎ *902 197 197*
⌚ *Mon.–Fri. 8am–10pm; Sat. 8.30am–2pm*

(international newspapers are on sale in the city center).

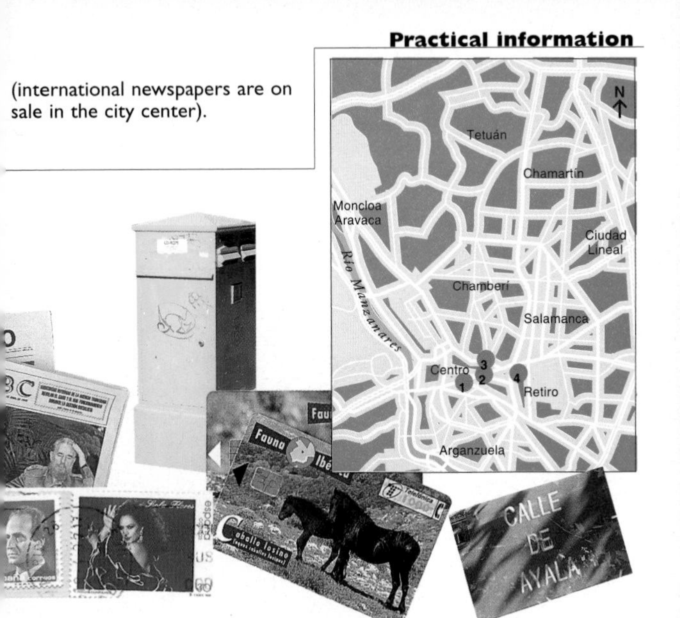

(some departments close earlier).

Neighborhood post offices
Mon.–Fri. 8.30am–8.30pm, some open 8.30am–2.30pm

Postal rates
To mail a letter weighing 20g: 35 Ptas (Spain); 70 Ptas (Europe); 114 Ptas (USA).

Getting around

Streets are numbered from the Puerta del Sol end. To ask the way, give the name of the neighborhood (Chamartín, Chamberí, Salamanca or Centro) or the name of the subway station.

Business hours

Stores
9.30am–2pm, 4.30–8pm
Opening times vary in summer.

Department stores
Mon.–Sat. 10am–9pm (1st Sunday in the month noon–8pm)

Tourist offices

Oficina Municipal de Turismo
Plaza Mayor 3, 28012
☎ 91 588 16 36
Mon.–Fri. 10am–8pm; Sat. 10am–2pm

Oficina de Información Turística de la Comunidad de Madrid
Duque de Medinaceli 2, 28014
☎ 91 429 49 51; or 91 429 31 77
Mon.–Fri. 9am–7pm; Sat.. 9am–1pm

Patronato Municipal de Turismo
Mayor 69, 28013
☎ 91 588 29 00
daily 9am–1pm

Información Turística General de España
☎ 91 300 600
Mon.–Fri. 8.30am–5.30pm; Sat.–Sun. 9am–6pm

Gays and lesbians

Colectivo de Gais y Lesbianas de Madrid
Fuencarral 37 primera planta, 28004
☎ 91 522 45 17
Mon.–Sat. 6–10pm

GAI-INFORM
☎ 91 523 00 70
Mon.–Fri. 5–9pm

Medical care

Municipal ambulances
☎ 91 588 44 00

Red Cross Ambulances
☎ 91 479 93 61

Pharmacies
Mon.–Fri. 8am–1.45pm; Sat. 9am–1.45pm
For a list of pharmacies, see *Guía del Ocio* (the weekly listings magazine), daily newspapers or pharmacy windows.

Useful phone numbers

Fire service (Cuerpo de bomberos)
☎ 080

Police (Policia)
☎ 091

Lost property
☎ 91 588 43 46

International codes
Calling Spain from abroad:
From the USA, dial 011 followed by 34 followed by the number.
From the UK, dial 00 followed by 34 then the number.
From Australia dial 0011 34, from New Zealand 0044 34.
To call abroad from Spain, dial the international prefix 001 for the USA, 0044 for the UK, 00353 for Ireland, 0061 for Australia, then the number.

Where to stay

Breakfast
Thick, hot chocolate or coffee and pastries filled with cream or jam is usually served. Some hotels also offer Spain's famous *churros*, long fritters made from doughnut batter ➡ 66. Order *café solo* for black coffee, *café cortado* for coffee with a dash of milk, and *café con leche* for a large cup of coffee with plenty of milk.

Reservations
Reserve rooms in advance. This is advised especially during the high season (*temporada alta*), from June to September and the week before Easter (*Semana Santa*).

Prices For all the hotels we list the number of rooms, the price range, the number of suites, the lowest price for a room, and the cost of the cheapest breakfast. Prices given are for a double room inclusive of taxes (VAT at 7%). Most of the large Spanish hotel chains (NH, Meliá or Tryp) and many independent hotels offer special low season and weekend rates.

43 Hotels

THE INSIDER'S FAVORITES

Hotel classification

Madrid offers a wide range of places to stay. *Hotels* listed here carry between one and five stars. *Hostales* are more modest hotels, also graded by a star system. *Pensiones* are family-run guest houses offering the cheapest accommodation.

Youth hostels

Madrid has two youth hostels. Information and reservations can be obtained from the REAJ (Spanish Youth Hostels Association):
Red Española de Albergues Juveniles
Alcalá 32, 28014
☎ 91 580 42 16
➠ 91 580 42 15

INDEX BY PRICE

HOTEL PRICE RANGES (DOUBLE ROOMS)
● under 19,000 Ptas
●● 19,000 Ptas–23,000 Ptas
●●● 23,000 Ptas–27,000 Ptas
●●●● 27,000 Ptas–36,000 Ptas
●●●●● Over 36,000 Ptas

In the area

A number of Madrid's great classic hotels lie close to the city's three major museums – Museo del Prado ➡ 96, Museo Thyssen-Bornemisza ➡ 96, and Centro Cultural Reina Sofia ➡ 98. ■ Where to eat ➡ 40 ■ After dark ➡ 70 ➡ 74 ➡ 76 ➡ 78 ■ What to see ➡ 94 ➡ 96

Where to stay

Ritz (1)

Plaza de la Lealtad 5, 28014 ☎ 91 521 28 57 ➡ 91 532 87 76

Banco de España *129 rooms* ●●●●● *29 suites 102,000 Ptas* *3300 Ptas* *Goya* ➡ 40

This spectacular white palace, built under the supervision of King Alfonso XIII and César Ritz and designed by Charles Mewes in 1910, created a revolution in the hotel business. Its elegance, grand public rooms and personal service make it Spain's most celebrated hotel. In summer, the terrace and garden are a popular meeting place for Madrid's smart set.

Palace (2)

Plaza de las Cortes 7, 28014 ☎ 91 360 80 00 ➡ 91 360 81 00

Banco de España *396 rooms* ●●●●● *44 suites 128,400 Ptas* *3200 Ptas* *La Cupola*

The Palace, built in 1912, has a much more modern ambience and attitude than its traditional rival, the Ritz. An ambitious renovation program is currently in progress, aimed at restoring the hotel to its former glory and equipping it with state-of-the-art facilities. It has a good Italian restaurant.

Villa Real (3)

Plaza de las Cortes 10, 28014 ☎ 91 420 37 67 ➡ 91 420 25 47

Banco de España, Sevilla *115 rooms* ●●●● *12 suites 69,550 Ptas* *2140 Ptas*

The Villa Real was only recently converted into a hotel. It blends well into this *belle-époque* corner of Madrid, harmonizing with its prestigious neighbors, the Spanish Parliament, the Palace Hotel and the Ritz. Fine antique furniture and marble bathrooms maintain its sense of period grandeur, but it also has the best facilities in terms of modern fixtures and fittings.

Tryp Reina Victoria (4)

Plaza de Santa Ana 14, 28014 ☎ 91 531 45 00 ➡ 91 522 03 07

Sol *201 rooms* ●●●● *4 suites 53,500 Ptas* *1650 Ptas*

The Reina Victoria's greatest claim to fame is that it is one of the favorite haunts of the bullfighting fraternity. Following recent renovations, this early 20th-century building can now boast elegant, modern facilities and interiors.

Not forgetting

■ **Regina (5)** Alcalá, 19, 28014 ☎ 91 521 47 25 ➡ 91 522 40 88 ●
■ **Suecia (6)** Marqués de Casa Riera 4, 28014 ☎ 91 531 69 00 ➡ 91 521 71 41 ●●●

■ Where to shop ➥ 126 ➥ 128 ➥ 132

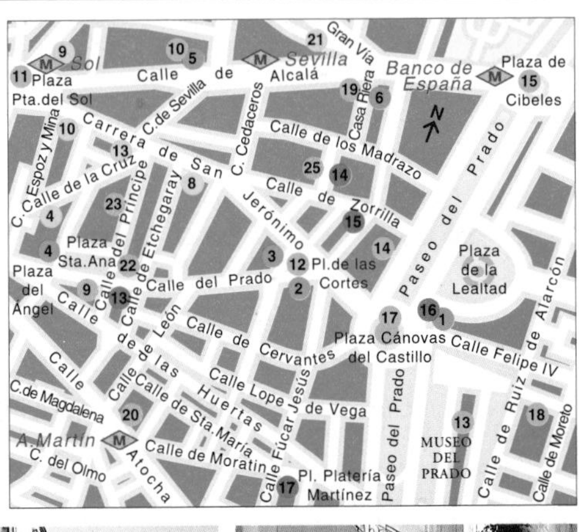

4

1

1

2

The beautiful cupola of the Palace, inaugurated in 1912 by Alfonso XIII, crowns a *belle-époque* rotunda.

2

4

Basic facts
This modern thoroughfare (built in 1910) cuts through the tangled streets of Old Madrid. ■ Where to eat ➥ 38 ■ After dark ➥ 72 ➥ 80 ■ What to see ➥ 90 ➥ 92 ➥ 94 ■ Where to shop ➥ 128 ➥ 132 ➥ 134 ➥ 136

Where to stay

Arosa (7)
Salud 21, 28013 ☎ 91 532 16 00 ➟ 91 531 31 27

M *Callao, Gran Vía* *139 rooms* ●● *1250 Ptas*

The Arosa is always undergoing an extensive program of modernization. The rooms are now very well sound-proofed and here it is essential. The hotel shares a building with the largest bookstore in Madrid, Casa del Libro ➥ 132, but the upstairs reception area and separate side entrance help to maintain discretion. There are two restaurants: one, inside the hotel, which is adequate; the other, La Joya de Jardines, a few yards away on Calle Jardines, is more adventurous.

Gaudí (8)
Gran Vía 9, 28013 ☎ 91 531 22 22 ➟ 91 531 54 69

M *Gran Vía 88 rooms* ●●● *2 suites 37,450 Ptas* *1500 Ptas*

A small, modern hotel tucked away behind the financial district of Calle Alcalá, the Gaudí is well suited to the business traveler. Unusually for accommodation in this area, the hotel has both a gym and a sauna.

Style Santo Domingo (9)
Plaza de Santo Domingo 13, 28013
☎ 91 547 98 00 ➟ 91 559 22 16

M *Santo Domingo* P *120 rooms* ●●● *1500 Ptas* @ *sdomingo@stnet.es*

In spite of its size, this brand new independent hotel can certainly be described as 'characterful'. Fine furniture, antiques and modern paintings blend well. The lounges retain the impressive granite walls of the apartment block that was once here.

Tryp Ambassador (10)
Cuesta de Santo Domingo 5, 28013
☎ 91 541 67 00 ➟ 91 559 10 40

M *Ópera, Santo Domingo* P *180 rooms* ●●● *2 suites 68,500 Ptas* *1800 Ptas*

A superb 19th-century mansion in which the Granada de Ega family once lived. It features an interior courtyard, covered by a glass roof, and a conservatory housing a charming restaurant. The Teatro Royal opera house ➥ 92 is located nearby.

Not forgetting

■ **El Coloso (11)** Leganitos 13, 28013 ☎ 91 559 76 00 ➟ 91 547 49 68 ●●

■ **Mayorazgo (12)** Flor Baja 3, 28013 ☎ 91 547 26 00 ➟ 91 541 24 85 ●

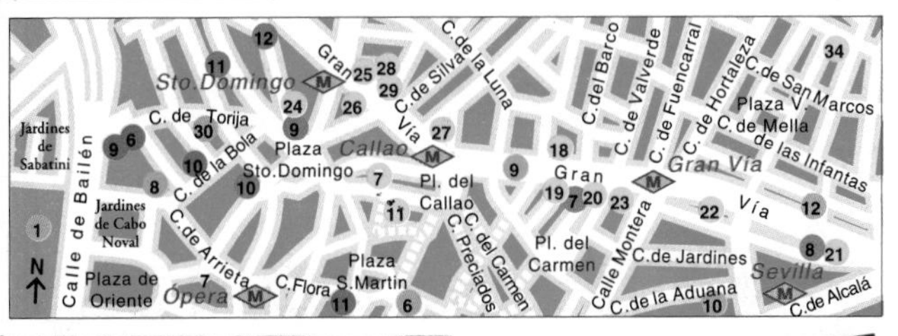
Jardines de Sabatini
Calle de Bailén
Jardines de Cabo Noval
Plaza de Oriente
Ópera
Sto. Domingo
C. de Torija
C. de la Bola
Plaza Sto. Domingo
C. de Arrieta
C. Flora
Plaza S. Martín
Gran Vía
C. de Silva
C. de la Luna
Callao
Pl. del Callao
C. Preciados
C. del Carmen
Pl. del Carmen
C. del Barco
C. de Valverde
C. de Fuencarral
C. de Hortaleza
C. de San Marcos
Plaza V.
C. de Mella
de las Infantas
Gran Vía
Calle Montera
C. de Jardines
C. de la Aduana
Sevilla
C. de Alcalá
N
1 6 6 7 7 8 8 9 9 9 10 10 10 10 11 11 11 12 12 18 19 20 21 22 23 24 25 26 27 28 29 30 34

0

HOTEL AROSA

7

7

8

9

9

In the area

Plaza de Colón, ideally situated for the Biblioteca Nacional and the restaurants of the Castellana and Calle Génova, has become the hub of Madrilenian life. ■ Where to eat ➡ 44 ➡ 52 ■ After dark ➡ 68 ➡ 72 ➡ 78 ■ What to see ➡ 104 ■ Where to shop ➡ 130 ➡ 140 ➡ 144

Where to stay

Santo Mauro (13)

Zurbano 36, 28010 ☎ 91 319 69 00 ➠ 91 308 54 77

Alonso Martínez, Rubén Dario *26 rooms ●●●●● 11 suites 49,220 Ptas* *2500 Ptas* *Belagua* ➡ *52* ➡ *68*

Built as a palace for the dukes of Santo Mauro, this elegant and imposing building was then used by a sequence of foreign embassies before being transformed into a luxury hotel in 1991. The original formal architecture coexists extremely well with the newly designed and fashionably modern interiors. The vast bedrooms that retain their great marble fireplaces have been decorated in a rather unusual style, which is not always to everyone's taste. The glass pavilion serving as entrance to the inner courtyard creates a light and graceful ambience. What was once the library is now a good restaurant, and the gardens and terrace provide an ideal meeting place as well as a delightful setting to rest or relax on a fine day.

NH Embajada (14)

Santa Engracia 5, 28010 ☎ 91 594 02 13 ➠ 91 447 33 12

Alonso Martínez 101 rooms ●● *1700 Ptas*

The ideally-located Embajada has an interesting and attractive design, which dates from the Madrilenian Belle Epoque, when the Spanish regional style with its Castilian and Andalusian features was highly prized. The style achieves its most distinctive expression in the wrought-iron balconies that adorn rooms facing the street. The rooms themselves are modern and functional, in the style of the Spanish chain NH, of which Embajada is a part.

Tryp Fénix (15)

Hermosilla 2, 28001 ☎ 91 431 67 00 ➠ 91 314 31 56

Serrano *214 rooms ●●●● 14 suites 57,250 Ptas* *1800 Ptas*

The distinctive style of the Tryp Fénix's reception area and its marble-clad lounges evokes the 1950s, a time when the hotel bar was a favorite watering-hole and meeting place of journalists, writers and bankers. Its name derives from the huge bronze imperial phoenix that perches on its rooftop. A few years ago, this venerable if somewhat aging establishment announced a long-awaited relaunch under the wing of the Spanish Tryp chain. The vast bedrooms, which are quiet and well-equipped, have been completely redecorated, and the hotel once again counts itself among the liveliest and most interesting in the capital. Note that the local branch of the Hard Rock Café, which occupies part of the ground floor of the building, has no direct access to the reception area, thereby preserving peace in the hotel.

Not forgetting

■ **NH Sanvy (16)** Goya 3, 28001 ☎ 91 576 08 00 ➠ 91 575 24 43 ●●●

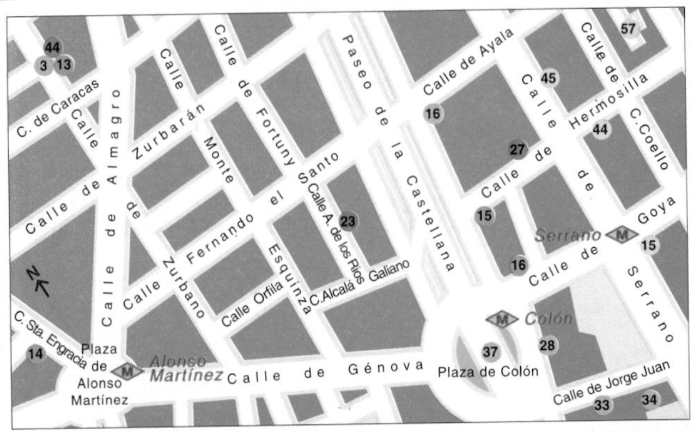
C. de Caracas
Calle
Calle de Almagro
Calle de Zurbarán
Calle de Fortuny
Paseo de la Castellana
Calle de Ayala
Calle de Hermosilla
C.Coello
Calle de Goya
Calle de Serrano
Monte el Santo
Calle A. de los Ríos
Calle Fernando
Esquinza
Calle Orfila
C.Alcalá Galiano
Calle Zurbano
Calle de Génova
Serrano
Colón
Plaza de Colón
Calle de Jorge Juan
C. Sta. Engracia
Plaza de Alonso Martínez
Alonso Martínez
44
3
13
57
45
16
44
27
23
15
15
16
14
37
28
33
34

14

13

16

In the area

The streets of this eastern section of Madrid are laid out on a grid plan, designed by the Marqués de Salamanca. The area that takes his name is today Madrid's most upmarket residential and shopping area. ■ Where to eat ➥ 44 ➥ 46 ➥ 48 ➥ 50 ■ After dark ➥ 70 ➥ 74 ➥ 80 ■ What to see ➥ 98

Where to stay

Villa Magna (17)

Paseo de la Castellana 22, 28046 ☎ 91 576 75 00 ➠ 91 431 22 86

M *Colón, Rubén Dario* 182 rooms ●●●●● 16 suites 96,300 Ptas 2950 Ptas *Tse-Yang, Le Divellec* ➥ 50
@ *villamagna@compuserve.com*

The Villa Magna is a modern hotel set in a park of ancient cedars that once belonged to an old palace on the Castellana. The rooms are exceptionally comfortable, and the lounges have a classical English elegançe, while the entrance and reception areas reflect a sense of calm opulence that relaxes the senses at the same time as it inspires confidence in the management. This is justified, and the Hyatt chain, which owns the Villa Magna, has excelled itself here in many respects, especially in the culinary field. It has placed Jacques Le Divellec in charge of the exceptional restaurant, and has also opened a branch of the Geneva-based Chinese restaurant, the Tse-Yang, in the hotel.

Wellington (18)

Velázquez 8, 28001 ☎ 91 575 44 00 ➠ 91 576 41 64

M *Velázquez, Principe de Vergara, Retiro* P 296 rooms ●●●●● 7 suites 53,300 Ptas 2200 Ptas *El Fogón* ➥ 46

This traditional hotel, in the heart of the elegant Salamanca district, has recently been modernized while retaining many of the most-loved features of its former style. Located close to the Ventas bullring ➥ 100, it has long been popular with bullfighters and their followers, and is always full during the Feria de San Isidro in May and June. The service is impeccable, the bedrooms are spacious, and – unusually for Madrid – there is also a swimming pool.

Gran Hotel Velázquez (19)

Velázquez 62, 28001 ☎ 91 575 28 00 ➠ 91 575 28 09

M *Velázquez* P 146 rooms ●●● 75 suites 34,500 Ptas 1600 Ptas

The Gran Hotel Velázquez, situated in the heart of the Salamanca district, attracts large numbers of visitors during the major art exhibitions held at the nearby Juan March foundation ➥ 74. It also hosts numerous social activities for a predominantly Spanish clientele. The huge rooms are attractively old-fashioned (1940s in style); the restaurant is adequate if not exceptional. An additional attraction is that tea is served daily in the *salón*.

Not forgetting

■ **Pintor (20)** Goya 79, 28001 ☎ 91 435 75 45 ➠ 91 576 81 57 ●●
Recently renovated
■ **Convención (21)** O'Donnell 53, 28009 ☎ (91) 574 84 00 ➠ 91 574 68 00 ●●

■ Where to shop ➥ 130 ➥ 138 ➥ 140 ➥ 144

In the area

The place for shopaholics and museum-goers, the Castellana is also an architectural showcase. Bullfighting enthusiasts can spend an afternoon at Las Ventas. ■ Where to eat ➥ 50 ■ After dark ➥ 68 ➥ 70 ➥ 72 ➥ 74 ➥ 80 ■ What to see ➥ 100 ➥ 106 ■ Where to shop ➥ 130

Where to stay

Emperatriz (22)

López de Hoyos 4, 28006 ☎ 91 563 80 88 ➟ 91 563 98 04

M *Rubén Darío* P *153 rooms* ●●●● *5 suites from 75,000 Ptas* *1800 Ptas*

Like its neighbor, the Inter-Continental ➥ 28, this comfortable, white-fronted hotel was built in the mid-1950s. It was refurbished in 1996, and the rooms today are bright and cheerful, with pale furniture, soft-colored drapes and three original vestibule panels by Eduardo Vicente, Madrid's chief style interpreter (also responsible for the frescos in the restaurant El Schotis ➥ 36).

Apartahotel Eraso (23)

Ardemáns 13, 28028 ☎ 91 355 32 00 ➟ 91 355 66 52

M *Diego de Léon* P *31 studio appartments* ● *850 Ptas*

The Eraso certainly lives up to the reputation of the Barcelona-based Husa hotel chain. Its affordable studio apartments, with lounge and kitchenette, are ideal for short visits or long stays in the Spanish capital. Although not ultra-luxurious, they are well maintained, modern and comfortable, with none of the impersonal atmosphere of so many *apartahotels*.

Rafael Ventas (24)

Alcalá 269, 28027 ☎ 91 326 16 20 ➟ 91 326 18 19

M *El Carmen* *110 rooms* ● *1 suite 26,725 Ptas* *1300 Ptas* @ hotel@rafaelventas.com

The *fin-de-siècle* version of the Wellington ➥ 24. The new Rafael is closer to the bullring ➥ 100, and numerous toreros and their impresarios have taken to staying in this steel-and-concrete establishment, as have their fans. The rooms are bright and pleasant.

NH Parque de las Avenidas (25)

Biarritz 2, 28028 ☎ 91 361 02 88 ➟ 91 361 21 62

M *Ventas, Parque de Avenidas* P *198 rooms* ●●●● *1 suite 32,100 Ptas* *2000 Ptas*

This is one of the most recent of the 12 hotels owned by the NH chain in Madrid, and one of the most successful in terms of its ultra-functional style. The rooms are spacious and comfortable, the small bar is lively, and the modern restaurant serves modern Basque cuisine. Well positioned midway between the bullring ➥ 100 and the residential district of Parque de las Avenidas.

Not forgetting

■ **Meliá Confort Los Galgos (26)** Claudio Coello 139, 28006 ☎ 91 562 66 00 ➟ 91 561 76 62 ●●●●

■ **NH Príncipe de Vergara (27)** Príncipe de Vergara 92, 28006 ☎ 91 563 26 95 ➟ 91 563 72 53 ●●

■ **Abeba (28)** Alcántara 63, 28006 ☎ 91 401 16 50 ➟ 91 402 75 91 ●

C. de María de Molina
Av. de América
N
C.de Brescia
C.del General Oráa
C. Diego de León
C. de Velázquez
C. de Serrano
Paseo de la Castellana
C. de Maldonado
Diego de León
C. de J. Bravo
N. de Balboa
Calle de Padilla
Calle de Fco. Silvela
C. de Ardemáns
C. Cartagena
C. de Azcona
Calle de Martínez Izquierdo
AV. DE LA PAZ
Los Toreros
Avenida de
C. de Londres
Ventas
Calle de Alcalá
El Carmen
8
39
6
22
26
27
7
1
41
14
33
16
17
38
23
18
28
25
27
26
24

25

24

22

In the area

This residential district parallels Salamanca, though it has no shopping avenue to compare with that of Calle Serrano. The site of embassies and ministries, it is also home to the charming Museo Sorolla. ■ Where to eat ➡ 52 ➡ 56 ■ After dark ➡ 68 ■ What to see ➡ 106

Where to stay

Castellana Inter-Continental (29)

Paseo de la Castellana 49, 28046
☎ 91 310 02 00 ➡ 91 319 58 53

Rubén Darío, Gregorio Marañón *285 rooms ●●●●● 20 suites 90,000 Ptas* *2800 Ptas* *albor@line/pro.es*

The Castellana Inter-Continental has recently been modernized, but it still boasts some of the rarest examples of tasteful 1950s style to be found in Madrid: the red and black marble facings are unique, and the courtyard garden features sculptures by Angel Ferrant – a member of 1950s avant-garde. The garden offers excellent, shaded dining – try the famous club sandwiches. An establishment with a big personality, much loved in Spain.

Miguel Ángel (30)

Miguel Ángel 20, 28010 ☎ 91 442 00 22 ➡ 91 442 53 20

Gregorio Marañón *232 rooms ●●●●● 30 suites 45,368 Ptas* *2500 Ptas*

The Miguel Ángel has a modern exterior combined with an elegant, classical interior that is impressively decorated with Baroque-style carpets and furniture. The well-proportioned bedrooms have recently been refurbished, the service is of a high standard and the management is professional – making this palace on the Castellana one of the most reliable addresses in Madrid. It also boasts a superb indoor swimming pool and gymnasium.

NH Zurbano (31)

Zurbano 79-81, 28003 ☎ 91 441 55 00 ➡ 91 442 91 48

Gregorio Marañón *264 rooms ● 10 suites 24,610 Ptas*

1700 Ptas

Vuelta de España drivers and other professional sporting teams often stay in this comfortable, NH-style hotel close to the Castellana. Its sporting reputation means that it is livelier and more colorful than many of the other hotels in the chain.

Style Escultor (32)

Miguel Ángel 3, 28010 ☎ 91 310 42 03 ➡ 91 319 25 84

Rubén Darío 59 rooms ●●● 2 suites 37,450 Ptas *1450 Ptas*

A small, basic but comfortable hotel, the Style Escultor looks out over the Glorieta Rubén Darío, now the most expensive residential square in town.

Not forgetting

■ **NH Prisma (33)** Santa Engracia 120, 28003 ☎ 91 441 93 77 ➡ 91 442 58 51 ●●

29

30

30

Statue of Gregorio Marañón, endocrinologist and Madrid historian.

29

In the area

The wide thoroughfare of the Paseo de la Castellana is lined with government ministries and hotels geared toward the business traveler. Two skycrapers – the 43-story Torre Picasso and the twin-towered Puerta de Europa – stand as symbols of Madrid's modernity.

Where to stay

Meliá Castilla (34)

Capitán Haya 43, 28020 ☎ 91 567 50 00 ➠ 91 567 52 51

Plaza de Castilla *899 rooms* ●●●● *14 suites 60,445 Ptas* *1600 Ptas* ➡ *82*

An uninspiring skyscraper from the outside, the Meliá Castilla rewards closer inspection. It offers attentive service, comfortable, tastefully decorated rooms, two reputable restaurants and a famous cabaret venue and nightclub.

Hotel Cuzco (35)

Paseo de la Castellana 133, 28046
☎ 91 556 06 00 ➠ 91 556 03 72

Cuzco *30 rooms* ●●● *8 suites 32, 100 Ptas* *1350 Ptas*

The names of the lounges (Tolteca, Maya, Azteca, Inca) are in keeping with that of the hotel which, unsurprisingly, refers to the Spanish Conquest of South America. Guests will love the richly decorated entrance hall with its allegorical 17th- and 18th-century tapestries, the comfortably modern bedrooms and the restaurant with its weekend 'family menu' offering special reductions for the under-11s.

Holiday Inn (36)

Plaza de Carlos Trías Beltrán 4, 28020
☎ 91 456 80 00 ➠ 91 456 80 01

Nuevos Ministerios 282 rooms ●●●● *31 suites 37,611 Ptas* *2400 Ptas*

A modern building, ideally located close to the Torre Picasso, Spain's highest skyscraper, opposite the Real Madrid stadium and the Palacio de Congresos, and right in the heart of Azca, Madrid's largest business complex ➡ 108. American-style comfort: large beds, a swimming pool, rooftop solarium and a gym.

Castilla Plaza (37)

Paseo de la Castellana 220, 28046
☎ 91 323 11 86 ➠ 91 315 54 06

Plaza de Castilla *234 rooms* ●●●● *7 suites 31,000 Ptas* *1900 Ptas*

This recently opened hotel (1994) lies at the foot of the two leaning towers of the Puerta de Europa ➡ 108, modern Madrid's most talked-about landmark. It is well equipped, and the ultra-modern rooms are softened by wooden fittings and plants. A tapas bar with a surprisingly good menu adds an unexpected, but welcome, Madrilenian touch.

Not forgetting

■ **Orense (38)** Orense 38, 28020 ☎ 91 597 15 68 ➠ 91 597 12 95 ●●●
■ **Aitana (39)** Paseo de la Castellana 152, 28046 ☎ 91 344 00 68 ●● *Recently renovated.*

■ Where to eat ➥ 60 ➥ 64 ■ After dark ➥ 68 ➥ 80 ➥ 82 ■ What to see ➥ 108 ■ Where to shop ➥ 142

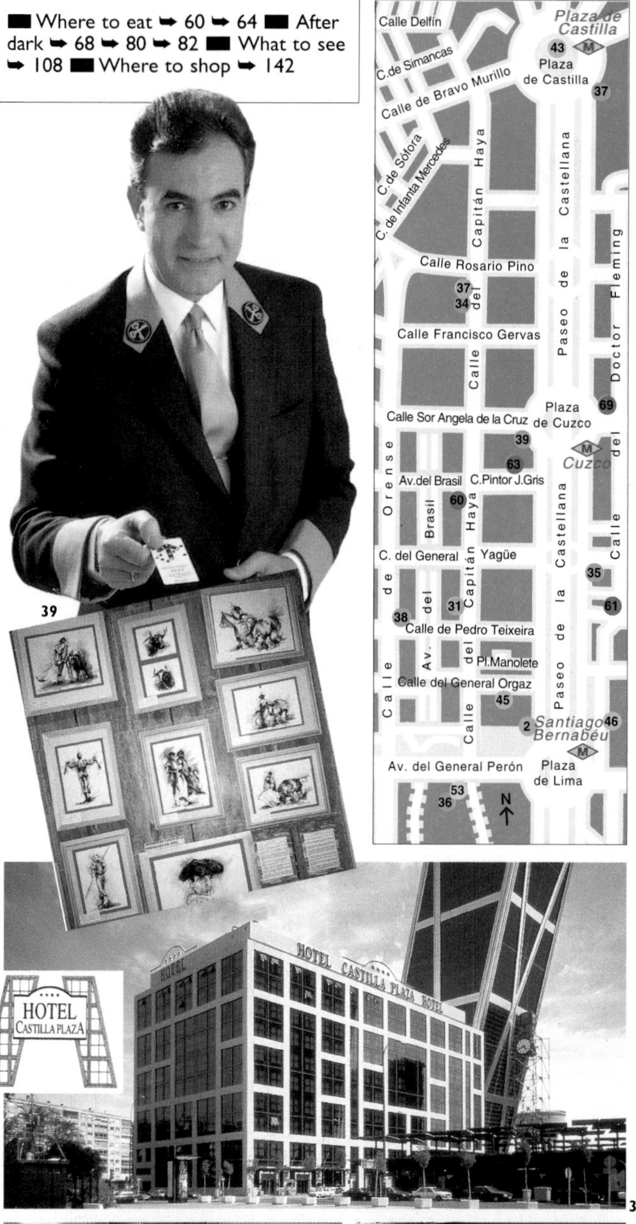

39

37

37

In the area

The Real Madrid district is a prime example of the Madrilenian 'boom' of the 1960s, when anarchic urban planning schemes were implemented. Both a shopping district and a residential area, its real treasures, tucked away at its center, are the *colonias*, with their villas and secluded gardens.

Where to stay

NH Eurobuilding (40)

Padre Damián 23, 28023 ☎ 91 345 45 00 ➠ 91 345 45 76

Cuzco *428 rooms ●●● 52 suites 33,000 Ptas* *2000 Ptas*

Occupying an entire block of houses just off the Castellana, this is more of a city than a hotel. If this may seem a disadvantage to those looking for a more intimate environment, this can be countered by the advantages of the impressive raised terrace-garden, with a beautiful outdoor pool – a rarity in Madrid – which combine to give Eurobuilding the edge over its competitors. In addition, the hotel has numerous conference rooms, restaurants, shops, the most famous bridge club in Madrid, and a renowned debating society. Many business travelers return here again and again for the hotel's impressive facilities.

La Residencia de El Viso (41)

Nervión 8, 28002 ☎ 91 564 03 70 ➠ 91 564 19 65

República de Argentina *12 rooms ●* *800 Ptas* *elviso@estancias.es*

La Residencia de El Viso is a remarkable cubist-style, salmon-pink villa that typifies the rationalist architecture of the 1930s. In addition to this architectural distinction, the hotel provides a green and quiet refuge from the noisy, bustling capital, even though it is situated right in the city center. Its small bedrooms are functional and modern. A garden-view restaurant serves fresh market produce.

Aristos (42)

Avenida Pío XII 34, 28016 ☎ 91 345 04 50 ➠ 91 345 10 23

Pío XII *24 rooms ●● 1 suite 24,000 Ptas* *1000 Ptas* *El Chaflán* *El Chaflán*

Situated at the end of an avenue that once marked the northern limits of the city, the Aristos has a deserved reputation as a charming place to stay for a romantic visit to Madrid. The rooms are impeccable, the garden delightful, and the restaurant excellent. Since the early 1990s, a burgeoning business district on the nearby M30 bypass has attracted a lively new clientele to this small hotel.

NH Habana (43)

Paseo de La Habana 73, 28036 ☎ 91 345 82 84 ➠ 91 457 75 79

Colombia *156 rooms ●●* *1700 Ptas*

Frequented especially by sportsmen and by Basque and Catalan business travelers, the Habana is the Charmartín representative of the ubiquitous NH hotel group. This establishment is modern and is also more luxurious than others in the chain. One attraction for sports enthusiasts is that the concierge has an amazing ability to procure tickets for even the most oversubscribed Real Madrid football matches ➠ 108.

■ Where to eat ➥ 36 ➥ 60 ➥ 64
■ After dark ➥ 70 ➥ 72 ■ What to see ➥ 108 ■ Where to shop ➥ 142

1

1

42

41

41

The Bauhaus and art deco movements have left their imprint on the El Viso area.

Tipping

Although service (12% of the total) is always included in the bill, it is usual to leave at least 5% more.

Where to eat

IVA

Some restaurants give prices inclusive of IVA (VAT at 7%); others add it to the total. The menu should state whether or not IVA is included.

Parking

It is not unusual for restaurants, especially the upmarket kind, to have doormen to park diners' cars for them. Otherwise parking is difficult in the narrow, winding streets of old Madrid.

Busy times

It is worth reserving a table, especially at lunchtime. The locals take a very late lunch (often not until around 2.30pm), but they no longer dine around midnight like they used to, preferring to eat around 9.30pm. Nevertheless, restaurants are quite accustomed to taking earlier reservations from foreign visitors.

73 Restaurants

THE INSIDER'S FAVORITES

INDEX BY TYPE

AND PRICE RANGE

● under 4000 Ptas
●● 4000 Ptas–5000 Ptas
●●● 5000 Ptas–6000 Ptas
●●●● 6000 Ptas–7000 Ptas
●●●●● over 7000 Ptas

Basic facts

In the 19th century, tascas were the wine leftovers used to concoct such basic dishes as the *cocido*, a stew made from cabbage, *chorizo* (spicy sausage) and chickpeas. The word 'tasca' is now applied to small restaurants, called *tascas ilustradas*. There is still a large number of these in Madrid, often

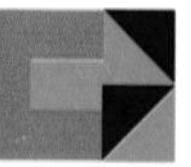

Where to eat

Casa Lucio (1)

Cava Baja 35, 28005 ☎ 91 365 32 52 ➠ 91 366 48 66

M *La Latina* ***Tasca*** ●●●● *Mon.–Fri., Sun. 1.15–3.45pm, 9pm–midnight; Sat. 9–11.30pm; closed in Aug*

This historic inn was renovated in the 1970s by the great Lucio Blázquez, who has transformed it into one of the best-known and most fashionable Madrilenian restaurants. The owner is a colorful character of such renown that he has been made the subject of a book, a copy of which he is proud to produce. The established ritual for most regulars begins with a plate of *patatas revolconas* (sautéd potatoes with scrambled eggs), followed by red meat, milk-fed roast lamb or fried hake, washed down by a carafe of Valdepeñas. To soak up the atmosphere, ask for a table in the main brick-vaulted dining room.

El Schotis (2)

Cava Baja 11, 28005 ☎ 91 365 32 30 ➠ 91 365 72 44

M *Tirso de Molina, La Latina* ***Tasca*** ●● *Mon.–Sat. 1–4.30pm, 8.30pm–12.30am; Sun. 1–4.30pm*

The splendid frescos depicting scenes from old Madrid (painted by Eduardo Vicente in the 1940s) add a lively touch to this *tasca*, a local-style restaurant which has influenced numerous other similar eating houses in the area. The waiters are 'old-timers' who have become co-owners and are most attentive. Try the stuffed sweet peppers and excellent red meats.

La Fuencisla (3)

San Mateo 4, 28004 ☎ 91 521 61 86

M *Tribunal* ***Tasca*** ●●● *Mon.–Sat. 1.30–4pm, 9pm–1am; closed in Aug.*

Modern paintings of questionable artistic merit and bullfighting mementoes adorn the walls of this tiny dining room. Señor and Señora De Frutos serve up excellent home cooking, which reflects the traditions of Segovia ➡ 120, their native town. While the proprietor presides over the front-of-house, as he has for the last 40 years or so, his wife creates meals in the kitchen. Try the grilled chops of milk-fed lamb or oven-baked *ventresca* (fillet) of tuna. The Rioja wines are exceptional.

De la Riva (4)

Cochabamba 13, 28016 ☎ 91 458 89 54

M *Colombia* ***Tasca*** ●● *Mon.–Fri. 1.30–6pm; closed in Aug.*

De la Riva has moved to the north of the city where, in a nondescript building in the modern district of Chamartín, its eponymous owner has re-created the atmosphere of a traditional *tasca*. When ordering, trust his advice as he recites the dishes of the day, among them *chipirones* (squid) in their ink, roasted fillet of veal, and the famous Castilian conger eel. This *tasca* is closed in the evenings.

plainly decorated with colored *azulejos,* (ceramic tiles), offering an atmospheric place to meet but little in the way of comfort.

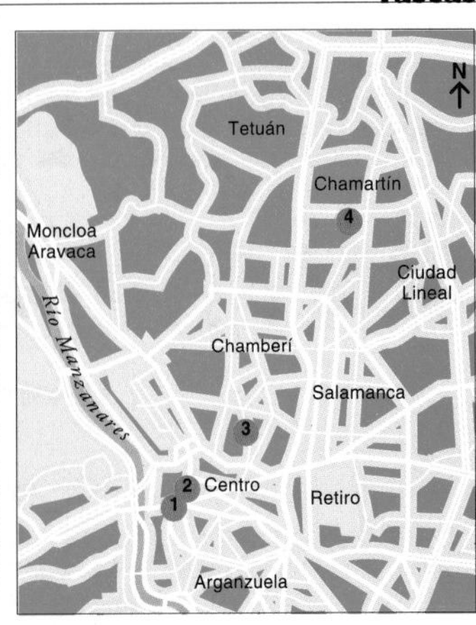

Lucio Blázquez makes a point of offering his customers those tables at which famous guests have sat.

In the area
Plaza Mayor, nestling between the Hapsburg district and the old working-class neighborhoods of Madrid, is a splendid architectural ensemble. From the 17th to the 20th centuries, it was the hub of the city, and many old stores remain. ■ Where to stay ➡ 20 ■ After dark

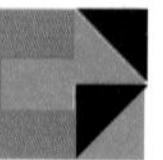

Where to eat

Botín (5)

Cuchilleros 17, 28005 ☎ 91 366 42 17 ➟ 91 366 84 94

M *Sol, Tirso de Molina* ***Castilian cuisine*** ●●● ▭ ◷ *daily 1–4pm, 8pm–midnight*

This traditional establishment, founded in 1725, was entered in the *Guiness Book of Records* as 'the oldest restaurant in the world'. Happily, though, its four floors, exposed beams, wood oven and Castilian decoration in no way resemble a dusty museum. Delicious milk-fed lamb and roasted suckling pig are served to a mixed clientele of tourists and Madrileños.

Caripén (6)

Plaza de la Marina Española 4, 28013 ☎ 91 541 11 77

M *Santo Domingo* ***French bistro cuisine*** ●● ▭ ◷ *Mon.–Sat. 9pm–3am*

In a genuine art deco dining room Daniel Boute serves up the best French-style bistro cooking in Madrid. The Caripén is also one of the Madrid's most appealing restaurants in another sense, because you can eat here well after midnight when most other restaurants have closed. Sample specialties such as mussels in a cream sauce, excellent and copious fresh pasta, deliciously fresh steak tartare, mouthwatering skate in black butter and, to round out the meal, a very good apple tart... The cellar has some good French wines including a wonderful, reasonably priced vintage Médoc.

La Esquina del Real (7)

Amnistía 2, 28013 ☎ 91 559 43 09

M *Ópera* ***French cuisine*** ●●● ▭ ◷ *Mon.–Fri. 2–4pm, 9–11.30pm; Sat. 8pm–midnight; closed Aug. 15–31*

Located a few yards from the Teatro Real ➡ 92, the Esquina del Real is one of Madrid's well-kept culinary secrets. The 17th-century building is one of the oldest in Madrid, with impressive granite walls that are nearly six feet thick. Marcel Margossian serves classic and resolutely French dishes, including Dublin Bay prawns with raspberry vinegar, delicious home-made foie gras, fricassée of veal sweetbreads, and as a specialty,. flambéd Tarte Tatin.

Not forgetting

■ **Bajamar (8)** Gran Vía 78, 28013 ☎ 91 548 48 18 ●●●●● *Sublime fish and shellfish, simply cooked. Expensive.*

■ **Entre Suspiro y Suspiro (9)** Plaza de la Marina Española 4, 28013 ☎ 91 542 06 44 ●●● *Genuine Mexican home cooking – a far cry from the local 'Tex Mex'.*

■ **La Bola (10)** Bola 5, 28013 ☎ 91 547 69 30 ● *A* Taberna *(inn) with an old-style* tasca *atmosphere* ➡ *36**. Serves up an excellent* cocido madrileño *(Madrilenian stew).*

■ **Cornucopia (11)** Flora 1, 28013 ☎ 91 547 64 65 ●● *Although Debora Hansen has left this Edwardian setting, there is still a distinctly New England flavor to this restaurant which is in fact more like a tearoom. European and American cuisine.*

➥ 68 ➥ 80 ■ What to see ➥ 92 ➥ 102 ■ Where to shop ➥ 126 ➥ 128 ➥ 134 ➥ 144

10

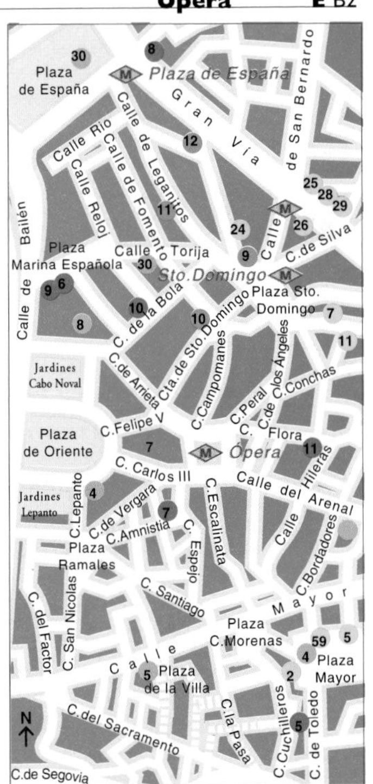

11

11

9

In the area

This is the artistic hub of Madrid, and the political heart of the capital, home to the Palacio de Congresos, scene of the attempted coup of February 23, 1981. ■ Where to stay ➡ 18 ➡ 20 ■ After dark ➡ 70 ➡ 72 ➡ 74 ➡ 76 ➡ 78 ■ What to see ➡ 94 ➡ 96 ➡ 98

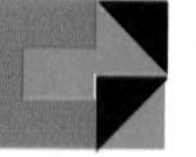

Where to eat

Viridiana (12)

Juan de Mena 14, 28014 Madrid ☎ 91 523 44 78 ➡ 91 532 42 74

Ⓜ *Retiro, Banco de España* **Modern Castilian cuisine** ●●●●● ⊟
🕑 *Mon.–Sat. 1.30–4pm, 9pm–midnight; closed Easter week, Aug., Christmas*

Everything here is dedicated to the memory of Luis Buñuel. The movie-mad proprietor Abraham García is a colorful character, always on the look out for new and exotic ingredients and techniques (the menu changes fortnightly), while remaining rooted in his native Castile. The result is the most inventive cuisine in Madrid. The cellar is exceptional, stocked with wines from around the world.

El Cenador del Prado (13)

Prado 4, 28014 ☎ 91 429 15 61 ➡ 91 369 04 55

Ⓜ *Sevilla* **Mediterranean cuisine** ●●●● ⊟ 🕑 *Mon.–Fri. 1.45–4pm, 9pm–midnight; Sat. 9pm–midnight; closed one week in Aug.*

Abandoning their haute cuisine, the Herranz brothers have opted for a cheaper, neo-Madrilenian version. Yet their clam and potato ragout, venison medallions with quince jelly, and chocolate stuffed with pear ice-cream never disappoint, and the three dining rooms are sumptuous.

Errota-Zar (14)

Jovellanos 3 (1st floor), 28014 ☎ / ➡ 91 531 25 64

Ⓜ *Banco de España, Sevilla* **Basque cuisine** ●● ⊟ 🕑 *Mon.–Sat. 1–4pm, 9pm–midnight; closed Easter week*

Errota-Zar belongs to Euskal Etxea, the home of Basque cuisine in Madrid. In this plush, traditional setting, the Olano family serves up excellent meats and popular Basque dishes, such as Tolosa kidney beans, almond cardoons, and Bay of Biscay cod.

Paradis Madrid (15)

Marqués de Cubas 14, 28014 ☎ 91 429 73 03 ➡ 91 429 32 95

Ⓜ *Banco de España* **Catalan cuisine** ●●● ⊟ 🕑 *Mon.–Fri. 1.30–4pm, 9pm–midnight; Sat. 9pm–midnight; closed Easter week, Aug., public holidays*

With its Catalan-style décor and old mosaic-tiled floor, this Madrid branch of the Barcelona-based restaurant chain is a worthy ambassador of the cuisine and wines of the principality: broad beans sautéd with squid, sea bream cooked on a hot slate, Catalan cream, Penedés and Priorato wines.

Not forgetting

■ **Goya (16)** Hotel Ritz, Plaza de la Lealtad 5, 28014 ☎ 91 521 28 57 ●●●●● *A splendid wood-paneled dining room overlooking Madrid's most beautiful summer garden.* Cocido, callos *(tripe)* a la madrileña... *the menu changes daily.*

■ **La Vaca Verónica (17)** Moratín 38, 28014 ☎ 91 429 78 27 ● *Decorated in the style of a Madrid mansion of the early 1900s. Featured on the lunchtime menu are salads, bourgeois dishes and excellent Argentinian meats.*

■ Where to shop ➥ 128 ➥ 132

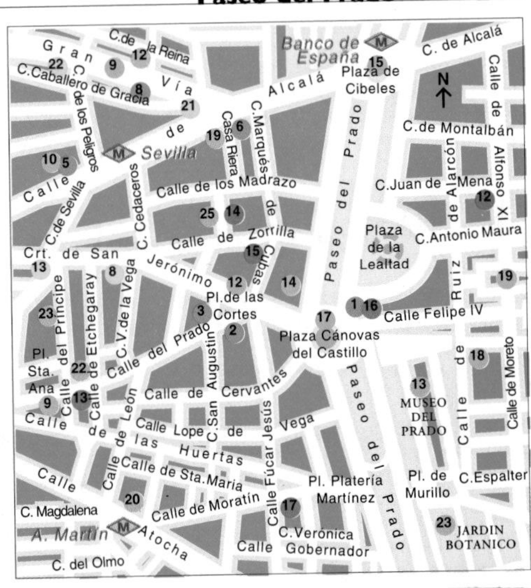

16

14

17

12

In the area

Cibeles is dominated by two symbols of Madrid – the fountain of Cybele, showing the goddess in a chariot, and the granite Puerta de Alcalá. ■ Where to stay ➡ 18 ➡ 20 ■ After dark ➡ 72 ➡ 74 ➡ 76 ■ What to see ➡ 94 ➡ 96 ➡ 98 ■ Where to shop ➡ 132 ➡ 138

Where to eat

San Carlo (18)

Barquillo 10, 28004 ☎ 91 522 79 88 ➡ 91 522 73 01

Ⓜ *Banco de España* **Modern Italian cuisine ●●●** ▭ 🕒 *daily 1–4.30pm, 9–11.30pm* 🍸

A newcomer in a category that is well represented but often disappointing in Madrid, the San Carlo offers authentic trans-alpine cooking. The impressive interior calls to mind the Teatro San Carlo in Naples, a city that was for a long time ruled by Spain. Light pizzas are served up in the first room; in the second, a modestly updated Italian cuisine, with fresh tomato sauce and beef *tagliata* with rocket. Musical evenings at weekends.

Nicolás (19)

Villalar 4, 28001 ☎ ➡ 91 431 77 37

Ⓜ *Banco de España, Retiro* **Creative Spanish cuisine ●●** ▭ 🕒 *Tue.–Sat. 1.30–4pm, 9pm–midnight; closed Easter week, Aug.*

Formerly a bistro in a working-class neighborhood, Nicolás has now become a comfortable restaurant with minimalist decor and Guinovart prints on the walls. The cuisine served up by Juan Antonio Méndez is as simple and elegant as ever: lamb sweetbreads in breadcrumbs, cassoulet of squid and chickpeas, duck's liver with pears, and perfect cod *ajoarriero* (in garlic).

La Gamella (20)

Alfonso XII 4, 28014 ☎ 91 532 45 09 ➡ 91 523 34 90

Ⓜ *Retiro* **Spanish and American cuisine ●●●** ▭ 🕒 *Mon.–Fri. 1.30–4pm, 9pm–midnight; Sat. 9pm–midnight; closed Easter week*

A truly postmodern eating house with scarlet walls. The restaurant, run by Richard Stephens, combines the best of Spanish and American cuisine. The latter is fairly predictable (steak tartare with bourbon, excellent cheesecake), while the former is more inventive (eggplant with Manchego cheese and Xérès brandy and a tomato coulis).

Horcher (21)

Alfonso XII 6, 28014 ☎ 91 522 07 31 ➡ 91 523 34 90

Ⓜ *Retiro* **Traditional German cuisine ●●●●●** ▭ 🕒 *Mon.–Fri. 1.30–4pm, 8.30pm–midnight; Sat. 8.30pm–midnight; closed in August*

The Horchers arrived in Madrid in 1943, when allied bombs were falling on the family restaurant in Berlin. A cozy conservative Saxon atmosphere in which to sample traditional German cuisine served up by Carlos Horcher: herrings with *kartoffelpuffer*, game, Viennese strudels.

Not forgetting

■ **Club 31 (22)** Alcalá 58, 28014 ☎ 91 531 00 92 ●●●●●
International cuisine with a classic finish served in a luxury-style canteen to a well-heeled clientele.

N
Calle de San Marcos
C. de Barbieri
Calle de las Infantas
Calle de la Reina
Gran Vía
C.Caballero de Gracia
Sevilla
Calle de Alcalá
Calle del Barquillo
Cuartel General del Ejército
Po. de Recoletos
Plaza de Cibeles
Paseo del Prado
Banco de España
C.de Salustiano Olozaga
C. Villalar
Calle de Serrano
C. de Columela
Retiro
Alcalá
Plaza de la Independencia
Calle de Alcalá
C. Alfonso XI
C.Valenzuela
Calle de Montalbán
Calle de Alfonso XII
Avenida Méjico
PARQUE DEL RETIRO
37
19
16
18
22
15
12
9
8
21
20
6

18

18

20

19

NICOLAS
Villalar, 4
Teléfono 431 77 37
28001 Madrid

In the area

This square, commemorating the discovery of America, and the nearby shopping street of Génova are presided over by the Torres Heron, twin towers linked by an incongruous green 'hat'. ■ Where to stay ➥ 22 ■ After dark ➥ 68 ➥ 72 ➥ 76 ➥ 78 ➥ 84 ■ What to see ➥ 104

Where to eat

Jockey (23)

Amador de los Ríos 6, 28010 ☎ ➠ 91 319 24 35

M *Colón* ***Classic Spanish and French cuisine*** ●●●●● *Mon.–Fri. 1–4pm, 9pm–midnight; Sat. 9pm–midnight; closed public holidays, Aug.*

The green, velvet benches and equestrian prints have been here since the restaurant opened in 1945. For over half a century, it has maintained its position at the top of Madrid's restaurant league under the direction of the Cortés family. The cuisine is ultra-conservative, but the well-roasted fatted chicken served up by chef Jesús Barbolla has definite appeal. Private dining rooms, and a clientele of bankers and politicians.

Ciao Madrid (24)

Argensola 7, 28004 Madrid ☎ 91 308 25 19

M *Alonso Martínez* ***Italian trattoria*** ● *Mon.–Fri. 1.30–3.45pm, 9.30pm–midnight; Sat. 9.30pm–12.30am; closed Easter week, Aug.* *Apodaca 20, 28004 ☎ (91) 447 00 36*

When it comes to authentic, family-run Italian *trattorias*, Ciao Madrid wins hands down. The decor is unremarkable and the service brisk, but the cooking is good and ranges from pasta (*gnocchi al pesto* and ravioli with zucchini) to meat dishes (carpaccio and a robust *cotechino* with lentils). The cellar stocks a good Rosso di Montalcino. The related establishment on Calle Apocada serves excellent pizzas.

El Mentidero de la Villa (25)

Santo Tomé 6, 28004 ☎ 91 308 12 85 ➠ 91 319 87 92

M *Alonso Martínez* ***Modern Franco-Spanish cooking*** ●● *Mon.–Fri. 1.30–4pm, 9pm–midnight; Sat. 9pm–midnight; closed Aug. 15–31*

The charming proprietor Mario Martínez has created a fairy-tale interior with the aid of *trompe l'oeil* murals and carousel horses. The culinary style is modern Franco-Spanish, featuring unusual but simple fish dishes and perfect cuts of lamb. An excellent cellar stocked with Spanish wines.

Al Mounia (26)

Recoletos 5, 28001 ☎ 91 435 08 28

M *Colón, Banco de España* ***Moroccan cuisine*** ●●● *Tue.–Sat. 1.30–4pm, 9–11.30pm*

The ornate decorative motifs conceived by Moroccan craftsmen are alone worth a visit, but the best North African restaurant in Madrid has other delights to offer: the *b'stella etheree* (Castilian lamb prepared Moroccan-style) is excellent and the couscous is light and flavorsome. The wines are expensive but not of the standard of the food.

Not forgetting

■ **La Alpargatería (27)** Hermosilla 7, 28001 ☎ 91 577 43 45 ●
Italian-style pasta, Argentinian beef and a no-fuss atmosphere. Modest prices.

■ **Pelotari (28)** Recoletos 3, 28001 ☎ 91 578 24 97 ●●●●●
Classic Basque cuisine with excellent beef grills.

■ Where to shop
➥ 136

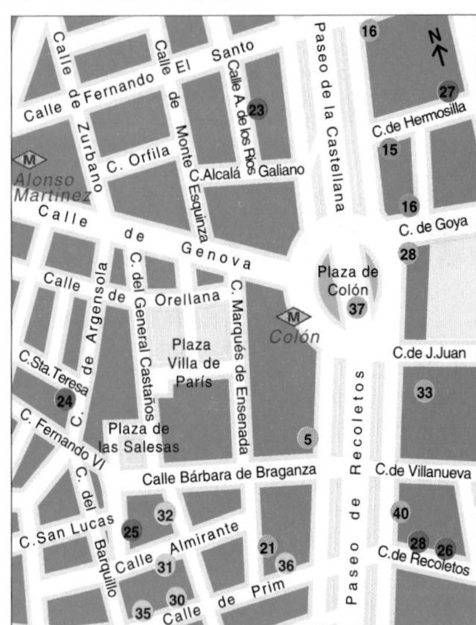

At Al Mounia the interior, atmosphere and food will transport you to the Maghreb. An essential 'detour' for those wanting to learn more about Spanish history while in Madrid.

26

26

In the area

Located north of Retiro Park, this part of the Salamanca district has developed into an upmarket shopping area specializing in designer items and luxury goods. It is here that the most prestigious commercial art galleries are located.

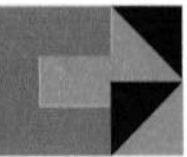

Where to eat

El Amparo (29)

Puigcerdá 8, 28001 ☎ 91 431 64 56 ➡ 91 575 54 91

M *Goya* ***Modern Spanish cuisine*** ●●●●● *Mon.–Sat. 1.30–3.30pm, 9–11.30pm; closed Aug. 11–17*

One of the finest and most innovative restaurants in Madrid, El Amparo was relaunched following the arrival as culinary adviser of Martín Berasategui, one of the most outstanding young chefs to emerge from the Basque Country in recent years. Several intimate dining areas are laid out on different levels around a covered interior courtyard. Choose from the prawn and wild mushroom salad, the white tuna and lobster mousse or the grilled turbot with spinach and a shellfish-and-saffron coulis. The menu also includes a selection of choice cuts of meat. Luis Miguel Martín, one of the best sommeliers in Madrid, runs a well-stocked wine cellar that includes bottles of *prioratos* and *riberas*, some of the latest labels to cause a stir.

La Paloma (30)

Jorge Juan 39, 28001 ☎ 91 576 86 92

M *Goya, Principe de Vergara* ***Creative gourmet cuisine*** ●●● *Mon.–Sat. 1.30–4pm, 9–11.45pm; closed Easter week, Aug., public holidays*

Segundo Alonso was head chef at El Amparo, but has now opened his own restaurant nearby. La Paloma is less luxurious, and not as beautifully decorated, but the menu is less expensive, while the service is impeccable, and Alonso's cooking is as robust and appealing as ever. This undisputed master of variety meats – notably pigs' trotters – excels equally at wood pigeon stuffed with foie gras, lasagna with spider crab and spinach and watercress coulis. He also creates some mouthwatering desserts.

Teatriz (31)

Hermosilla 15, 28001 ☎ 91 577 53 79

M *Serrano* ***Italian cuisine*** ●●● *daily 1.30–4pm, 9pm–1am; closed in Aug.* Y

A fashionable restaurant where many of the regulars are being squeezed out by crowds of newcomers visiting this old theater – often less for its superb cuisine than for its extraordinary modern decor, designed by Philippe Starck in the early 1990s. Not least among its wonders must be a visit to the *servicios* (W.C.s), in the center of which stands a throne-like fountain of gold, marble and silver, all bathed in a bluish light – you could be forgiven for thinking this was a nightclub.

Not forgetting

■ **La Trainera (32)** Lagasca 60, 28001 ☎ 91 576 05 75 ●●●●
A rustic tasca serving up excellent seafood. A good Jabugo (cured ham) for meat-lovers, plus langoustines, sole and turbot, all delicately prepared.

■ **El Fogón (33)** Hôtel Wellington, Villanueva 34, 28001 ☎ 91 575 44 00 ●● *A good hotel restaurant serving up classic Spanish dishes. Service is smooth.*

■ Where to stay ➡ 24
■ Where to shop ➡ 130
➡ 138 ➡ 140 ➡ 144

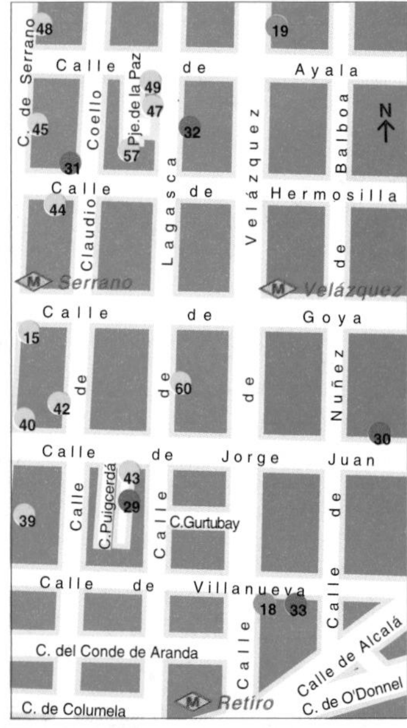

29

31

The Teatriz (above) was designed by Philippe Starck, the French architect and interior designer, who attaches great symbolic importance to shapes and spaces.

In the area

Goya is a large upmarket residential district, much of it built in the early 1900s. Its northern perimeter is marked by a splendid plaza dedicated to Salamanca – the man behind this urban grid-plan. The district stretches south to Retiro Park, and is also the most direct route to the bullring.

Where to eat

El Buey I (34)

General Pardiñas 10, 28001 ☎ 91 431 44 92

M *Príncipe de Vergara* ***Grills*** ● ▭ ◷ *daily 1–4pm, 9pm–midnight*

Despite its origin as a 'formula' restaurant, El Buey I has managed to rise above the negative connotations of such a label, as the clientele attests. The long, narrow dining room, resembling a railroad dining-car, is always packed. Diners flock here for the tender slabs of beef roasted over a wood fire, served up in unusually generous portions. A good *estofado de ternera* (beef stew) helps vary the meat theme, but beef is not the only ingredient on the menu. There is onion soup as a starter, a choice of specials (the game and mushroom lasagna is excellent), and lemon sorbet to finish off with, all washed down with a good Duero *ribera* house wine.

Combarro (35)

José Ortega y Gasset 40, 28001 ☎ 91 577 82 72 ➠ 91 435 95 12

M *Nuñez de Balboa* ***Fish and shellfish*** ●●●●● ▭ ◷ *Mon.–Sat. 1–4.30pm, 8pm–midnight; Sun. 7pm–2am* ⧉ *Reina Mercedes 12, 28020 Tel. 91 554 77 84 Fax. 91 534 25 01*

Did the stone for the façade really come from Galicia? It did according to Manuel Domínguez Limeres who, after almost twenty years in the north of the city where he has won the acclaim of the profession, has opened a second restaurant under the same name. The new Combarro merely enhances his reputation. The very freshest seasonal produce is meticulously prepared to create traditional Galician dishes – from baked bass to *coquilles Saint-Jacques* – while the vast wine cellar is well stocked with excellent French and Spanish wines.

Castelló 9 (36)

Castelló 9, 28001 ☎ / ➠ 91 435 91 34

M *Príncipe de Vergara* ***Modern Spanish cuisine*** ●●● ▭ ◷ *Mon.–Sat. 1.30–4pm, 9pm–midnight; closed Easter week, public holidays*

Castelló 9 provides a smart setting in which to sample Franco-Spanish food in the style of the Jockey genre ➡ 44. For particular specialties, try the wild-mushroom omelette with lobster or the hake tartare with caviar; neither will disappoint.

El Pescador (37)

José Ortega y Gasset 75, 28006 ☎ 91 402 12 90 ➠91 401 30 26

M *Lista* ***Fish and shellfish*** ●●●● ▭ ◷ *Mon.–Sat. 1–4pm, 8.30pm–midnight; closed Easter week, Aug.*

The rustic setting of El Pescador, with fishing nets hanging from the ceiling, conjures up the dockside taverns of Spain's northern ports. Here, you can sample the same seafood cooking as at O'Pazo ➡ 56, but at slightly lower prices. Enormous fresh sole served up *lenguado Evaristo*-style is unbeatable.

Where to stay ➥ 24
After dark ➥ 70 ➥ 74 ➥ 82 What to see ➥ 98

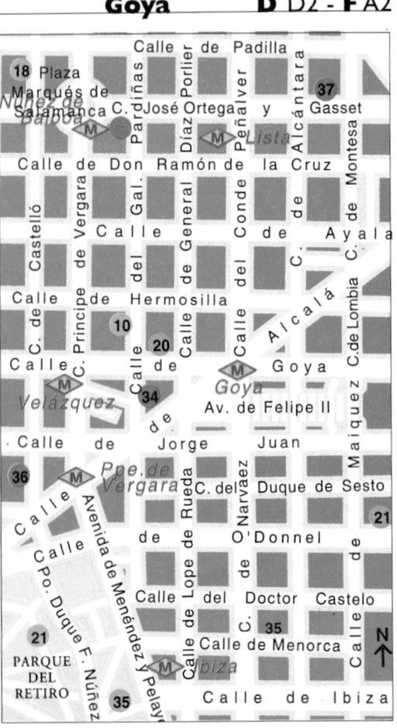

37

37

In the area

An extension of the shopping district of Serrano, this is the most attractive section of the Castellana. ■ Where to stay ➡ 24 ➡ 26 ➡ 28 ■ After dark ➡ 68 ➡ 70 ➡ 72 ➡ 74 ➡ 80 ■ What to see ➡ 106 ■ Where to shop ➡ 130 ➡ 140

Where to eat

Suntory (38)

Paseo de la Castellana 36-38, 28046 ☎ 91 577 37 34 ➠ 91 577 44 55

Ⓜ *Rubén Darío* ***Japanese cuisine*** ●●●● ▭ ⏲ *Mon.–Sat. 1.30–3.30pm, 8.30–11.30pm; closed public holidays*

With its minimalist décor and maximally attentive service, this exceptional restaurant is a worthy ambassador of the famous Japanese chain which now has branches worldwide. Talented chef Ken Sato presides over three different dining areas (sushi bar, Teppan Yaki, Shabu-Shabu). The superlative quality of the fish and shellfish in the local markets is a source of delight to Japanese chefs in Madrid, and allows them to create exquisite sushi, red tuna sashimi and Mediterranean-prawn tempura. An unforgettable experience, even though it is an expensive one.

Pedro Larumbe (39)

Serrano 61, 28001 ☎ 91 575 11 12 ➠ 91 576 60 19

Ⓜ *Rubén Darío, Núñez de Balboa* ***Creative cuisine*** ●●●● ▭ ⏲ *Mon.–Fri. 1.30–4pm, 9pm–midnight; Sat. 9pm–midnight; closed public holidays*

Pedro Larumbe, the Navarrese chef who used to preside over the kitchen at the Cabo Mayor ➡ 64, now has his own restaurant, with his own name. The three dining rooms (the stunning Patio Andaluz, the Salón Pompeyano and the Salón Fundador) have retained the *belle époque* interior of the former headquarters of the *ABC* newspaper ➡ 130. The cuisine is appropriately *fin de siècle* too: warm lobster salad with almond mayonnaise or casserole of *kokotxas* (hake cheeks). The wine list is good, if still on the young side.

Le Divellec (40)

Hotel Villa Magna, Paseo de la Castellana 22, 28046
☎ 91 576 75 00 ➠ 91 431 22 86

Ⓜ *Rubén Darío, Serrano* ***French cooking, fish and shellfish*** ●●●●● ▭ ⏲ *daily 1–4pm, 8.30–11.30pm*

The Hyatt chain chose Jacques le Divellec to relaunch the Berceo, at the Hotel Villa Magna, making it one of the most attractive dining venues in Madrid. Decked out in wood, deep-blue fabrics and beautiful Chinese lamps, its magnificent banquet rooms have breathtaking views of the city. After Thierry Buffeteau, it is now Frédéric Fétiveau who has embraced the challenge of creating a seafood-based, French-style cuisine in a city renowned for its fish and shellfish. Since his arrival in 1996 the restaurant has developed innovative dishes such as oven-baked mullet with eggplant and pine-nut ravioli and a julienne of crisp chives.

Not forgetting

■ **La Giralda III (41)** Maldonado 4, 28006 ☎ 91 577 77 62 ●●●●
Fried fish and Andalusian dishes served up in a relaxed décor. Cuisine similar to that of nearby Giralda I (Claudio Coello 24): fluffy rice with clams or hake in sherry.

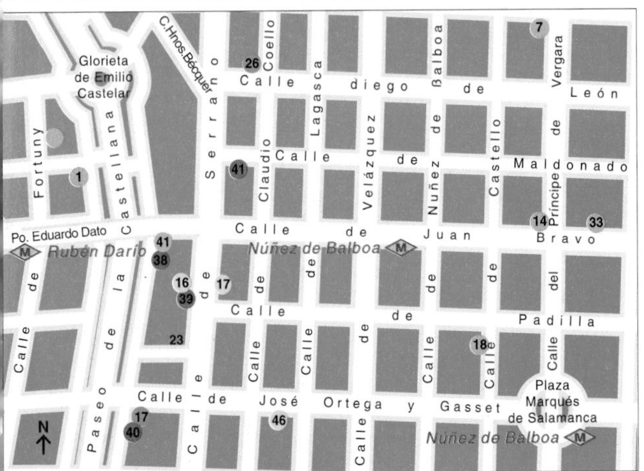

The Pedro Larumbe with its stately entrance hall, sophisticated Salón Fundador and banqueting area, La Redacción.

39

39

40

40

In the area

The three most desirable neighborhoods – Salamanca, Chamberí and Chamartín – converge on the verdant Plaza del Doctor Marañón. The area combines noisy thoroughfares and peaceful oases, such as the area around the Museo Nacional de Ciencías Naturales, or the tiny garden of

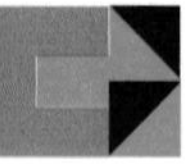

Where to eat

Zalacaín (42)

Álvarez de Baena 4, 28006 ☎ 91 561 48 40 ➟ 91 561 47 32

Rubén Darío, Gregorio Marañón ***Haute cuisine*** ●●●●● *Mon.–Fri. 1.30–3.45pm, 9–11.45pm; Sat. 9–11.45pm; closed Easter week, Aug., public holidays*

Since the Zalacaín opened in 1974 it has been the undisputed leader among the top restaurants in Madrid. Although in its early days it cut a radical figure in what was then a traditional field, chef Benjamín Urdiaín's cuisine is today regarded as classic. The interior is reminiscent of a rich 19th-century bourgeois residence, the service is impeccable, and the intelligent wine advice of Custodio Zamarra is a bonus. Memorable culinary encounters include hake sprinkled with thyme, warm salad of young pigeon and foie gras, turbot on a soubise of wild mushrooms and herb butter, crunchy chocolate and warm pineapple desert – each dish is presented with care. The prospect of dining on the new veranda is a pleasant additional attraction.

El Bodegón (43)

Pinar 15, 28006 ☎ 91 562 88 44 / 91 562 31 37 ➟ 91 562 97 25

Rubén Darío, Gregorio Marañón ***Modern Basque cuisine*** ●●●●● *Mon.–Fri. 1.30–4pm, 9pm–midnight; Sat. 9pm–midnight; closed public holidays, Aug.*

The elegant yet simple cuisine of Hilario Arbelaitz, who advises El Bodegón from his peaceful retreat in the Basque province of Guipúzcoa (in Oyarzun, Zuberoa), is interpreted admirably in Madrid by chef José Machado. The modern paintings of proprietor Plácido Arango, one of Spain's great collectors, are a treat, while the menu offers a mouthwatering feast for the palate. Snout of Zuberoa veal, soft-boiled eggs on pickled vegetables, oven-baked hake with red pepper coulis or mille feuille with creamed rice and cinnamon ice-cream are on a par with the masterpieces of the Centro Nacional de Arte Reina Sofia ➡ 98.

Belagua (44)

Hotel Santo Mauro, Zurbano 36, 28010
☎ 91 319 69 00 ➟ 91 308 54 77

Alonso Martínez ***Modern Basque-Navarran cuisine*** ●●●●● *Mon.–Sat. 1.30–3.30pm, 8.30–11pm; closed Easter week, public holidays* ➡ 68

A magnificent town-house interior ➡ 22 with postmodern touches. The cuisine varies with chefs. Several special dishes are worth a mention: foie gras sautéd with celery and redcurrants, partridge *en escabeche* (marinated in vinegar with bay leaves) and veal snout with fried chickpeas. In summer the restaurant opens its pleasant terrace. A word of caution: prices are steep.

Not forgetting

■ **Doña (45)** Zurbano 59, 28010 ☎ 91 319 25 51 ● *A delightfully roguish cuisine reminiscent of the Casa Benigno* ➡ *58*. *In 1996, the Doña changed its décor and its menu which became resolutely Mediterranean. The lobsters, prawns and sardines prepared by chef Emilio Serrano are complemented by one of the 89 Spanish wines from the well-stocked cellar.*

the Museo Sorolla. ■ Where to stay ➥ 22 ➥ 26 ➥ 28 ■ After dark ➥ 68 ➥ 70 ■ What to see ➥ 106

44 The gardens of the Santo Mauro (above) provide the Belagua with a superb summer setting. At tables under the white pergola you can have a full meal, while on the terrace you can sample items from the *pica pica* menu (tapas ➥ 70).

In the area

To the east, Glorieta Cuatro Caminos, once a working-class neighborhood, is now home to the middle classes. To the west, the university district is now surrounded by a new business zone.

■ Where to stay ➡ 28 ■ After dark ➡ 82 ■ What to see ➡ 102

Where to eat

Las Cuatro Estaciones (46)

Paseo San Francisco de Sales 41, 28003
☎ 91 553 63 05 ➠ 91 553 32 98

M *Guzmán el Bueno* ***Creative gourmet cuisine*** ●●●● *June–Sep: Mon.–Fri. 1.30–4pm, 9pm–midnight / Oct.–May: Mon.–Fri. 1.30–4pm, 9pm–midnight, Sat. 9pm–midnight / closed Jan. 1, Easter week, Aug.*

Francisco Arias reigns over this modern, flower-decked dining space. Although it opened in 1981, the somber colors give it the air of a 1970s disco, but dancing is far from the thoughts of the diners as they tuck into some of the best food in Madrid, served up by young Francisco Vicente. From ravioli with asparagus to bull's tail with breadcrumbs and sautéd potatoes, or cod cased in pastry, the choice is wide-ranging and imaginative. Impeccable service at all times.

Las Batuecas (47)

Avenida Reina Victoria 17, 28003 ☎ 91 554 04 52

M *Guzmán el Bueno, Cuatro Caminos* ***Spanish cuisine*** ● *Mon.–Fri. 1–4pm, 9–11pm; Sat. 1–4pm*

The building and its interior are unremarkable, but the wholesome and unpretentious cuisine are certainly noteworthy. This *casa de comidas* (literally, 'meal house') has proved itself time and again. Las Batuecas opened its doors in 1954 and has survived by virtue of its above-average *comidas* – a culinary genre that, sadly, is becoming increasingly rare. The clientele remains faithful from one generation to the next, dining out here on home cooking at low prices: traditional specialties include fried whiting, squid in its own ink, omelette with potatoes (*tortilla española*) and asparagus accompanied by *callos* (tripe) *a la madrileña*. A first-class eatery.

San Mamés (48)

Bravo Murillo 88, 28003 ☎ 91 534 50 65

M *Cuatro Caminos* ***Spanish cuisine*** ●●● *Mon.–Fri. 1.30–4pm, 8.30–11pm; Sat. 2.30–4pm; closed public holidays, Aug.*

Nine tables are crammed into two small rooms decorated with multi-colored *azulejos* (ceramic tiles): signs that this is a good, honest *tasca* ➡ 36. Santiago García, however, is not content with serving up basic *tasca* cuisine. Occasionally too grand (take the fillet with duck liver, for example), the cooking is perfect when it relies on regional recipes: hotpot of haricot beans, black pudding and chorizo from Ávila, or sautéd meadow mushrooms and tripe *a la madrileña*.

Not forgetting

■ **Sal Gorda (49)** Beatríz de Bobadilla 9, 28040 ☎ 91 553 95 06 ●
The dining area resembles a bourgeois dining room and the cuisine is suitably in keeping: superb menestra *of fresh vegetables, excellent roast beef,* bacalao ajoarriero *(salt cod with garlic) and apple tart. Service is attentive, and the prices reasonable.*

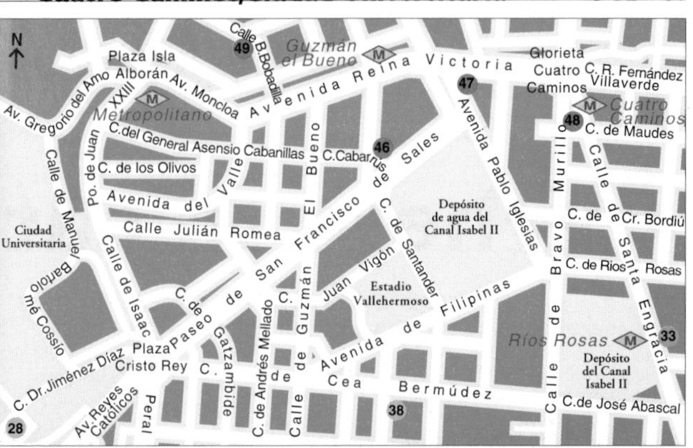
N
Plaza Isla
Alborán
Av. Gregorio del Amo
Av. Moncloa
Avenida Reina Victoria
Calle B.Bobadilla
Guzmán el Bueno
Glorieta Cuatro Caminos
C. R. Fernández Villaverde
Cuatro Caminos
C. de Maudes
Juan XXIII
Metropolitano
C.del General Asensio Cabanillas
C.Cabarrús
C. de los Olivos
Po. de Juan
Calle de Manuel Bartolomé Cossío
Ciudad Universitaria
Avenida del Valle
Calle Julián Romea
El Bueno
San Francisco de Sales
Avenida Pablo Iglesias
Depósito de agua del Canal Isabel II
Calle Bravo Murillo
C. de Cr. Bordiú
C. de Ríos Rosas
Calle de Santa Engracia
Calle de Isaac Peral
C. de Santander
Juan Vigón
Estadio Vallehermoso
Avenida de Filipinas
Ríos Rosas
Depósito del Canal Isabel II
C.de José Abascal
C. de Andrés Mellado
Calle de Guzmán
C. Gatzambide
Cea Bermúdez
Plaza Cristo Rey
C. Dr. Jiménez Díaz
Av. Reyes Católicos
28
33
38
46
47
48
49

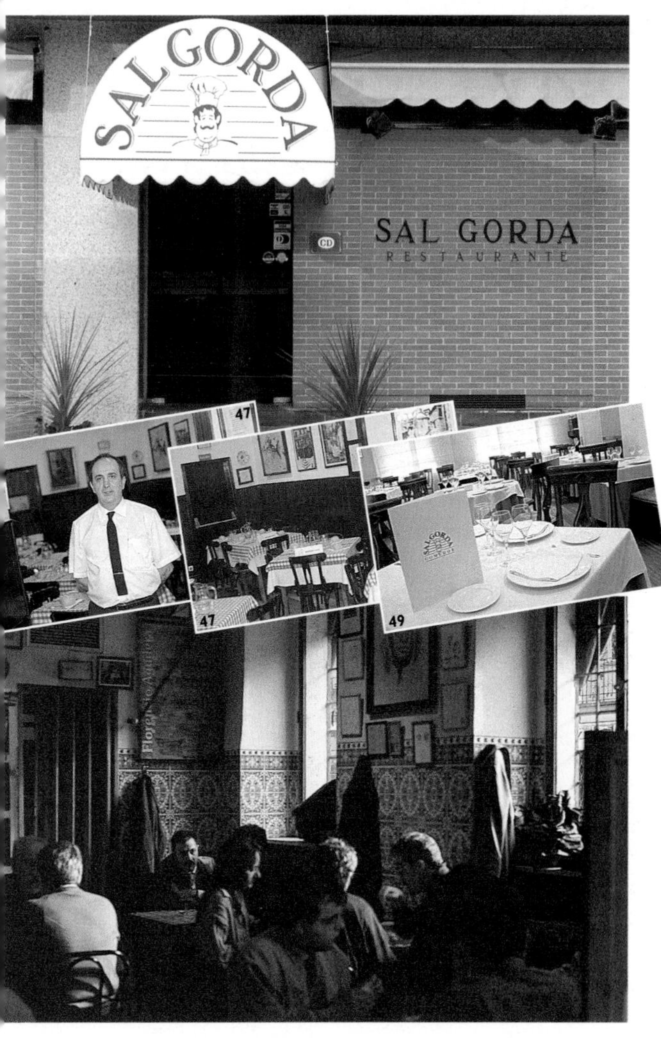
SALGORDA
SAL GORDA
RESTAURANTE
47
47
49

In the area

This immense ministerial complex, begun in the 1930s and completed under General Franco, together with the Azca commercial complex, its contemporary equivalent, form the hub of the modern city's expansion. The 'Manhattan of Madrid', this second city center is where the

Where to eat

O'Pazo (50)

Reina Mercedes 20, 28020 ☎ 91 553 23 33 ➠ 91 554 90 72

Ⓜ *Nuevos Ministerios, Alvarado* ***Fish and seafood*** ●●●● ▭ ◷ *Mon.–Sat. 1–4pm, 8.30pm–midnight; closed in Aug.*

Evaristo García – a fishmonger in his youth and now a big name in Spain's upmarket fish trade – supplies the best restaurants in the land. In this English-style dining room, one corner of which is a library, he is in his element. His chef Francisco Monje prepares simple, perfectly cooked fish and shellfish. The oven-baked turbot with olive oil and vinegar is exquisite.

Goizeko Kabi (51)

Comandante Zorita 37, 28020 ☎ 91 533 01 85 ➠ 91 533 02 14

Ⓜ *Alvarado* ***Basque cuisine*** ●●●●● ▭ ◷ *June 16–Sep. 15: Mon.–Fri. 1.30–4pm, 8.30pm–midnight, Sat. 8.30pm–midnight / Sep. 16–June 15: Mon.–Sat. 1.30–4pm, 8.30pm–midnight*

The Madrid branch of the famous Bilbao restaurant. The squid with onions, red meat, fried hake or woodcock roasted in Jesús Santos' old brandy are in the best Biscay tradition. English-style décor, but a small room. Book in advance.

Gaztelupe (52)

Comandante Zorita 32, 28020 ☎ 91 534 90 28 ➠ 91 554 65 66

Ⓜ *Nuevos Ministerios, Estrechos* ***Rotisserie, Basque specialties*** ●●● ▭ ◷ *June 16–Sep. 15: Mon.–Sat. 1.30–4pm, 8.30pm–midnight, Sun. 1.30–4pm / Sep. 16–June 15: Mon.–Sat. 1.30–4pm, 8.30pm–midnight*

The emphasis here is on the spectacular – or, if you like, 'Hollywood' – version of the popular Biscay inns, with all the expected classics of the genre: tender kidney beans from Tolosa, *zancarrón* (ragout) of veal, *marmitako* (a soup of tuna, potatoes and green peppers), and rice pudding. Very good wines.

Babel (53)

Alonso Cano 60, 28003 ☎ 91 553 08 27

Ⓜ *Ríos Rosas* ***Armenian specialties, grilled meats*** ●● ▭ ◷ *Mon.–Fri. 1.30–4pm, 8.30pm–midnight; Sat. 8.30pm–midnight; closed Aug.*

The regulars know what to expect with Armik Hamparzoumian: perfect roasts of Galician beef, which have made this one of Madrid's best meat-eating establishments, and exotic hors d'oeuvres, such as the tender Armenian-style eggplants. Good red wines.

Not forgetting

■ **Da Nicola (54)** Orense 4, 28020 ☎ 91 555 76 37 ● *Huge underground premises offering good, authentic Italian cuisine at low prices.*

■ **Alborán (55)** Ponzano 39, 28003 ☎ 91 399 21 50 ●● *A tiny dining room in which to enjoy good Andalusian seafood.*

multinational corporations are located. ■ After dark ➥ 86 ■ What to see ➥ 108

Restaurante GOIZEKO KABI ANTES GAZTELUBIDE

51

55

51

O'Pazo (above) is among the fish and seafood restaurants that have earned Madrid its gastronomic reputation. Though situated at the center of the Iberian peninsula, nearly 200 miles from the nearest sea, Madrid is considered by seafood aficionados to be the best 'port' in the country.

In the area

From 1930 until 1970 this was an inner suburb consisting of *colonias*, or small developments of detached houses. Despite being engulfed by the city, these still survive, lending the area a touch of greenery and an air of calm. ■ Where to stay ➡ 32 ■ After dark ➡ 74

Where to eat

Príncipe y Serrano (56)

Serrano 240, 28016 ☎ 91 458 62 31 ➡ 91 458 86 76

Ⓜ *Concha Espina, Colombia* ***Modern Castilian cuisine*** ●●●● ▭ ◷
Mon.–Fri. 2–4pm, 8.30pm–midnight; Sat. 8.30pm–midnight; closed in Aug. ✪

The view of lawns and flower beds, seen through the restaurant's bay window, make it difficult to believe that you are dining in central Madrid. Service is attentive, the setting classic and luxurious, and yet Príncipe y Serrano is still affordable, thanks to intelligent management by Salvador Gallego's two daughters. Gallego, the 'guru' of haute cuisine in the Sierra of Madrid, keeps a discreet eye on this, the second of his family establishments. The cuisine is simple yet sophisticated, in the very best Spanish tradition – try the *txangurro* (spider crab cocktail), or boned oxtail in flaky pastry. The cellar is interesting, with some very good and unusual Iberian wines, such as Veigadares, a vat-fermented white wine from Galicia.

Casa Benigna (57)

Benigno Soto 9, 28002 ☎ 91 413 33 56 ➡ 91 416 93 57

Ⓜ *Concha Espina* ***Mediterranean cuisine and Scandinavian specialties*** ●●●● ▭ ◷ *daily 1.30–4pm, 9.30–11.45pm*

The bright colors of this simple bistro and the landscape paintings on the wall divert attention from the low ceiling, which might otherwise seem oppressive. By the side of his mother, ever present beside the stoves, Norberto Jorge (who comes from Alicante but has lived for 20 years in Norway and still commutes between Madrid and Oslo) offers some of the most exquisitely prepared dishes in town. The dual influence – resulting in dishes that could be termed Hispano-Scandinavian – produces a unique menu. For instance, the marinated herring with horseradish contrasts with sumptuous vegetarian paellas, prawns *en papillote* and scampi *al ajillo* (in garlic mayonnaise). There is always an excellent fish of the day and the international wine list includes some interesting finds at a democratic range of prices.

La Atalaya (58)

Joaquín Costa 31, 28002 ☎ 91 562 87 45

Ⓜ *República Argentina* ***Cantabrian cuisine*** ●● ▭ ◷ *Tue.–Sat. 1–4.30pm, 9pm–midnight; Mon. 1–4pm; closed public holidays and one week in Aug.*

The walls of La Atalaya are covered with modern paintings – the owners come from Santander, a city where virtually every restaurant and bar resembles an art gallery. The atmosphere is restrained but hospitable and the cuisine comes straight from Spain's verdant north, with specialties such as *maganos* (minuscule squid) prepared with onions, and fried anchovies stuffed with *piquillos*. At lunchtime, La Atalaya offers a cheap but interestingly authentic menu, based on the rustic dishes of Cantabria (the region south of the Bay of Biscay in the province of Santander). Choose a Thursday or a Saturday for your visit in order to savor *cocido montañés*, a hearty cabbage soup with haricot beans, sausage and black pudding.

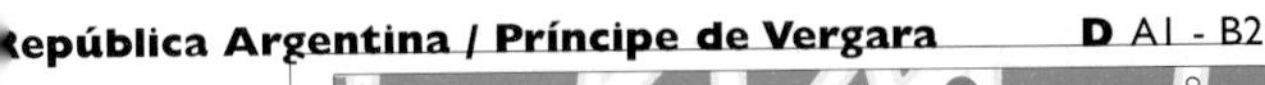

What to see ➥ 108
Where to shop ➥ 142

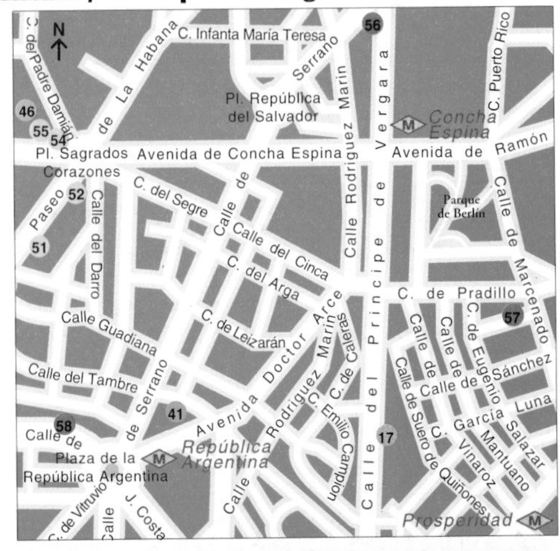

Norberto Jorge runs the Casa Benigna ('gentle house') like the Sancho, his other Oslo restaurant, with a master's hand. Here he is the chef as well as the owner, and sometimes even provides the evening's entertainment by playing the guitar.

57

58

58

In the area
The Palacio de Congresos and the immense Bernabéu football stadium, home of Real Madrid, extend the city northward. The shops of the Castellana and of the streets running parallel rival those of the Serrano district. ■ Where to stay ➡ 30 ■ After dark ➡ 80

Where to eat

El Comité (59)

Plaza de San Amaro 8, 28020 ☎ 91 571 87 11 ➡ 91 435 43 27

M *Santiago Bernabéu* ***Creative gourmet cuisine*** ●●● *Mon.–Fri. 1.30–4pm, 9pm–midnight; Sat. 9pm–12.30am; closed in Aug.*

Old photos of revolutionary parties and women's charitable committees adorn the walls of this bistro, where Agnès Masso and her French chef Claude Maison d'Arblay offer elegant dishes to a devoted clientele. These include monkfish with mascarpone and a red wine sauce and julienne of fried pears, followed by hazelnut Charlotte with a coffee-flavored coulis.

La Tahona (60)

Capitán Haya 21, 28020 ☎ 91 555 04 41 ➡ 91 556 62 02

M *Cuzco* ***Castilian cuisine*** ●● *Mon. –Sat. 1–4pm, 9pm–midnight; Sun. 1–4pm; closed in Aug.*

Madrid has several Hollywood-style restaurants, but La Tahona, designed to resemble a basilica, is inimitable. A branch of the restaurant chain created in Aranda de Duero, and home to tender, Castilian milk-fed lamb, the place is itself a temple dedicated to the glory of this traditional Spanish roast.

Príncipe de Viana (61)

Manuel de Falla 5, 28036 ☎ 91 457 15 49 ➡ 91 457 52 83

M *Santiago Bernabéu* ***Basque and Navarin cuisine*** ●●●●● *Mon.–Fri. 1–4pm, 9–11.45pm; Sat. 9–11.45pm; closed Easter week, Aug., public holidays*

Ramón Quintanilla, the chef who trained here before launching another successful restaurant, has returned to the fold in order to maintain the highest quality of popular cuisine in the city. In this distinctive and cheerful setting, the *menestra* of fresh spring vegetables and oven-baked fish merit the highest culinary accolades. Attentive service.

El Cenachero (62)

Manuel de Falla 8, 28036 ☎ 91 457 59 04

M *Santiago Bernabéu* ***Mediterranean cuisine*** ●● *Mon.–Fri. 1.30–4pm, 9.30pm–midnight; Sat. 9.30pm–midnight; closed in Aug.*

This kind of small, unpretentious restaurant, perfect for an intimate dinner, is rare in Madrid. El Cenachero offers the flavors of maritime Andalusia (in Malaga a *cenachero* is a port peddler), interpreted delicately by chef Alberto Chicote: broad beans and snow peas with smoked duck breast, tomatoes stuffed with crab, tuna with a compote of tomato and basil, and sea bream with oven-roasted vegetables. Exceptional quality at reasonable prices.

Not forgetting

■ **Asador de Roa (63)** Pintor Juan Gris 5, 28039 ☎ 91 555 39 28 ●●
Castilian cuisine. Specialties: milk-fed oven-roasted lamb and roast piglet.

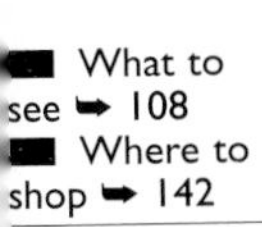
What to see ➥ 108
Where to shop ➥ 142

59

0

2

60

'...in true Spanish inns, naturally you can eat and drink, but you also enjoy what others bring to the place.'
Abraham Bengio

In the area

The Ciudad Lineal – a model district of villas and broad, pine-shaded avenues dating from the early 1900s – has been dramatically altered by sprawling urban developments. Mayor Arturio Soria would no longer recognize his own town. Despite this, the district is still very pleasant.

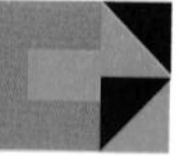

Where to eat

Casa d'a Troya (64)

Emiliano Barral 14, 28043 ☎ 91 416 44 55

M *Avenida de La Paz* ***Galician cuisine*** ●● *Mon.–Sat. 1.30–3.30pm, 8.30–11pm; closed July 15–Aug. 31, Christmas, public holidays*

With the exception of a fine rustic-style slate façade, the setting is unremarkable and resembles that of an ordinary restaurant in a new suburb. However, appearances are deceptive because this is a high temple of Galician tradition. Pilar Vila serves octopus, *camarones* (small shrimps), hake, pork knuckle with turnip tops, and almond tart of the highest quality, yet at reasonable prices, using produce sent daily from northwestern Spain. Understandably the regular clientele is devoted so be sure to book well in advance.

La Misión (65)

José Silva 22, 28043 ☎ 91 519 24 63 ➠ 91 416 26 93

M *Arturo Soria* ***Classic Basque cuisine*** ●●●● *Mon.–Fri. 1.30–4pm, 9pm–midnight; Sat. 9pm–midnight; closed Easter week, Aug.*

The charming décor, complete with pink stucco and exposed beams, conjures up the image of a Spanish 17th-century mission in California. Yet the cuisine at La Misión makes no allusions to new-wave Californian cuisine. Indeed it is firmly rooted in Hispanic tradition, with a heavy Basque accent. Our gastronomic recommendation is the excellent oven-baked turbot, one of the star dishes on the menu.

Nicomedes (66)

Moscatelar 18, 28043 ☎ 91 388 78 28 ➠ 91 388 78 28

M *Arturo Soria* ***Estremaduran specialties, creative cuisine*** ●●● *Sun.–Mon. 1.30–4pm; Tue.–Sat. 1–4pm, 9–11pm*

A modern villa with huge bay windows opening onto a flower-filled garden, the restaurant of Elena and Concha Suárez has a strong New World flavor, with 1940s jazz playing gently in the background. The cuisine is thoroughly modern, and incorporates imaginative touches from the region of Extremadura. Especially memorable dishes include Iberian pork and the exquisitely soft farm cheese, *Torta del Casar*, made from ewe's milk. The service, presided over by the two sisters, is charming and friendly, and the cellar boasts a fine selection of many of the best 'new' Spanish wines.

Don Víctor (67)

Emilio Vargas 18, 2843 ☎ 91 415 47 47 ➠ 91 320 93 10

M *Arturo Soria* ***Fish, Galician cuisine*** ●●●●● *Mon.–Fri. 1–4.30pm, 9–11pm; Sat. 9–11pm; closed in Aug.*

Don Víctor's modern bistro is one of the few culinary options available in a new business district still badly served by restaurants. The Galician owners offer superb fish and excellent red meats roasted in a crust of coarse salt. The high quality is reflected in the check.

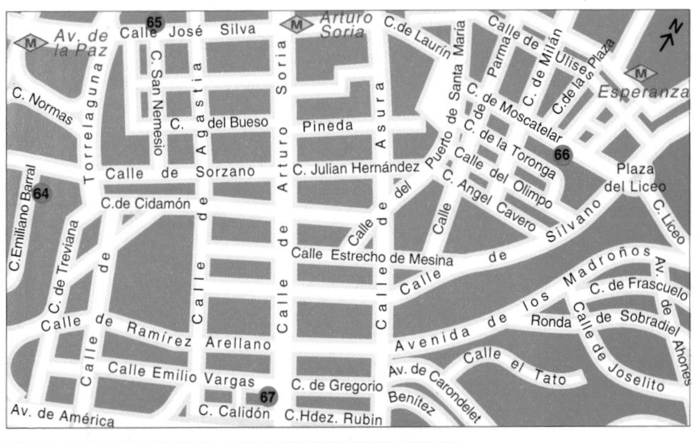

Av. de la Paz
Calle José Silva
Arturo Soria
C.de Laurín
Calle de Milán
Ulises
C.de la Plaza
Esperanza
C. Normas
Torrelaguna
C. San Nemesio
C. del Bueso
Agastia
Calle de Arturo Soria
Pineda
Calle de Asura
C. de Santa María
Parma
C. de Moscatelar
C. de la Toronga
Calle del Olimpo
C. Angel Cavero
C. Julian Hernández
Calle del Puerto de Mesina
Plaza del Liceo
C. Liceo
Silvano
C.Emiliano Barral
Calle de Sorzano
C.de Cidamón
C. de Treviana
Calle Estrecho de Mesina
Avenida de los Madroños
C. de Frascuelo
Calle de Sobradiel
Ahones
Ronda de Joselito
Calle de Ramírez Arellano
Calle Emilio Vargas
C. de Gregorio Benítez
Av. de Carondelet
Calle el Tato
C. Calidón
C.Hdez. Rubin
Av. de América
64
65
66
67

65

66

66

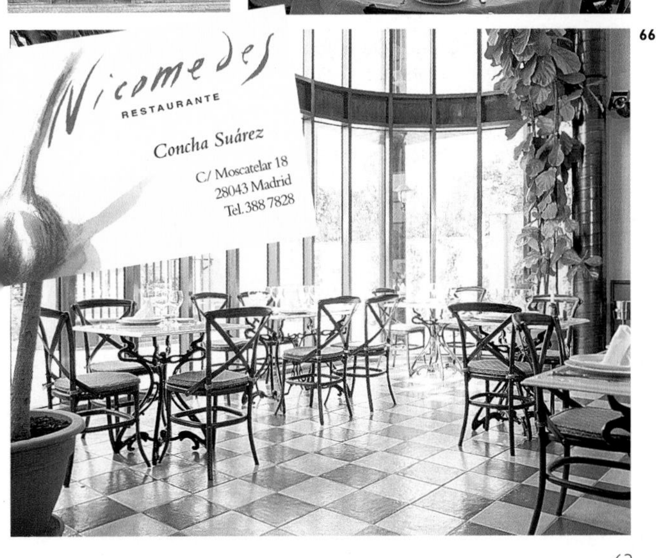

Nicomedes
RESTAURANTE
Concha Suárez
C/ Moscatelar 18
28043 Madrid
Tel.388 7828

In the area

The shaded streets of this quiet district are frequented mainly by office workers who, at various times of day, leave their work to chat or relax at the tables of the local terrace bars. ■ Where to stay ➡ 30 ➡ 32
■ After dark ➡ 70 ➡ 80

Where to eat

El Olivo (68)

General Gallegos 1, 28036 ☎ 91 359 15 35 ➡ 91 345 91 83

Ⓜ *Cuzco, Plaza de Castilla* **Mediterranean cuisine** ●●●● *Tue.–Sat. 1–4pm, 9pm–midnight; closed Aug. 15–30*

The vocation of this olive-green restaurant is clear: virgin olive oils and Xérèz wines constitute its main culinary theme. Born in Bordeaux and raised in Andalusia, Jean-Pierre Vandelle's Franco-Spanish background produces some superb results. Don't miss the springtime specialty, lamprey in Ribera del Duero wine, or the monkfish *a la plancha* (grilled on a hot plate) with a black olive coulis.

Aldaba (69)

Avenida Alberto Alcocer 5, 28036 ☎ 91 345 21 93 ➡ 91 350 83 03

Ⓜ *Cuzco* **Basque and Navarin cuisine** ●●●● *Mon.–Fri. 1–4pm, 9pm–midnight; Sat. 9pm–midnight; closed in Aug.*

This intimate little restaurant was renovated by the team from Zalacaín ➡ 52, headed by José Luis Pereira. It lays on some of the best cuisine in Madrid, with an emphasis on regional and market produce: cod salad with a compote of tomatoes and spiced oil, and lasagna of monkfish and king prawns with sage.

Cabo Mayor (70)

Juan Ramón Jiménez 37, 28036 ☎ 91 350 87 76 ➡ 91 359 16 21

Ⓜ *Cuzco* **Creative cuisine** ●●●● *Mon.–Sat. 1–4pm, 9pm–midnight; closed Easter week, Aug. 15–31, public holidays*

The cavernous, nautical-themed interior of this restaurant is decorated in the style of a Santander farmhouse. The son and daughter of founder Victor Merino maintain the tradition of modern regional cuisine, aided by chef Carlos Barasoain's passion for spices: try the turbot with asparagus and squid or supreme of young pigeon.

Asador Frontón (71)

Pedro Muguruza 8, 28036 ☎ 91 345 36 96

Ⓜ *Cuzco* **Basque grilled meats and fish** ●●● *Mon.–Sat. 1–4pm, 9pm–midnight; Sun. 1–4pm* *Jesús y María 1, 28012 ☎ (91) 369 23 25*

Madrid is a meat-eater's paradise. With its superb Basque-style grilled meats and slabs of beef, the Frontón is the front runner in this field. The fish is equally good. A busy and noisy atmosphere. Book ahead.

Not forgetting

■ **Sacha (72)** Hurtado de Mendoza 11, 28036 ☎ 91 345 59 52 ●● *Galician cuisine served up by Pitila Hormaechea and son Sacha: clams with creamed turnips, partridge with mushrooms and rice.*
■ **Alborada (73)** Henri Dunant 23, 28036 ☎ 91 359 18 42 ●● *From Tuesday to Saturday, simple, fresh ingredients and Mediterranean flavors prepared by the former chef of El Olivo.*

69

As you go down into the Cabo Mayor (below), look up at the bronze sculptures (left) of children preparing to leap into the water to fish out the coins thrown there by passers-by – a once-familiar scene in Santander.

70

72

71

La Filmoteca Española
International movies in the original language.
Cine Dore *Santa Isabel 3, 28012 ☎ (91) 369 11 25*

After dark

Listings magazines
To check out day-to-day cultural events:
La Guía del Ocio, *weekly from news-stands.*
¿ Que Hacer en Madrid ?, *free monthly from the tourist office in Plaza Mayor (bilingual Spanish-English).*

Open to all
There are no private clubs in Madrid. Some places try to discourage customers by putting up *aforo completa* (full) notices, but no door can resist the determined night owl.

'Vamos de juerga' say Madrileños as they prepare for a night on the town. Not too fond of private parties, they cram the countless bars. They say there are more bars in one Madrid neighborhood than in the whole of Switzerland.

Chocolate con churros
Follow an old city tradition and indulge in this late-night treat: long, crunchy fritters dunked in a steaming cup of thick hot chocolate.
Chocolatería San Ginés *Pasaje de San Ginés 5, 28013* ☎ *91 365 65 46*
Oct.–May: Tue.–Thur. 7pm–10pm; Fri.–Sun. 7pm–7am; July-Aug: Tue.–Sun. 10pm–7am; June, Sep, Tue.–Thur. Midnight–7am, Fri.–Sun. 7pm–7am.

49 Nights out

THE INSIDER'S FAVORITES

Cultural events calendar

May–June Madrid City Rock Festival *Mastertrax* ☎ *91 304 95 17*
Madrid Dance Festival *Información del Ayuntamiento* ☎ *010*
Summer (Sunday Concerts by the Banda Municipal in the Parque del Retiro) *Información del Ayuntamiento* ☎ *010*
July Johnny Walker Music Festival *Caja de Cataluña* ☎ *902 38 33 33*
July–Sep. Summer in the City *Información del Ayuntamiento* ☎ *010*
Sep.–Oct. Autumn Festival *Información del Ayuntamiento* ☎ *010*
Oct.–April Chamber and polyphonic music concerts *Auditorio Nacional de Música* ☎ *91 337 01 00*
Nov. Jazz festival *Caja de Cataluña* ☎ *902 38 33 33*

INDEX BY AREA

Basic facts

With the arrival of the first fine days of summer, which is always early in Madrid, the capital's inhabitants take to the streets, and re-acquaint themselves with their summer haunts. Chairs and parasols spill out onto the sidewalk as the *terrazas* re-open between April and June. This is

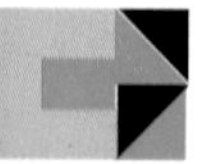

After dark

Terraza Bulevar (1)

Paseo de la Castellana 37, 28046 ☎ 91 308 51 45 / 91 308 52 58

Rubén Darío May 15–Sep. 30: daily noon–5am Serrano 41–45, 28001 ☎ (91) 578 18 65 ; Paseo de la Castellana 12, 28046

Summer visitors to Madrid are drawn inexorably to the colorful crowds filling the *terrazas* of the Castellana, the city's vital artery. Lately El Bulevar has become *the* spot to visit on a summer's night, frequented by stars and personalities such as Richard Gere, Michael Jackson and Samantha Fox. Any day of the week, however, the movers and shakers from the world of business, bullfighting, sports or showbiz come to drink here. After celebrity spotting at the Bulevar, wander down the Castellana for a drink at the terrace bars of the Bolero, Embassy or Castellana 8 ➡ 72. Here you can sample the beach-style holiday atmosphere of Madrid, complete with blaring music.

Fortuny (2)

Fortuny 34, 28010 ☎ 91 310 18 49

Rubén Dario daily 1.30pm–6am Mon.–Thur. 1.30–4pm, 9pm–12.30am; Fri.–Sun. 1.30–4pm, 9pm–1.30am ☎ 91 319 05 88

The Fortuny occupies a 19th-century mansion (1896) that offers a unique setting less than 100 yards from the Castellana. The three-story building, whose vast terrace holds up to 1,000 people, stands in a district of former private mansions that now house foreign embassies. Guests can simply enjoy a drink, dine in the lively restaurant or hold a private function. Since it opened in May 1997, Fortuny has been one of Madrid's most popular venues. From the vaguely to the seriously glamorous, as well as the simply curious, all come to enjoy the cool freshness of the magnificent garden.

Hotel Santo Mauro (3)

Zurbano 36, 28010 ☎ 91 319 69 00

Alonso Martínez May–Sep.: daily 10–3am Belagua ➡ 52

In summer the delightful garden of the hotel Santo Mauro ➡ 22 is transformed into a *terraza*. One part is reserved for restaurant diners, while the other contains a bar. Shaded by magnificent chestnut trees, this is one of the most elegant and intimate places for a romantic rendezvous in the city, or simply for an opportunity to enjoy a relaxed drink with friends.

Not forgetting

■ **Cafe de Oriente (4)** Plaza de Oriente 2, 28013 ☎ 91 541 39 74
In May this is one of the best terrazas in the city. Service is impeccable. A classic Madrileño café in a newly pedestrianized area.

■ **El Espejo (5)** Paseo de Recoletos 31, 28004 ☎ 91 308 23 47
Like the famous Café Gijon further down the Paseo, El Espejo terraza recreates the ambience of a belle-époque literary café. The splendid glass pavilion is worthy of admiration in its own right.

where the *Madrileño* puts the world to rights over a coffee or cool drink, and where the visitor can taste an authentic slice of Madrid life.

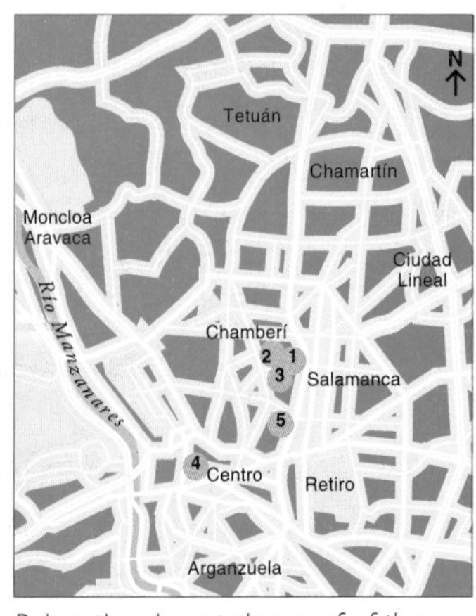

Below the elegant glass roof of the famous *belle-époque* pavilion of El Espejo, it is sometimes difficult to find a seat.

5

4

Basic facts

Various anecdotes are used to explain the origin of tapas. One theory is that *tapear* – getting a bite to eat – became popular in the reign of Charles III, when in the army it became obligatory to have something to eat with a drink in order to 'moderate' the effect of the alcohol.

After dark

José Luis (6)

Serrano 89-91, 28006 ☎ 91 563 09 58

Rubén Darío daily 9–1am Paseo de la Habana 4, 28036 ☎ 91 562 75 96; Paseo San Francisco de Sales 14-16, 28003 ☎ 91 442 67 90; Rafael Salgado 11, 28036 ☎ 91 458 80 28; Teatro Real ➡ 78

For years now, the tapas served up at José Luis have been an unmissable treat come snack-time. When you don't feel up to a full-blown meal and are looking for a relaxed atmosphere, there is always a José Luis nearby. The four branches in Madrid tend to be permanently packed, proof of the quality of the *pinchos* (literally, 'little pieces of something'), which are both varied and copious. Sirloin, hake, crab salad, fritters, salmon or potato *tortillas* are all popular, but the list is endless.

Handicap (7)

General Oráa 56, 28006 ☎ 91 562 21 59

Diego de León Mon.–Sat. 1–4pm, 8pm–1am; closed public holidays, Aug.

The owner was a dancer at the Paris Lido in the 1950s, has performed for the Queen of England and was a triumph at Las Vegas. A fan of French refinement, his restaurant resembles a tiny Parisian bistro. Yet this is not to say that Juan Contreras has turned his back on Spain when it comes to culinary matters, for it was he who introduced to Madrid those tiny baguettes, called *bocadillos* (then later *pulgas*), which serve as a base for smoked meats, pâtés, black pudding or sirloin steak with Dijon mustard. His 'astronaut potatoes' (fried potatoes with scrambled eggs)

11

9

Another, more simple, explanation is that to *tapear* is a natural urge for the Spanish.

and *Kung-fu* (marinaded tuna with mayonnaise and vinaigrette) have been a resounding success. The cramped premises can be a problem at busy times, but this is no reason to miss out on the experience.

Punto Cero (8)

Serrano 93, 28006
☎ 91 561 27 89

M *Rubén Darío, Avenida América*
daily 7–2am

A shopping street, a nearby business school, a pleasant owner and a wide range of *pinchos*, both hot and cold: all this explains why the Punto Cerro is full at 9pm every evening. Here, a glass of wine becomes a reason to *tapear*, which later on becomes an excuse for a full-blown meal. Outdoor seating between April and September – sometimes later – when the crowded *terraza* is noisy, but convivial.

Not forgetting

Cervecería Alemana (9) Plaza Santa Ana ☎ 91 429 70 33
To tapear *in this bar, or in the next-door Cerveceria Santa Ana or Naturbier, is one of the delights of Madrid.*

La Daniela (10) General Pardiñas 21, 28028 ☎ 91 575 23 29
An authentic Spanish taberna *serving excellent tapas: stuffed olives, bread rubbed with garlic or topped with fresh tomato.*

Las Cumbres (11) Avenida Alberto Alcocer 32, 28036
☎ 91 458 76 92 *To be sampled seated or at the bar:* Jabugo *(cured ham), oxtail, cheese, home-made fritters, squid, lettuce hearts with anchovies. A little corner of Andalucía!*

10

8

Basic facts

Every day of the week from about 8pm in the evening, when the tapas hour is over, hundreds of places open their doors to those wanting to *ir copas* (have a drink) and listen to some music. This is the time of the night when the *Madrileños* meet up with friends and launch into

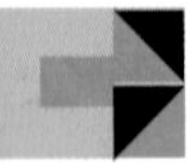

After dark

Cock (12)

Reina 16, 28004 ☎ 91 532 28 26

M *Gran Vía, Banco de España* ⌚ *Mon.–Thur. 7pm–3am, Fri.–Sat. 7pm–4am* ● *950 Ptas*

This cocktail bar never disappoints. This is partly due to its charming surroundings – the high ceiling and old oak furniture that are the dominant features of its elegant 1920s interior. The key to its success is also the *mojitos* and other delicious cocktails that can be sampled here. It attracts a mixed clientele from a spectrum that can range from politicians to actors of stage or screen.

Honky-Tonk (13)

Covarrubias 24, 28010 ☎ 91 445 68 86 ➠ 91 445 68 86

M *Bilbao, Alonso Martínez* ⌚ *daily 9pm–5am* ● *800 Ptas–900 Ptas* *Sun.–Fri. after midnight, rock, blues, fusion* *Honky-Tonk Café*

After nine years as one of the city's top venues, the Honky Tonk is still one of the best disco-bars in Madrid. Its formula: good cocktails and other drinks, live bands and exhibitions of photos and paintings. Its program satisfies lovers of country music, swing, jazz, rock or blues; as if this is not enough, it also features magicians and one-person shows. It attracts a regular crowd of sports personalities, actors and night owls, between the ages of 18 and 45.

El Viso Madrid (14)

Juan Bravo 31, 28006 ☎ 91 562 23 79 ➠ 91 562 23 79

M *Diego de Léon* ⌚ *daily 9pm–5am* ● *900 Ptas* *Wed. 10.30pm*

One of the latest bars to hit the scene. It was bought recently by the owners of the El Viso terrace bar, and the regular clientele followed. It is known less for its hi-tech décor than for the animated crowds jamming its entrance. Upstairs, there is a quiet area for chatting. The ground level is the place to parade or people-watch, and you can let your hair down on the downstairs dance floor.

Gayarre (15)

Paseo de la Castellana 118, 28046 ☎ 91 564 25 15

M *Nuevos Ministerios* ⌚ *Mon.–Thur. 6pm–3am; Fri., Sat. 6pm–4am* ● *1000 Ptas*

This former cinema opened as a bar in 1992. The spacious premises are decorated with bowls of fruit and rustic kitchen utensils and the candlelight and gentle background music combine to create an atmosphere that is popular with the over-35s. ★ Twice a week, but never the same day, a surprise buffet is served up free of charge.

Not forgetting

■ **Castellana 8 (16)** Paseo de la Castellana 8, 28046 ☎ 91 431 30 54 A *warm welcome and intimate ambience in this bar.*

animated conversations, setting the world to rights.

16

Basic facts
When it comes to classical music, Spain is known more for its opera than for its symphonic orchestras. Nowadays, however, the choice during the season (October to June) is seemingly limitless. Concerts are held almost daily, either in the capital's main concert halls or in more unusual

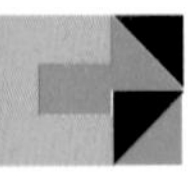

After dark

Auditorio Nacional de Música (17)
Príncipe de Vergara 146, 28002 ☎ 91 337 01 00

M *Cruz del Rayo* **Concerts** *7.30pm; 10.30pm* **Information** *daily 8am–10pm* **Box office** *Mon. 5–7pm, Tue.–Fri. 10am–5pm, Sat. 11am–1pm (for some concerts 100 tickets are on sale 1 hr before the show)* ● *4200–8100 Ptas* **Concerts Ibermusica** ☎ 91 359 09 64

Founded in 1988, the auditorium contains two halls, one for symphonic music and the other for chamber music, with 2200 and 700 seats respectively. In the former, which is almost rectangular in shape, the ceiling has been designed to achieve maximum acoustic effect, and to allow different sections of the orchestra to be heard more precisely. The semi-circular chamber hall is designed to maintain proximity between orchestra and audience. The National Auditorium is home to the Spanish National Orchestra (the *Orquestra Nacional de España,* or ONE) and its associated choir, who play here from October to June. In tandem, the group Ibermúsica organizes the *Orchestras del Mundo* between October and May, featuring major international orchestras. Though in theory reserved for season-ticket holders, some of the upmarket hotels should be able to procure tickets. Elsewhere in the capital, the *Pro-Música* cycle and programs at the Polytechnic, Complutense and Autónoma universities are usually of interest. Finally, the concerts organized by the *Orquestra Nacional de España* and the *Liceo de Cámara* between October and June offer music lovers of all types the opportunity to enjoy both chamber and polyphonic music.

Fundación Juan March (18)
Castelló 77, 28006 ☎ 91 435 42 40 ➠ 91 576 34 20

M *Núñez de Balboa* *Sep.–June : Mon.–Sat. 10am–2pm, 5.30–9pm; Sun., public holidays 10am–2pm* ● *free*

Renowned for its exhibitions of contemporary art, the Fundación Juan March, one of the leading cultural centers in the city, also hosts numerous chamber music concerts.

Círculo de Bellas Artes (19)
Marqués de Casa Riera 2, 28014 ☎ 91 360 54 00

M *Banco de España* **Exhibitions** *Tue.–Fri. 5–9pm; Sat. 11am–2pm, 5–9pm; Sun. 11am–2pm* ● *100 Ptas* **Movies, theater, concerts** *telephone or see the magazine* Minerva *for details* ● *prices vary*

This multifunctional cultural institution offers a literary café, exhibition spaces, an arts cinema, workshops and conferences, plays and top-notch concerts. Ask for a program.

Not forgetting
■ **Teatro Monumental (20)** Atocha 65, 28012 ☎ 91 429 81 19
Home of the Orchestra and Choir for Spanish Radio and Television (OCTRVE). Also used by the Orchestra and Choir of the Comunidad de Madrid.

venues. Check the programs of the major museums, for instance, as they occasionally host classical concerts.

Basic facts
Taking into consideration all the national, municipal, private and public venues in the capital, Madrid is home to more than 30 different theaters. This means that it is possible to take in a first-rate production every evening. The repertoire is sufficiently wide-ranging to accommodate all

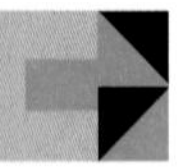

After dark

Teatro María Guerrero (21)

Tamayo y Baus 4, 28004 ☎ 91 310 29 49 ➠ 91 319 38 36

M *Chueca, Colón* **Performances** *Sep.–July: Tue.–Sat. from 8pm, Sun. from 7pm* **Box office** *Tue.–Sat. 11.30am–1.30pm, 5–8pm* **Reservations by telephone** *902 488 488* ● *1650 Ptas–2600 Ptas*

Inaugurated in 1885 as the Teatro de la Princesa, this building is one of the best examples in Madrid of a 19th-century wrought-iron structure. The classical façade conceals a neo-Mudéjar theater which can accommodate a large audience. When it was purchased by the Spanish State, the theater was renamed Teatro María Guerrero, after the great Spanish actress who performed here for many years in the early part of this century. It is now home to Spain's Centro Dramático Nacional. The program covers the different trends in international and contemporary Spanish drama. The theater basement has a café that is quiet and friendly, frequented by both actors and theatergoers.

Teatro Español (22)

Príncipe 25, 28012 ☎ 91 429 62 97 ➠ 91 429 62 50

M *Sevilla* **Performances** *Tue.–Thur., Sun. 7pm; Fri.–Sat. 7pm, 10.30pm* **Box office** *daily 11.30am–1.30pm, 5–8pm* ● *up to 2200 Ptas*

One of the oldest theaters in Europe, the Teatro Español is, with the María Guerrero, one of the most important theaters in the city. It was inaugurated as an open-air theater in 1583, and was known as the Corral de La Pacheca, or Corral del Príncipe. In 1745 it was given a roof, and was renamed Teatro del Príncipe. In 1849 it became the Teatro Español, and many of the new Romantic plays were premiered here. It became a municipal theater in 1975. In 1980 it was enlarged to accommodate 763 spectators. The program features contemporary Spanish works.

Teatro de la Comedia (23)

Príncipe 14, 28012 ☎ 91 521 49 31 ➠ 91 522 46 90

M *Sol* **Performances** *Sep.–June: Mon.–Tue., Thur.–Sat. 8pm; Sun. 7pm* **Box office** *daily 11.30am–1.30pm, 5–6pm* ● *from 1300 Ptas; Thur. –50%*

Housed in a 19th-century building, the Teatro de la Comedia is the home of Spain's Compañía Nacional de Teatro Clásico. This was created in order to fill a gap in the city's theater program – that of a sorely needed classical repertoire. As a result, since 1985 works by Spanish Golden Age authors such as Calderón de la Barca, Lope de Vega and Tirso de Molina have been resurrected in Madrid, and performed before the 619 spectators that the Teatro de la Comedia can accommodate.

Not forgetting

■ **Teatro de Bellas Artes (19)** Marqués de Casa Riera 2, 28014 ☎ 91 532 44 37 *A theater linked to the Círculo de Bellas Artes* ➠ *74.* *Run by director José Tamayo, it reflects both his personality and that of his troupe, the Campañía Lope de Vega, which performs also in major theaters around the country. A repertoire of Spanish authors.* ■ **Teatro Nuevo Apolo (24)** Plaza Tirso de Molina 1, 28012 ☎ 91 369 06 37 *Popular shows and musicals.*

tastes, from the traditional to the avant-garde.

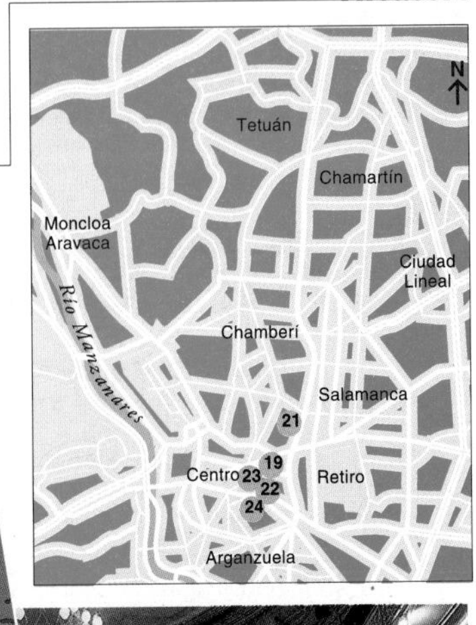

23

Luces de Bohemia by Don Ramón del Valle Inclán, directed by José Tamayo at the Teatro de Bellas Artes.

19

2

23

Basic facts

The *zarzuela* is a form of light opera unique to Spain and not to be missed. Like other Mediterranean countries, Spain has a strong vocal tradition and some superb singers. It excels equally at dance with the world-class Ballet Nacional de España.

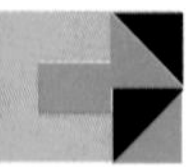

After dark

Teatro de la Zarzuela (25)

Jovellanos 4, 28014 ☎ 91 524 54 00 ➟ 91 429 71 57

M *Banco de España, Sevilla* **Performances** *Nov.–July: Tue.–Sun. 8pm* ● *1200 Ptas–4500 Ptas* **Box office** *daily noon–6pm; performance days noon–8pm*

This beautiful theater stages an exclusive program of *zarzuela*, the light romantic operetta so popular in Madrid. Its annual repertoire consists of a dozen or so carefully selected works (often repeated by popular demand) and at least one little-known piece. The scenery is often spectacular and the productions extremely imaginative. The theater also presents individual singers and organises series of *lieder*.

Teatro Real (26)

Plaza de Oriente 1, 28013 ☎ 91 516 06 60 ➟ 91 516 06 51

M *Opera* **Performances** *Oct.–July* **Box office** *daily 10am–2pm, 5–8pm* ● *Operas 2000 Ptas – 20000 Ptas; Recitals and concerts 500 Ptas – 5000 Ptas; Ballets 1000 Ptas – 16000 Ptas* *José Luis* ➡ *70* *every morning 300 Ptas*

Opened in 1850 by Queen Isabel II, the Teatro Real enjoyed its golden age during the second half of the 19th century. It was closed in 1925 and finally restored to its former glory in 1997 when it was entirely renovated. A multi-level scene mechanism enabling it to present three plays concurrently without having to change the sets has placed it at the cutting edge of technology and made it a world-class opera venue. It has a seating capacity of 1700 and excellent acoustics wherever you are sitting and whatever you are watching – opera, ballet or a concert. The Teatro Real also has a fashionable restaurant and tearoom, while its private rooms stage regular exhibitions of works of art loaned by the Museo del Prado ➡ 96, the Centro Nacional de Arte Reina Sofia ➡ 98 and the Patrimonio Nacional.

Teatro Calderón (27)

Atocha 18, 28012 ☎ 91 369 14 34

M *Tirso de Molina* **Performances** *Sep.–July: Tue.–Sat. 8pm; Sun. 7pm* **Box office** *daily 11am–2pm, 4–9pm* ● *3000 Ptas–8000 Ptas*

Bought by the municipality in 1996, this theater hosts a program of events ranging from popular *zarzuelas* (in the summer) to well-known operas (during the rest of the year). Its repertoire features popular operas such as *Madama Butterfly* or *La Bohème*, Spanish operettas such as *Bohemios* or *La Alegría de la Huerta* and moving recitals by Isabel Pantoja.

Not forgetting

■ **Centro Cultural de la Villa (28)** Plaza de Colón, 28001 ☎ 91 575 60 80 *Hidden beneath the monument to Columbus and the fountains of this square* ➡ *104* *is a remarkable purpose-built cultural center which, from time to time, hosts* zarzuela *and flamenco shows* ➡ *80**. It is also the home of Banda Sinfonica Municipal of Madrid. See program for details.*

Rigoletto

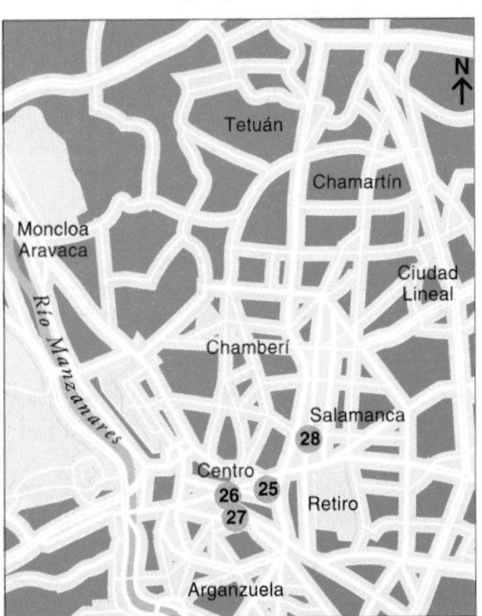
N
Tetuán
Chamartín
Moncloa
Aravaca
Ciudad
Lineal
Río Manzanares
Chamberí
Salamanca
28
Centro
26
25
27
Retiro
Arganzuela

Teatro de
LA ZARZUELA

25

CULTURAL DE LA VILLA DE MADR

CENTRO CULTURAL DE LA VILLA
Ayuntamiento de Madrid

Basic facts

Nearly every performing company in Spain ends its tour by coming to Madrid, including the country's best flamenco and *sevillana* shows. Seize an opportunity to spend an evening in a *tablao* (literally, 'stage') or *sala rociera*. In a *tablao*, or Andaluz bar, you will be applauding the footwork of

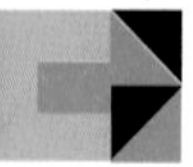

After dark

Corral de la Morería (29)

Morería 17, 28005 ☎ 91 365 84 46

M *Latina, Ópera* ⌚ *daily from 9pm* **Performance** *10.45pm–2am* ● **Dinner performance** *11,000 Ptas* **Bar performance** *4000 Ptas* ▭

Hidden away at the Corral de la Morería in the Castilian district of Las Vistillas is one of the more surprising flamenco *tablaos*, both for its long tradition and for the purity of its performance. The ballet that founded the place in 1956 included famous dancers such as Pastora Imperio. Other great names, such as Antonio Gades, La Chunga and Lucero Tena, followed. The star of the moment is Blanca del Rey. The small room is ideally suited to the smouldering intimacy of a flamenco dance, while the Castilian-style décor is sober and elegant.

Café de Chinitas (30)

Torija 7, 28013 ☎ 91 559 51 35

M *Santo Domingo* ⌚ *Mon.–Sat. dinner served from 9pm* **Performance** *10.30pm–2am* ● **Dinner performance** *9500 Ptas* **Bar performance** *from 4300 Ptas* ▭

Art and history interweave to great effect in this 17th-century palace, now renovated and decorated with valuable paintings, sculptures in bronze and marble, bullfighting memorabilia and a superb collection of Manila shawls ➡ 128. The famous dancer La Chunga appeared at its opening in 1969. Since then, flamenco stars such as Manuela Vargas, Enrique Morente, José Mercé and Pastora Vega have performed here.

Al Andalus (31)

Capitán Haya 19, 28020 ☎ 91 556 14 39

M *Cuzco* ⌚ *daily 10.30pm–6am; closed 15 days in July.–Aug.* ● *Sun.–Wed. 2000 Ptas; Thur.–Sat. 3000 Ptas (with one drink)* ▭

Al Andalus is more of a *sala rociera* than a *tablao*, where you can dance passionate *sevillanas* or athletic rumbas with the *rocieros*. It is impossible to stay seated. Al Andalus transports you to the lively streets of Andalusia with the bar's southern *mosaicos* (Andalusian tiles), white-washed balconies, flowers, roasts and the fiesta flamenca.

Corral de la Pacheca (32)

Juan Ramón Jiménez 26, 28036 ☎ 91 359 26 60

M *Plaza Castilla, Cuzco* ⌚ *daily 9pm–2.30am* ● **Dinner performance** *9500 Ptas–12,500 Ptas* **Bar performance** *4200 Ptas* ▭

A famous *tablao* on two floors. The ballets performed here are of the highest standard. The *bailaoras* (female dancers) are splendidly costumed in spotted dresses and colored shawls.

Not forgetting

■ **Almonte (33)** Juan Bravo 35, 28006 ☎ 91 563 54 04 *Somewhere to practise the* sevillana, *rumba or salsa!*

the audience; in a *sala rociera* you may find yourself joining in with the dancers on the floor.

29

30

29

9

30

29

Basic facts

You will find fewer cabarets in Madrid than any other European capital. A reason for this could be that the Spanish, who are by nature fidgety and talkative, are restless spectators. Those that do exist, however, are worth seeing. The shows are invigorating and of a high quality. Madrid

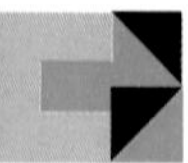

After dark

Berlín Cabaret (34)

Costanilla de San Pedro 11, 28005 ☎ 91 366 20 34

La Latina *Mon.–Thur. 11pm–5am; Fri.–Sat. 11pm–6am*
***Performances** from 1.30am ● 1200 Ptas*

An evocation of the Prohibition era, with exotic shows, near-naked women, drag-queens, dancing, magic tricks, plenty of humor and a dose of 1930s social satire. The Berlin Cabaret is the perfect place for a drink in a unusual setting. It is not a traditional cabaret, nor a café, but a bar, dance club and meeting-place all rolled into one. In short, somewhere to be thoroughly entertained.

Florida Park (35)

Paseo de coches del Retiro, 28009 ☎ 91 573 78 05

Ibiza *Mon.–Sat. from 9pm **Performance** 10.30pm–3am ● **Dinner performance** 9500 Ptas **Bar performance** 4500 Ptas*

Located right in the heart of the Parque del Retiro ➡ 98, Florida Park was for a long time the place to hear major Spanish and international artists such as Lola Flores, Chavela Vargas, Liza Minelli, Plácido Domingo and Diana Ross. Today, flamenco ➡ 80 and other types of Spanish dance music are on the program, and the orchestra is as happy to play old bolero and salsa classics as it is to play the latest tunes.

Clamores Jazz (36)

Albuquerque 14, 28010 ☎ 91 445 79 38

Bilbao *Sun.–Thur. 5pm–3am, Fri.–Sat. 5pm–4am, Sun. dancing from 10pm, ● 500 Ptas* *Tue.–Sat. ● prices vary*

Jazz, country, salsa and blues are just some of the different types of live music on offer at the Clamores. Here, you can hear Ismaël Serrano, Jayme Marqués, Pedro Iturralde, Jorge Drexler, Lonnie Smith, Billy Brooks and many others. Should you wish to seize the microphone, a pianist will accompany you until the audience gives in and applauds.

Scala Meliá (37)

Rosario Pino 7, 28020 ☎ 91 571 44 11

Plaza de Castilla *Tue.–Sat. from 8.30pm **Performances** Tue.–Fri. 10.45pm; Sat. 10.45pm–12.30am ● **Dinner performance** 10200 Ptas **Bar performance** 5300 Ptas*

A spectacular setting, with a skating rink, swimming pool, water cascades, bridges, floating staircases, hydraulic platforms, featuring exotic beauties, dancers, musicians and other artistes, always of a high standard. Excellent variety shows. An unusual venue that is a must for night owls.

Not forgetting

■ **Galileo Galilei (38)** Galileo 100, 28015 ☎ 91 534 75 57
Café concerts. An extensive program featuring a variety of shows. Salsa evenings.

has a selection of off-the-beaten-track venues offering everything from live concerts to exotic shows in good-humored spirit.

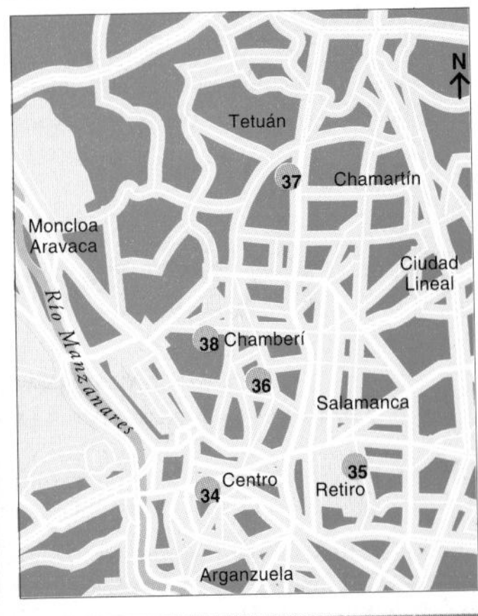

36

37

36

34

Basic facts

When people talk of Madrid as the 'party capital', they are usually referring to the huge number of clubs and their one great advantage over their European counterparts: their long hours. The clientele is varied, though there are some places where the 'urban tribe' look is *de rigueur*.

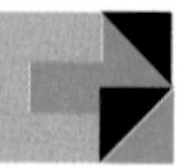

After dark

Joy Eslava (39)

Arenal 11, 28013 ☎ 91 366 54 39 ➠ 91 366 54 40

M *Sol* ⏲ *daily 11.30pm–6am* ***Performances*** *Thur.–Sun. around 2am*
● *Sun.–Wed. 1500 Ptas; Thur.–Sat. 2000 Ptas*

The star of the Madrid scene, Joy Eslava is housed in a former variety theater. The interior has retained its tiered balconies, which overlook the dance floor, and its 19th-century Romantic décor, and serves as a backdrop for social gatherings, cultural events, fashion shows, movie premieres and concerts. The clientele is the most cosmopolitan of all Madrid night spots, comprising movie stars, theater actors, dancers, literary figures, politicians, TV personalities and members of Madrid's jet-set.

Empire (40)

Paseo de Recoletos 16, 28001 ☎ 91 435 84 50

M *Colón* ⏲ *daily 11pm–5am* ● *Fri.–Sat. 1500 Ptas, Sun.–Thur. 1000 Ptas*

The Empire is a mix of traditional and modern, in both its clientele and its décor. It once played host to luminaries such as Gloria Estefan, Prince, Omar Shariff, Antonio Banderas, Pedro Almodóvar and Steven Seagal. It has preserved its theatrical charm, and still draws a mixed crowd. Plenty of *marcha* (ambience) and good music.

Pachá (41)

Barceló 11, 28004 ☎ 91 446 01 37

M *Bilbao* ⏲ *Wed.–Thur. 12.30pm–6am; Fri.–Sat. 11.30pm–6am* ● *Wed.–Thur., Sun. 1500 Ptas; Fri.–Sat. 2000 Ptas (with one drink)*

'When you go by Pachá, don't forget to visit Madrid.' This famous saying tells you a lot about the reputation of this club with *Madrileños* and visitors alike. Attractive people, good music, and a packed dance floor – Pachá has become the late-night legend of Madrid.

Nells (42)

López de Hoyos 25, 28006 ☎ 91 562 49 54

M *Avenida de América, Cruz del Rayo* ⏲ *Tue.–Sat. midnight–6am* ● *5000 Ptas*

This small, recently opened club, with its élite clientele, is to Madrid what private clubs are to other European capitals. This is where the beautiful people meet: mostly over-25s, jackets but no ties, glamorous, well-dressed women and good music. ★ At weekends, book a table in advance to avoid being suffocated at around 3am. On Tuesdays there is a flamenco *fiesta* ➠ 80, usually by invitation only.

Not forgetting

■ **Palacio de Gaviria (43)** Arenal 9, 28013 ☎ 91 526 60 69
A gorgeous 19th-century palace hosting tea dances, disco nights and salsa evenings.

N
Tetuán
Chamartín
Moncloa Aravaca
Ciudad Lineal
Río Manzanares
42
Chamberí
41
Salamanca
40
39 43
Centro
Retiro
Arganzuela
Joy
43

Bono museo
You can buy a pass for the Centro Cultural Reina Sofía, the Prado and Museo Thyssen-Bornemisza at any of the three museums • 1050 Ptas

What to see

Bus tours

Privately-operated buses run regularly between Palacio Real and Plaza de Colón. Take the whole tour, or get off at any stop and take the next bus.
Madrid Vision *Avenida Manoteras 14, 28050 ☎ (91) 767 17 43*
• *1600 Ptas for a panoramic tour, 2000 Ptas for one day, 2500 Ptas for two days.*

46 Sights

THE INSIDER'S FAVORITES

Guided tours

Asociación de Guías de Madrid
Genova 3, 28004
☎ 91 308 17 66
Mon.–Fri. 8am–7pm; Sat. 9am–1pm
• *Pick your own itinerary. From 12000 Ptas for a three-hour walking tour for up to 30 people.*

Helicopter trips

You can hire a helicopter from ***Empresa Hispanica de Aviación*** *Aeropuerto de 4 Vientos, Avenida del Valle 13, 28003 ☎ 91 553 85 01*
• *162400 Ptas for a one-hour flight, maximum 5 people.*

INDEX BY TYPE

"And finally, Madrid! That beloved city, welcoming you into its arms like a lover! A city that still offered the traveler a uniquely gentle way of life. A city of contrasts with its Plaza Mayor, its Género chico, its skyscrapers and its local bistros still haunted by the shadowy figure of Federico García Lorca!" *Alejo Carpentier*

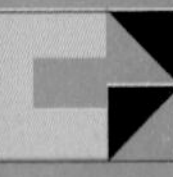

What to see

Born from water

The fortress of Mayrit ('source of water') was built by the Moors in the rich, fertile valley of the Mazanares river facing the Sierra Guadarrama. The Muslim city stood on the present site of the Palacio Real. Today, all that remains of the Moorish occupation are a few remnants of the outer wall and the Mudéjar tower of the Iglesia San Pedro El Viejo. Recaptured by Alfonso VI in the 11th century, Mayrit was converted to Christianity and renamed Magerit. Gradually, the city developed around the original Moorish walls, forming a dozen or so parishes that functioned as separate districts.

A royal capital

There was nothing to suggest that Madrid was destined to become a capital. In the 16th century, it still resembled a medieval town with its cob buildings, its narrow, winding streets leading to small, enclosed market squares, and only 4,000 inhabitants. However, in 1561, Philip II, son of Charles V, chose it as his capital with the intention of making it a cosmopolitan city that would absorb all regional differences. But Madrid still lacked the buildings equal to its city status.

A monumental city

The Hapsburg dynasty (1516–1700) built the Plaza Mayor ➡ 92, constructed churches and laid out gardens. During the reign of the Bourbons (1701–1808), vast palaces (Palacio Real ➡ 90), promenades (Paseo del Prado ➡ 96) and gardens (Parque del Retiro ➡ 98) were built to celebrate the absolute power of the monarchy. In the 19th century, the face of Madrid was radically altered as the Castro plan rationalized urban development. Monumental squares were constructed and new districts based on a regular grid layout (e.g. Salamanca) were built alongside the old districts of the city center. The city's population had by now reached 250,000. The early 20th century saw the construction of the city's main thoroughfares – the Castellana and the Gran Vía – and such modern buildings as the impressive Palacio de Communicaciones ➡ 96 and the Compañía Telefónica ➡ 94.

Francoism

Vhen the parties of the left came to power in 1936, they fought bitterly .mongst themselves while the Carlists, Falangists and Monarchists formed n alliance. With the outbreak of civil war, Barcelona fell in early January 939 but Madrid held out until March 28. General Franco seized power and uled until his death in 1975. His severe centralist government drastically ltered the face of Madrid. The carefully preserved city center was marred y towers (Torre de España) and an increasing number of business districts Nuevos Ministerios ➡ 108), while the outskirts were overrun by ormitory towns. Madrid's population tripled in the space of forty years.

The districts of Madrid

he city of Madrid is in fact composed of a large number of 'villages'. In he narrow, winding streets of the old working-class districts of La Latina, .avapiès, Malasaña and Chueca, isolated from the hustle and bustle of the rand boulevards, time seems to stand still. But not for long! After dark, he narrow streets become the preserve of the districts' night birds. To he north lies modern Madrid with the business centers of the Castellana nd the elegant middle-class districts of Salamanca and Chamberí. The nain thoroughfares of the Paseo del Prado, the Gran Vía and the Castellana bridge the gaps between these vastly different areas of the city.

The festival tradition

here are over 10,000 bars in Madrid, not counting nightclubs and *tascas*. lthough the summer heat undoubtedly contributes to the city's frenetic festyle, the fall of Franco marked the end of dictatorship and moral arassment, and gave rise to a more liberal approach. This found its best orm of expression in the festivals of the 1980s when the *movida* was born. lowever the festival tradition dates from much earlier. Since time nmemorial the people of Madrid have always celebrated their popular aints: Isidro, the plowman, the city's patron saint since the 11th century, and ne Virgen de la Almudena, who watches over the city. The countless public olidays associated with these festivals are an integral part of life in Madrid.

In the area

The history of *La Villa* (Madrid) begins here, for it was on this site in the 9th century that Muhammad I erected his *Kasbah*. Though the settlement expanded over the centuries, the rocky promontory overlooking the Manzanares river – now little more than a trickle – has remained the

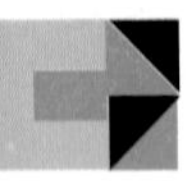

What to see

Palacio Real (1)

Bailén, 28005 ☎ 91 542 00 59 ➟ 91 542 69 47

Opera *Oct. 1–Mar 31: Mon.–Sat. 9.30am–5pm, Sun. 9am–2pm / Apr. 1–Sep 30: Mon.–Sat. 9am–4pm, Sun. 9am–3pm; closed on official ceremony days* ● *850 Ptas; over 65s, students, children 350 Ptas; Wed. free* *950 Ptas*

The Palacio Real (Royal Palace) is one of the most majestic monuments in the city. It was built on the ruins of the Alcázar (fortress) of Madrid, destroyed by fire in 1734. Completed in 1764, in the reign of Charles III (1759–88), the palace was designed by Italian architect Gianbattista Sacchetti, and construction was supervised by architects Ventura Rodríguez and Francisco Sabatini. The neoclassical structure was modified to suit the difficult terrain – a hill sloping steeply to the Manzanares river. Away from the river, on the other side of the palace, is the Plaza de Oriente. An equestrian statue of Philip IV – a superb piece of 18th-century sculpture by Pietro Tacca – stands at its center.

Inside the palace, highlights include the Throne Room, which has a superb view of the Campo del Moro, the sumptuous Dining Room (Comedor), the Porcelain Room, the Sala Gasparini, the grand staircase (each step cut from a single block of marble), and the Chapel, which has a remarkable collection of stringed instruments. In the various rooms hang paintings by Velázquez, Goya, El Greco, Rubens and Tiepolo. The palace's collection of tapestries is the largest in Europe, and charts the development of this decorative art from its Gothic origins to the late-18th century. One of the most impressive exhibits in the palace is the Armería Real (Royal Armoury), which exhibits weaponry from the Middle Ages through to the modern day. If there is time, try to visit the Farmácia (Royal Pharmacy), which has a display of Talavera ceramic jars, and the Museo de Carruajes (Carriage Museum), which houses a collection of 18th- and 19th-century vehicles (access is via the Sabatini gardens).

The Palace Gardens, or Campo del Moro, are attached to the west wing of the palace. Laid out under Isabel II (1833–68), they reflect the English landscape style that was popular in Madrid at the time. Note the splendid fountains, as well as the fantastic view of the palace's west face. Access to the gardens is via a grand flight of steps; another, toward the north side, leads down to the French-style Sabatini gardens, embellished with statues and fountains. These formal gardens were laid out in the reign of Alfonso XII (1874–85).

Not forgetting

■ **Catedral de la Almudena (2)** Mayor 90, 28005 daily 10am–2pm, 6–8pm *Work on the cathedral began in 1874. The plans were modified so many times during construction, however, that it was consecrated only in 1992.*

■ **El Viaducto (3)** Calle Bailén/Calle Segovia, 28071 *This viaduct is one of the city's marvels of civil engineering. Built in 1932 along 'rationalist' lines, it straddles the canyon-like Calle Segovia, and links the Royal Palace with the southern part of the city.*

main residence for all Spanish monarchs, except the present king, Juan Carlos.

After dark ➥ 68 ➥ 80

1

The State Dining Room is one of the palace's most magnificent rooms.

3

In the area
This district in Old Madrid, a warren of streets and famous squares (once the setting for official ceremonies and public events) is one of the most beautiful and unspoiled areas of the city. ■ Where to stay ➡ 20 ■ Where to eat ➡ 38 ■ After dark ➡ 68 ➡ 80 ➡ 84

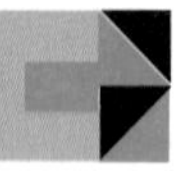

What to see

Plaza Mayor (4)

M *Sol, La Latina*

The Plaza Mayor is the largest square in the historic center of Madrid. Its present appearance is the result of work by Juan de Villanueva (1789–1811), the architect of the Prado ➡ 96. It comprises a medieval marketplace (adjacent streets are named after confraternities and guilds), the *Casa de la Panadería* (headquarters of the bakers' guild) and the *Casa de la Carnicería* (headquarters of the butchers' guild). The square evolved into the social hub of the city, hosting public spectacles, jousts and even bullfights ➡ 100. Today its shops, restaurants and architecture draw many visitors. The front of the Casa de la Panadería is decorated with frescoes by Carlos Franco depicting the classic symbols of Madrid: allegories of water and the countryside, *majos* and *majas* (elegant 17th-century men and women), *toreros* and 'cats' (the nickname given to the *madrileños*).

Plaza de la Villa (5)
☎ 91 588 10 00

M *Ópera, La Latina* ⏲ *Casa de la Villa / Casa de Cisneros Mon. 5–7pm* ● *free* *Patronato municipal de turismo* ☎ *91 588 29 00*

The buildings around Plaza de la Villa (Town Square) include several examples of the architectural style favored by the Hapsburgs. The *Ayuntamiento* (Town Hall) – also called the *Casa de la Villa* – is built on two levels around a patio, and flanked by pinnacle towers decorated with coats of arms. Inside, the grand staircase, the *Patio de Cristales*, the former chapel and the *Allegory of 2nd of May* (Francisco de Goya) merit close inspection. The *Casa de Cisneros*, built in 1537, is one of the finest examples of the Plateresque style (from *platero*, the Spanish word for silversmith), characterized by its intricate detail. Opposite the *Ayuntamiento* is the tower of Los Lujanes. It has two portals – one Gothic and the other, with an overreaching arch, that is typically Moorish. The statue in the center of the square represents Alvaro de Bazán, admiral of the 'invincible' Armada of Philip II (1556–98).

Not forgetting

■ **Monasterio de las Descalzas Reales (6)** Plaza de las Descalzas 3, 28013 ☎ 91 542 00 59 ⏲ Tue.–Sat. 10.30am–12.30pm, 4–5.30pm *A convent housing a rich collection of paintings, sculptures, tapestries and reliquaries. One of the finest Baroque collections in Spain.*

■ **Iglesia San Ginés (7)** Arenal, 28013 ☎ 91 366 48 75 ⏲ Sep.–June: daily 9am–1pm, 6–9pm / July.–Aug.: daily 9am–1pm, 7–9pm *The Iglesia San Ginés was rebuilt in the 17th century. Its Capilla del Cristo (Christ's chapel) houses paintings and sculptures reflecting 17th-century Spanish art, including El Greco's* Christ Cleansing the Temple.

■ **Monasterio de la Encarnación (8)** Plaza de la Encarnación 1, 28013 ☎ 91 542 00 59 ⏲ Wed., Sat., Sun. 10.30am–12.45pm, 4–5.30pm *An Augustin convent. Parts of the cloisters are open to the public. A remarkable collection of 17th-century Madrid School paintings. An impressive and ornate reliquary.*

Where to shop ➥ 126 ➥ 128 ➥ 144

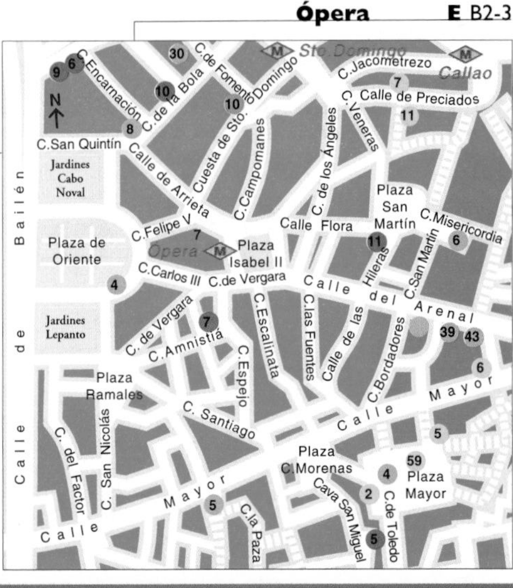

7

In the area

The opening up of the Gran Vía was the first major urban project of the early 1900s. A cosmopolitan symbol of the city, it includes some beautiful 1920s architecture. ■ Where to stay ➡ 18 ➡ 20 ■ Where to eat ➡ 40 ➡ 42 ■ After dark ➡ 70 ➡ 72 ➡ 74 ➡ 76 ➡ 78

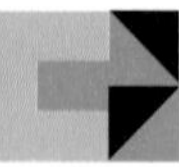

What to see

Gran Vía (9)

Gran Vía, Callao, Plaza de España

The Gran Vía is a broad, mile-long thoroughfare that links Plaza de Cibeles ➡ 96 with Plaza de España ➡ 102. Work was carried out in three phases, each corresponding to a different section. Along the first section, from the Plaza de Cibeles to Red de San Luis (at the intersection of Calle de Fuencarral and Calle de Hortaleza), the buildings resemble Parisian apartment blocks of the late-19th century. The Edificio Metrópolis (no. 39), located at the corner of Gran Vía and Calle de Alcalá, typifies this exuberant and theatrical style. On Calle de Alcalá (no. 42) to the left of it, is the Círculo de Bellas Artes ➡ 74, a striking building designed by architect Antonio Palacios. From the Red de San Luis the buildings resemble, on a reduced scale, the first skyscrapers of Chicago. The Compañía Telefónica building (no. 28), housing Spain's national telephone company, was the first skyscraper to be erected in Madrid, though its façade is more Madrid Baroque than avant-garde. Closing this second section of the Gran Vía are three unusual buildings: Palacio de la Prensa; Palacio de la Música; and the Callao Cinema. The brick Palacio de la Prensa (no. 46) was the fist Madrid apartment block to be given an art deco façade, revealing its debt to German Expressionism. Huge cinema posters conceal the curious façade of Palacio de la Música (no. 35), whose decorative details were inspired by the Madrid Baroque. The Art–Deco interior of the Callao Cinema is worth seeing. The third section of the Gran Vía begins at the curved corner of the Edificio Carrión (no. 78), which now houses the Capitol Cinema (no. 41). It ends at the pared-down Edificio Coliseum (no. 78), yet another cinema. This last section is the most colorful part of Madrid.

Real Academia de Bellas Artes de San Fernando (10)

Alcalá 13, 28014 ☎ 91 522 14 91

Sevilla, Sol **Museum** *Mon., Sat.–Sun. 9am–2.30pm; Tue.–Fri. 9am–7pm* ● *Mon.–Fri. 400 Ptas; children 150 Ptas; over-65s, students, Sat.–Sun. free* **Exhibitions** *Mon., Sat.–Sun. 10am–2pm, Tue.–Fri. 10am–2pm, 5–8pm* ● free

The second most important museum in Madrid after the Prado ➡ 96. The collection includes thirteen canvases by Francisco de Goya, numerous 17th-century sculptures and paintings (Zurbarán, Murillo, Pedro de Mena, Rubens and Van Dyck), a series of Italian paintings from the 16th century (including the only Archimboldo in Spain) and a series of academic paintings from the 18th, 19th and 20th centuries.

Not forgetting

■ **Puerta del Sol (11)** *The geographical center of Madrid and, up until the 1950s, the scene of historic events. Statues of* Mariblanca *and the* oso *and* madroño *(bear and arbutus tree), which feature on the city's coat of arms. Monument dedicated to King Juan Carlos.*

■ **Plaza de las Cortes (12)** *The Chamber of Deputies (1850) is the most important building on this square. Designed by Pascual y Colomer, it has a colonnaded portico and a classical pediment.*

■ Where to
hop ➥ 126
➥ 128 ➥ 130
➥ 132

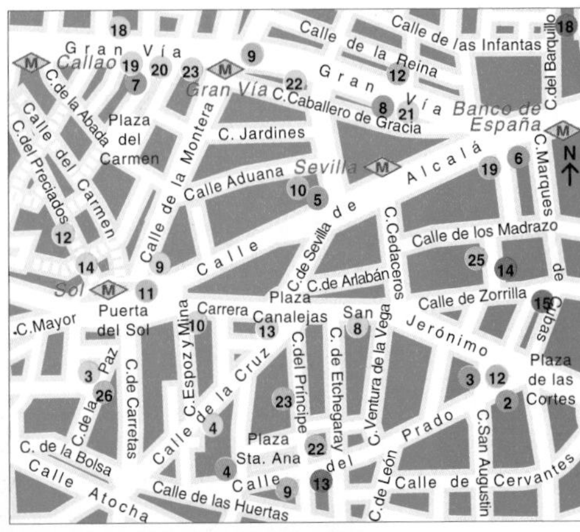

9

12

At the beginning of this century an entire district was demolished to make way for the Gran Vía. The Compañía Telefónica building was erected in 1929 by Ignacio Cárdenas. It rises to a height of 266 feet.

12

In the area

This shady avenue is often referred to as the Paseo del Arte (literally, the 'Art Walk'), and with good reason, for it is home to Madrid's great art museums. ■ Where to stay ➥ 18 ■ Where to eat ➥ 40 ➥ 42 ■ Where to shop ➥ 138

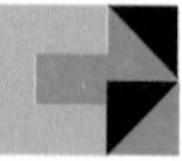

What to see

Museo del Prado & Casón del Buen Retiro (13)

Paseo del Prado, 28014 ☎ 91 330 28 00 ➟ 91 330 28 58

M Atocha, Banco de España ⌚ Tue.–Sat. 9am–7pm; Sun., public holidays 9am–2pm ● 500 Ptas; students 250 Ptas; over-65s, children free

Designed in 1785 by Juan de Villanueva, the building houses one of the world's leading art museums. The collections (originally part of the Spanish royal art collection) cover three great schools of painting. The Spanish School numbers among its works many El Grecos, the world's largest Velázquez collection (over sixty canvases, including his most famous painting *Las Meninas*) and works by Goya (court portraits and 'dark paintings'). The glorious Italian collection includes works by Fra Angelico, Raphael and Titian. The Flemish School has some superb pieces by Bosch and Rubens. The Prado also contains around 500 sculptures of Graeco-Roman, Renaissance and Baroque origin. The nearby annexe was once the ballroom of the palace of El Casón del Buen Retiro. Now run by the National Museum of Modern Art, it contains Spanish sculptures and paintings from the 19th century.

Museo Thyssen-Bornemisza (14)

Paseo del Prado 8, 28014 ☎ 91 420 39 44 ➟ 91 420 27 80

M Banco de España ⌚ Tue.–Sun. 10am–7pm ● 700 Ptas; over-65s, students 400 Ptas; children free

Since 1992 the Palacio de Villahermosa has housed the superb private collection of baron von Thyssen-Bornemisza. Over 800 works of western art are on display in the museum. Among them are *Saint Catherine of Alexandria* by Caravaggio, Venetian views by Canaletto, *Venus and Cupid* by Rubens and *Easter Morning* by Caspar David Friedrich. There is a good collection of Impressionist and post-Impressionist art, an impressive canvas by Mark Rothko, a leading American Abstract Expressionist, and an eclectic display of Soviet avant-garde works.

Not forgetting

■ **Plaza de Cibeles (15)**
A Castilian square designed by Ventura Rodríguez in 1775. Fountain dedicated to the goddess of nature, Cibeles.

■ **Puerta de Alcalá (16)** Plaza de la Independencia, 28001
Symbol of Enlightenment Madrid. A neoclassical granite gate by Francisco Sabatini (1778).

■ **Plaza de Cánovas del Castillo (17)**
The twin sister of Cibeles, by Ventura Rodríguez (1780). Fountain dedicated to Neptune.

■ **San Jerónimo el Real (18)** Moreto 4, 28014 ☎ 91 420 35 78
⌚ daily 9am–1pm, 5–8.30pm
Built over the ruins of a monastery. The church was erected under the Catholic Monarchs and was modified in the 19th century. Juan Carlos I was crowned here.

■ **Museo del Ejército (19)** Méndez Núñez 1, 28014 ☎ 91 522 89 77
⌚ Tue.–Sat. 10am–2pm *An extensive military collection.*

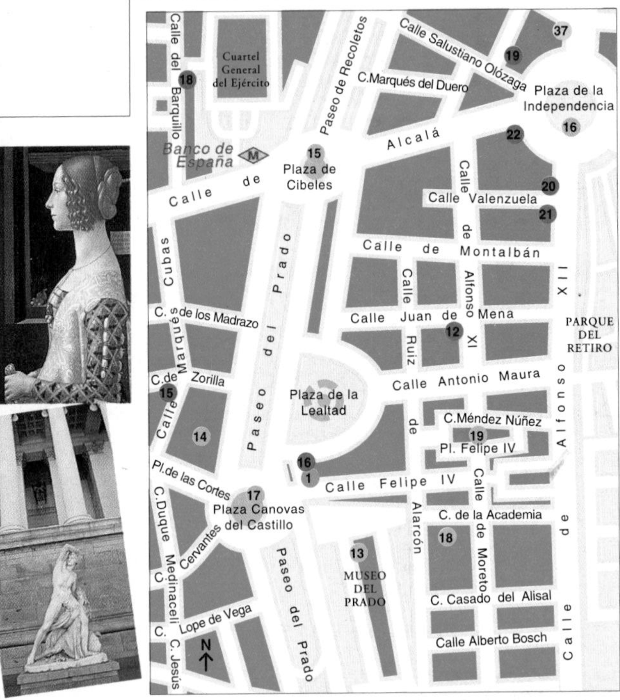
Calle del Barquillo
Cuartel General del Ejército
Paseo de Recoletos
Calle Salustiano Olózaga
C.Marqués del Duero
Plaza de la Independencia
Banco de España
M
Alcalá
Plaza de Cibeles
Calle de
Calle Valenzuela
Calle de Alfonso XI
Calle de Montalbán
Cubas
Paseo del Prado
C. de los Madrazo
Calle Ruiz de Alarcón
Calle Juan de Mena
Alfonso XII
PARQUE DEL RETIRO
C. Marqués
C.de Zorrilla
Calle Antonio Maura
Plaza de la Lealtad
C.Méndez Núñez
Pl. Felipe IV
Pl.de las Cortes
Calle Felipe IV
Calle de Moreto
C. de la Academia
Plaza Canovas del Castillo
C.Duque Medinaceli
Cervantes
MUSEO DEL PRADO
C. Casado del Alisal
Calle Alberto Bosch
C. Lope de Vega
C. Jesús
Calle de
N
37
19
18
22
16
15
20
21
12
14
19
16
1
17
18
13

Fundación
COLECCION THYSSEN-BORNEMISZA

14

14

19

In the area

The Glorieta (roundabout) of Charles V, known simply as Atocha, marks the city's southern perimeter. The Centro Cultural Reina Sofía completes the so-called 'Golden Triangle' bordered on its other sides by the Prado and Thyssen-Bornemisza museums.

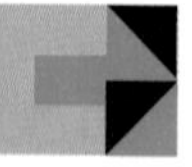

What to see

Museo Nacional Centro de Arte Reina Sofía (20)

Santa Isabel 52, 28012 ☎ 91 467 50 62 ➟ 91 467 84 31

M *Atocha* ⏲ *Mon., Wed.–Sat. 10am–9pm; Sun. 10am–2.30pm* ● *500 Ptas; students 250 Ptas; over-65s, children, Sat. after 2.30pm, Sun. free*
Reservations ☎ *91 527 72 05*

Designed by Francisco Sabatini in 1776, this former hospital today houses Madrid's National Museum of Contemporary Art. The 19th-century and 20th-century collections include the famous *Guernica* by Picasso, a number of important Spanish Surrealist and avant-garde works, including early works by Dalí, Miró paintings from the 1970s, and a fine collection of Cubist sculptures by Julio González. Major works by Antoni Tàpies and by Spain's two greatest living sculptors, Jorge de Oteiza and Eduardo Chillida are also on show. The museum hosts regular retrospectives of both major artists and up-and-coming talent.

Parque del Retiro (21)

M *Retiro, Príncipe de Vergara, Atocha, Ibiza* ⏲ *24 hours* ***Palacio de Velázquez*** ☎ *91 573 62 45* ● *free*

The garden of the palace of the same name, built as a pleasure retreat for Philip IV (1621–55) ➥ 96. Retiro Park was opened to the public in 1869 by Isabel II, in exchange for a rent of 5 Ptas a year. In the center is a boating lake presided over by a monument to Alfonso XII which features an equestrian statue of the king by Mariano Benlliure and some magnificent examples of 19th-century Spanish sculpture. Exhibitions were held in the park buildings up until 1882. Today, the only two buildings still used for this purpose are Palacio de Velázquez and Palacio de Cristal. The latter is an iron-and-glass structure inspired by London's Crystal Palace and designed as a huge hothouse. Both palaces are decorated with *azulejos* (enamelled ceramic tiles) by Daniel Zuloaga.

Not forgetting

■ **Estación de Atocha (22)** Plaza del Emperador Carlos V, 28012
19th-century railway architecture, transformed by Rafael Moneo in 1992. The old wrought-iron structure was designed by Alberto del Palacio with the aid of Gustave Eiffel, and housed a winter garden. Opposite is the Ministry of Agriculture, a 19th-century building decorated with azulejos *(ceramic tiles) and a large sculptural group.*

■ **Jardín Botánico (23)** Plaza de Murillo 2, 28014 ☎ 91 420 30 17
⏲ daily 10am–8pm *A remnant of Charles III's grand scheme for a scientific complex. Buildings and gateways by Juan de Villanueva. A peaceful botanical garden in which to examine a huge variety of plant species.*

■ **Observatorio Astronómico (24)** Alfonso XII 3 et 5, 28014
☎ 91 527 01 07 ⏲ Mon.–Fri. 9am–2pm *Part of the Botanic Garden. Built in 1790, and reconstructed in 1978.*

■ **Museo de Etnología (25)** Alfonso XII 68, 28014 ☎ 91 530 64 18
⏲ Tue.–Sat. 10am–7.30pm, Sun. 10am–2pm *The building dates from 1875. Exhibits from Africa, Asia and the Americas, including an interesting collection from the Philippines.*

■ Where to eat ➡ 40
■ Where to shop ➡ 144

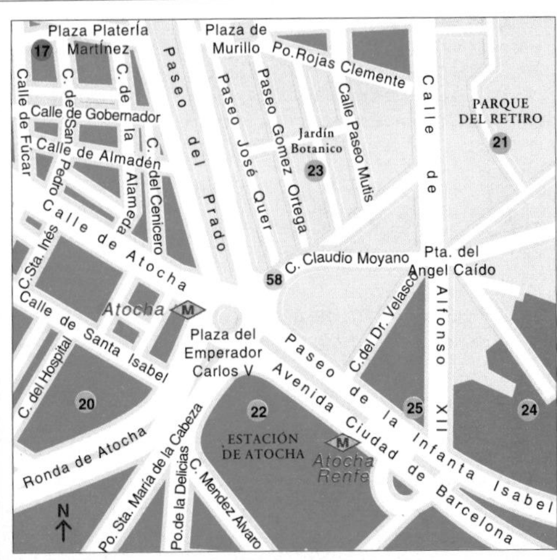

23

Shown in New York until 1981, *Guernica* returned to Spain after Franco's death in accordance with Picasso's wishes.

20

20

In the area

Some of the most animated scenes in Madrid are to be witnessed around Plaza de las Ventas on *corrida* (bullfight) days. Crowds of aficionados and devoted enthusiasts fill the streets after the fight.

Where to stay ➥ 26

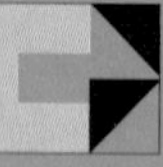

What to see

Plaza Monumental de las Ventas (26)
Alcalá 237, 28028 ☎ 91 356 22 00

Ventas ◷ ***Corridas** Mar.–Oct. : Sun. 7pm **Feria de San Isidro** May–June: daily 7pm ● 400 Ptas–15,000 Ptas; Victoria 3, 28012 ☎ 91 521 12 13 (tickets reserved in advance cost 20% more)*

This unusual building, erected in 1931, encloses one of the largest bullfighting arenas. Outside are monuments dedicated to two famous bullfighters, killed in the ring. The Feria of San Isidro (patron saint of Madrid) pits the most famous *toreros* and *novilleros* (novice bullfighters) against the most redoubtable fighting bulls or *novillos* (young bulls).

Museo Taurino (27)
Alcalá 237, 28028 ☎ 91 725 18 57

Ventas ◷ *Tue.–Fri., Sun. 9.30am–2.30pm ● free*

This collection comprises costumes and bullfighting memorabilia from the 17th century to the present day. These include lithographs by Goya, a costume worn by the legendary Manolete on the day he was gored by a bull named Islero, the Papal Bull of Pius V (1567) banning corridas, and posters signed by Miquel Barceló and Eduardo Arroyo.

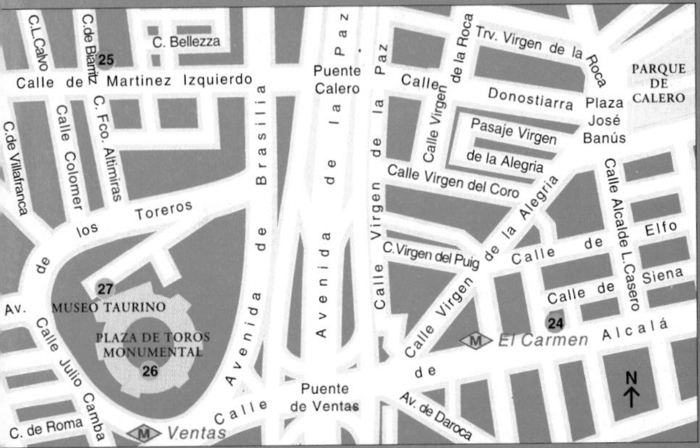

The traditional *corrida* involves six bulls and six *toreros*. It opens with a fanfare of trumpets and cymbals, after which the *alguacilillos*, or mounted constables, gallop in at the head of the *toreros* and their *cuadrillas* (teams of assistants). Each of the six fights is divided into three 'acts'. In the first *tercio* (third), the *torero* uses his pink cape to attract the bull while testing his temperament, condition and charge. The *suerte de varas* (*pic*-ing of the bull) is where the picador, mounted on a padded horse, applies his pic to the bull, causing it to bleed and thus to lose strength. In the second *tercio*, known as that of the *banderilleras* (short barbed sticks decorated with ribbons and colored paper), the *banderilleros* must test the bull and correct any defects in its line of charge. In the final *tercio*, called the *faena*, the *torero* faces the bull alone. Using his *muleta* (scarlet cape), he calls the bull, sidesteps it and forces it to turn around him by a series of skilful passes – performed increasingly slowly – and by retreating or standing still close to the bull's horns. When the matador's preliminary work is complete, he must kill the bull, going in over the horns to administer a clean, fatal blow.

In the area

This huge landscape park in the English tradition was laid out in the early 1900s, and stretches from Plaza de España to the Ciudad Universitaria. It is fringed with museums and unusual monuments. The scene of repeated clashes during the Civil War, it is now overlooked by skyscrapers.

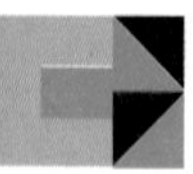

What to see

Museo de América (28)

Reyes Católicos 6, 28040 ☎ 91 543 94 37 ➡ 91 577 67 42

M *Moncloa* ⏲ *Tue.–Sat. 10am–3pm; Sun., public holidays 10am–2.30pm* ● *500 Ptas; students 250 Ptas; over-65s, children, Sun. free*

The Museum of America documents the relationship between Spain and the American continent. Part of the collection comes from the *Real Gabinete de Historia Natural*, created in the 18th century. It is made up of objects brought back from scientific expeditions and from early excavations in Peru and the Mayan ruins of Palenque, and a selection of Mexican sacred objects, and subsequent acquisitions. The museum is organized into five sections: *Los Instrumentos del Conocimiento* examines myths and ideas about America from Columbus to the Enlightenment; *La Realidad de América* is devoted to the continent's geography and landscape, and its native peoples and populations; and *La Sociedad* looks at how the indigenous societies organized themselves. *La Religión* displays the Paracas Mummy and the Quimbayas Treasure, which is the most important pre-Hispanic collection of American gold objects. Finally, *La Comunicación* examines means of communication, and displays the jewel in the museum's crown – the Tro-Cortesian Codex, one of four Mayan manuscripts in existence, its hieroglyphs depicting scenes of daily life.

Ermita de San Antonio de la Florida (29)

Glorieta de San Antonio de la Florida 5, 28008
☎ 91 542 07 22 ➡ 91 588 86 79

M *Príncipe Pío* ⏲ *Tue.–Fri. 10am–2pm, 4–8pm; Sat.–Sun. 10am–2pm* ● *300 Ptas; over-65s, students, children 150 Ptas; Wed., Sun. free*

Designed by Italian architect Felipe Fontana, the hermitage contains Francisco de Goya y Lucientes (1746–1828) largest cycle of frescos together with the artist's remains. The *Miracles of St Anthony*, which decorates the cupola, pendentives and transept, depicts Saint Anthony of Padua in Lisbon, where he brings a dead man back to life to testify to the innocence of his supposed assassin, the saint's father Don Martín de Bulloes. The church also houses the artist's remains. To preserve the frescos, a similar hermitage was built nearby in 1928 for church services.

Not forgetting

■ **Plaza de España (30)** *Two skyscrapers – a testament to Madrid's economic buoyancy during the early years of dictatorship.' Edificio España (1948–53) and the Torre de Madrid (1957) dominate the square. In the center of the plaza is a monument to Cervantes.*

■ **Templo de Debod (31)** Parque de la Montaña, 28008 *An Egyptian temple dating from the 4th century* BC *given to the city to thank its people for their contribution toward saving the temples of Nubia.*

■ **Museo Cerralbo (32)** Ventura Rodríguez 17, 28008 ☎ 91 547 36 46
⏲ Tue.–Sat. 9.30am–2.30pm; Sun. 10am–2pm
The residence and collection of Enrique de Aguilera y Gamboa, an aristocrat and respected archeologist. The museum provides an insight into the life of a late-19th-century nobleman.

■ Where to eat ➥ 38
■ After dark ➥ 86

28

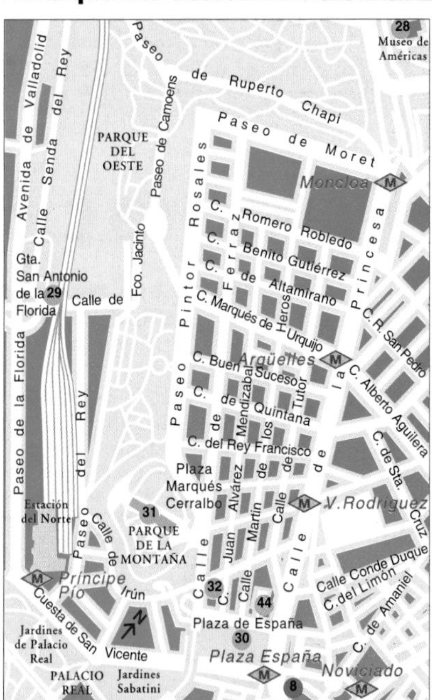

32

32

Cervantes looks down upon his two most famous creations: Don Quixote and Sancho Panza.

In the area

Here, in one of the liveliest districts in Madrid, you can take in a museum or simply mingle with the crowds in Plaza de Alonso Martínez.

■ Where to stay ➥ 22 ■ Where to eat ➥ 44 ■ After dark ➥ 68 ➥ 78 ➥ 84 ■ Where to shop ➥ 130 ➥ 136 ➥ 138 ➥ 140

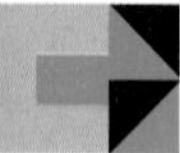

What to see

Biblioteca Nacional (33)

Paseo de Recoletos 20, 28001 ☎ 91 431 37 59 ➥ 91 577 56 34

M *Colón, Serrano* 🕒 *Mon.–Fri. 9am–9pm; Sat. 9am–2pm* ● *free, day pass for reading rooms available*

The building housing the National Library and Archeological Museum (1866–92) was the most important structure built during the reign of Isabel II, and one of the first to use metal. The steps leading up to the library are decorated with 19th-century statues representing the fathers of the Castilian language. The pediment features an allegory of Arts and Letters with statues representing Study, Glory and Fame, and in the vestibule a statue by French sculptor Coullault Valeradu represents the polymath Don Marcelino Menéndez y Pelayo. The National Library has about 11 million volumes, one-third of which are housed in the main reading room. It also possesses a series of early printed books, manuscripts and prints, including engravings by Dürer.

Museo Arqueológico Nacional (34)

Serrano 13, 28001 ☎ 91 577 79 12 ➥ 91 431 68 40

M *Colón, Serrano* 🕒 *Tue.–Sat. 9.30am–8.30pm; Sun. 9.30am–2.30pm* ● *500 Ptas; over-65s, students, children 250 Ptas; Sat. afternoon, Sun. morning free* ☎ *91 578 02 03*

A vast collection of over 200,000 artifacts dating from prehistoric times to the 19th century. These include: a reproduction of the Altamira cave paintings, the gigantic bones of an elephant from Classical Antiquity, Iberian sculptures dating from the pre-Roman era, Roman mosaics from Las Estaciones, and the Treasure of Guarrázar – Visigothic votive crowns dating from the 7th century. Islamic culture is represented by lamps from the Alhambra in Grenada and by mosaics from the city of Medina Azahara in Córdoba. Finally, the Romanesque works of Maestro Mateo are among the jewels of the museum. Recent reorganization has transformed the museum into a first-rate institution with an educational slant.

Not forgetting

■ **Museo Munícipal (35)** Fuencarral 78, 28004 ☎ 91 588 86 72
🕒 Tue.–Fri. 9.30am–8pm; Sat.–Sun. 10am–2pm *The finest Baroque portal in Madrid. The former hospice, now a Municipal Museum, houses a scale model of 1830s Madrid, the work of chronicler Ramón de Mesonero Romanos and of Ramón Gómez de la Serna, Madrid's most devoted poet.*

■ **Museo Romántico (36)** San Mateo 13, 28004 ☎ 91 448 10 71
🕒 Tue.–Sat. 9am–3pm; Sun. 10am–2pm *Spanish Romanticism, in the form of paintings, objects and documents displayed in a neoclassical building dating from the 18th century.*

■ **Plaza de Colón (37)**
A neo-Gothic statue of the legendary navigator and a rather unsuccessful sculptural group. The fountains represent Columbus' three ships.

Alonso Martínez
Plaza Alonso Martínez
Calle de Sagasta
C.M.Silvela
C.Orfila
C.Alcalá Galiano
Po.de Castellana
Serrano
Calle
Calle de Goya
Calle de Genova
Pl.Sta. Bárbara
C. Serrano Anguita
Lequerica
C.Mejía
C.de Larra
Apodaca
C.de Churruca
C.de Fuencarral
Calle Barceló
C.Beneficencia
Calle San Mateo
Trv. San Mateo
C.Santa Teresa
Calle Fernando VI
C. de Argensola
C.del General Castaños
Orellana
C.Marqués Ensenada
Pl.Villa de Paris
Plaza de Colón
Colón
Jardines del Descubrimiento
C.de Jorge Juan
Serrano
Po. de Recoletos
C. Bárbara de Braganza
C.de Villanueva
Tribunal
Calle C.San Lorenzo
Calle Belén
C. de Hortaleza
C.de Zurbano

33
34
34
35
MUSEO MUNICIPAL DE MADRID

In the area

Fast becoming a major hub, this square is surrounded by various ministries and administrative centers. It is an amalgam of architectural styles, including some exceptionally fine 19th-century buildings.

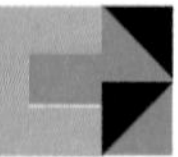

What to see

Museo Nacional de Ciencías Naturales (38)

José Gutiérrez Abascal 2, 28006
☎ 91 561 86 00 ➠ 91 564 50 78

Gregorio Marañon *Tue.–Fri. 10am–6pm; Sat. 10am–8pm; Sun. 10am–2.30pm* ● **Museum** *400 Ptas, over-65s, students, children 300 Ptas* **Exhibition** *200 Ptas; over-65s, students, children 100 Ptas* ☎ *(91) 564 61 69*

Madrid's Natural Science Museum has been elevated to the rank of a world-class educational institution by the renovation of these palaces, built for the 1881 National Exhibition of Industry and the Arts. It houses a public library and a collection of over 3,500,000 artifacts. The permanent exhibits are organized around three principal themes: The History of the Earth and Life; To the Rhythm of Nature; and The Museum of the Museum. The insect collection is remarkable for its wide variety of species; the dinosaur section has a complete skeleton of a megathere dating back over two million years; and the vertebrates section includes such exhibits as the African Elephant and the Marsupial Wolf of Tasmania. Invertebrates are represented by a vast collection of molluscs from the Philippines and Cuba.

Museo Lázaro Galdiano (39)

Serrano 122, 28006 ☎ 91 561 60 84 ➠ 91 561 77 93

Rubén Darío, República Argentina *Tue.–Sun. 10am–2pm* ● *400 Ptas; students 200 Ptas; over-65s, children, free on Sat.*

The private art collection of writer and editor José Lázaro Galdiano (1862–1947), is kept in the mansion he commissioned for his wealthy wife Doña Paula Florido. The collection includes *Head of The Savior*, attributed to Leonardo da Vinci, and works by Goya and other European artists, especially British painters. The museum also houses a collection of French 14th-century ivory sculptures; Spanish, Italian, Byzantine and Limoges enamels; religious gold and silverwork, and jewelry; Renaissance medals and bronzes. Textiles and fans complete this unusual collection.

Not forgetting

■ **Museo Sorolla (40)** Paseo General Martínez Blanco 37, 28010 ☎ 91 310 15 84 Tue.–Sat. 10am–3pm; Sun. 10am–2pm
The former home, with contents, of the painter Joaquín Sorolla y Bastida (1863–1923). A selection of works by the artist, generally considered to be Spain's best Impressionist painter. A delightful garden decorated with azulejos *(ceramic tiles), fountains and pools.*

■ **Museo de Escultura al Aire Libre (41)** Paseo de la Castellana 41, 28046 *A small open-air museum located under the flyover that links the calles of Juan Bravo and Eduardo Dato. A remarkable piece of civil engineering, the bridge was considered a model of urban design in the early 1970s. Displayed here are the works of 15 Spanish sculptors; notable among them are the* Sirena Varada *by Eduardo Chillida (comprising six tonnes of concrete suspended from the bridge), the mobile by Eusebio Sempere,* Mère Ubu *by Joan Miró, and* Al otro lado del muro *by José María Subirachs.*

Where to stay ➥ 26 ➥ 28
Where to eat ➥ 50 ➥ 52
After dark ➥ 68 ➥ 70
Where to shop ➥ 130

Al otro lado del muro by José María Subirachs (1972).

In the area

The walk from Nuevos Ministerios to the Plaza de Castilla is like a journey through time, beginning with the architecture of the Franco dictatorship and finishing with the purest expressions of modernism. A curtain of stone, glass and metal stretches across these northern districts.

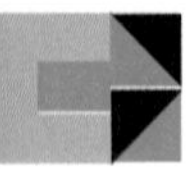

What to see

Azca (42)
Paseo de la Castellana 79, 28046

M *Nuevos Ministerios, Santiago Bernabéu*

A commercial center covering some 500 acres ➡ 142, the Azca complex sprang up during the final years of the Franco dictatorship. The building that best typifies the avant-garde architecture of the 1970s is the skyscraper designed by Javier Sáenz de Oiza, its smooth bronze-glass walls serving as a symbol of economic might over the people (and a nod to Frank Lloyd Wright). The Torre Europa and Torre Picasso are equipped with a fiber-optic network controlling light, temperature and communication systems, and the Torre Picasso, designed by Minoru Yamasaki (architect of the World Trade Center in New York), is the tallest skyscraper in Madrid. The Windsor tower by Genaro Alas and Pedro Casariego (Raimundo Fernández Villaverde, 65) is distinguishable by its cylindrical, smooth-surfaced structure. The most eye-catching Azca building is the Sollube, which has a 'chain-mail' structure of aluminium and white lacquer and a green-glass exterior.

Puerta de Europa (43)
Plaza de Castilla, 28046

M *Plaza de Castilla*

These two leaning towers rise to a height of over 370 feet, and tilt toward one another at an angle of 14.3°, forming a sort of *puerta* (door). Their green, smoked-glass surfaces reflect the surrounding buildings and the Madrid skyline. For architectural experts, the Puerta de Europa is the definitive skyscraper, arguably the most important architectural motif of the 20th century. The two towers seem to defy gravity, appearing locked in conflict. They are home to hundreds of offices.

Nuevos Ministerios (44)
Plaza de San Juan de la Cruz, 28003

M *Nuevos Ministerios*

The idea of bringing together the various government ministries within a single complex was the brainchild of the Spanish Republic. The project was completed under Franco at the end of the 1940s. This may explain the incongruous existence of a monument to the socialist Minister of Public Works, Indalecio Pieto, together with a monument to the dead dictator himself.

Not forgetting

■ **Palacio de Congresos y Exposiciones (45)** Paseo de la Castellana 99, 28046 ☎ 91 337 81 00 ⏲ 8am–8pm *A conference center and entertainment venue. The frieze by Joan Miró was added to the façade in 1980.*
■ **Estadio Santiago Bernabéu (46)** Paseo de la Castellana 104, 28046 ☎ 91 344 00 52 *Home of the Real Madrid football club. A model of 1940s 'sports architecture'.*

Where to stay ➥ 30 ➥ 32 ■ Where to eat ➥ 60 ➥ 64 ■ After ark ➥ 68 ➥ 72 ➥ 80 ➥ 82 ■ Where o shop ➥ 142

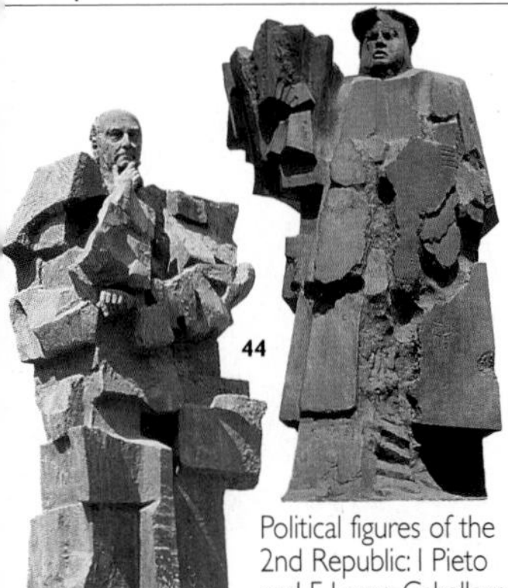

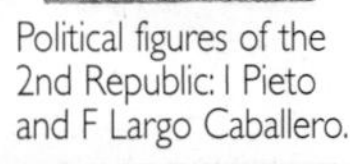
Political figures of the 2nd Republic: I Pieto and F Largo Caballero.

Paradores de turismo
State-owned buildings, usually former castles, palaces or monasteries, converted into luxury hotels. Book in advance. *Requena 3, 28013 Madrid* ☎ *(91) 516 66 66* ➠ *(91) 516 66 57 or (91) 516 66 58*

Further afield

22 Days out

Sports and pastimes

Airships
Globos y dirigibles Boreal
☎ *91 561 39 68*

Cycling
Federación Madrileña de Ciclismo
☎ *91 320 44 95*

Golf
Federación de Golf
☎ *91 556 71 34*

Paragliding
Hombre Pájaro
☎ *91 532 82 50*

Hiking
Taller de naturaleza Las Acacias
☎ *91 465 45 99*

Bungee jumping
Sport Adrenalin
☎ *91 365 19 23*

Horseback-riding
Individual lessons, courses and rides.
Posta de Corpes
Cañada de "El Arenal" - Cadalsos de los Vidrios (Par la C-501, carretera Plasencia)
☎ *91 861 14 16*
● *2200 Ptas for 1 hour*

Skiing
Navacerrada, Valcotos and Valdesqui are the three ski resorts closest to Madrid.
Information:
ATUDEM
(Asociación Turística de Estaciones de Esquí y Montaña)
☎ *91 359 15 57*

INDEX BY SUBJECT

Basic facts

San Lorenzo del Escorial, Aranjuez and Alcalá de Henares are part of the Comunidad de Madrid, one of Spain's 15 autonomous local authorities. Segovia and Toledo belong to Castilla y León and Castilla-La Mancha respectively.

Further afield

2

5

5

10

16

20

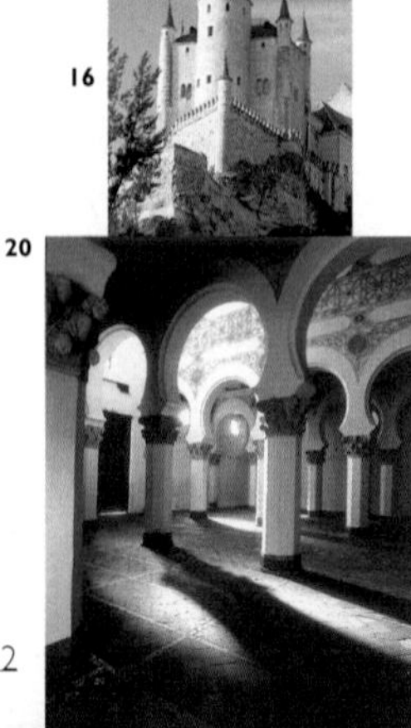

Segovia (13–17)

56 miles northwest of Madrid

C-8b train, from Atocha or Chamartín Stations journey time 1 hr 49 mins ● *One-way ticket 750 Ptas*

La Sepulvedana from Patio de la Florida 11, 28003 ☎ *91 530 48 00 Journey time 1 hr 30 mins* ● *One-way ticket 765 Ptas*

N–VI and N–603

If you have time, leave the N–VI at Collado Villalba and take the C–601 across the Sierra to Puerto de Navacerrada ➡ 111, a busy ski resort, and down to Valsaín and Granja de San Ildefonso.

Tourist office

Plaza Mayor 10, 40001
☎ *921 46 03 34*

San Lorenzo de El Escorial (5–8)

31 miles northwest of Madrid

C-8a train from Atocha or Chamartín Stations Journey time 50 mins ● *One-way ticket 430 Ptas*

Herranz from La Moncloa ☎ *(91) 890 41 00 Journey time 1 hr* ● *One-way ticket 380 Ptas*

N–VI and M–505

Tourist office

Florida Blanca 10, 28200
☎ *91 890 15 54*

Toledo (18–22)

44 miles south of Madrid

C-3 train from Atocha Station Journey time 1 hr 15 mins ● *One-way ticket 615 Ptas*

From Estación Sur, Méndez Álvaro, 28045 ☎ *91 527 29 61 Journey time 1 hr 30 mins* ● *One-way ticket 570 Ptas*

N–401 Park by the city walls

Tourist office

Puerta Visagra, 45003
☎ *925 22 08 43*

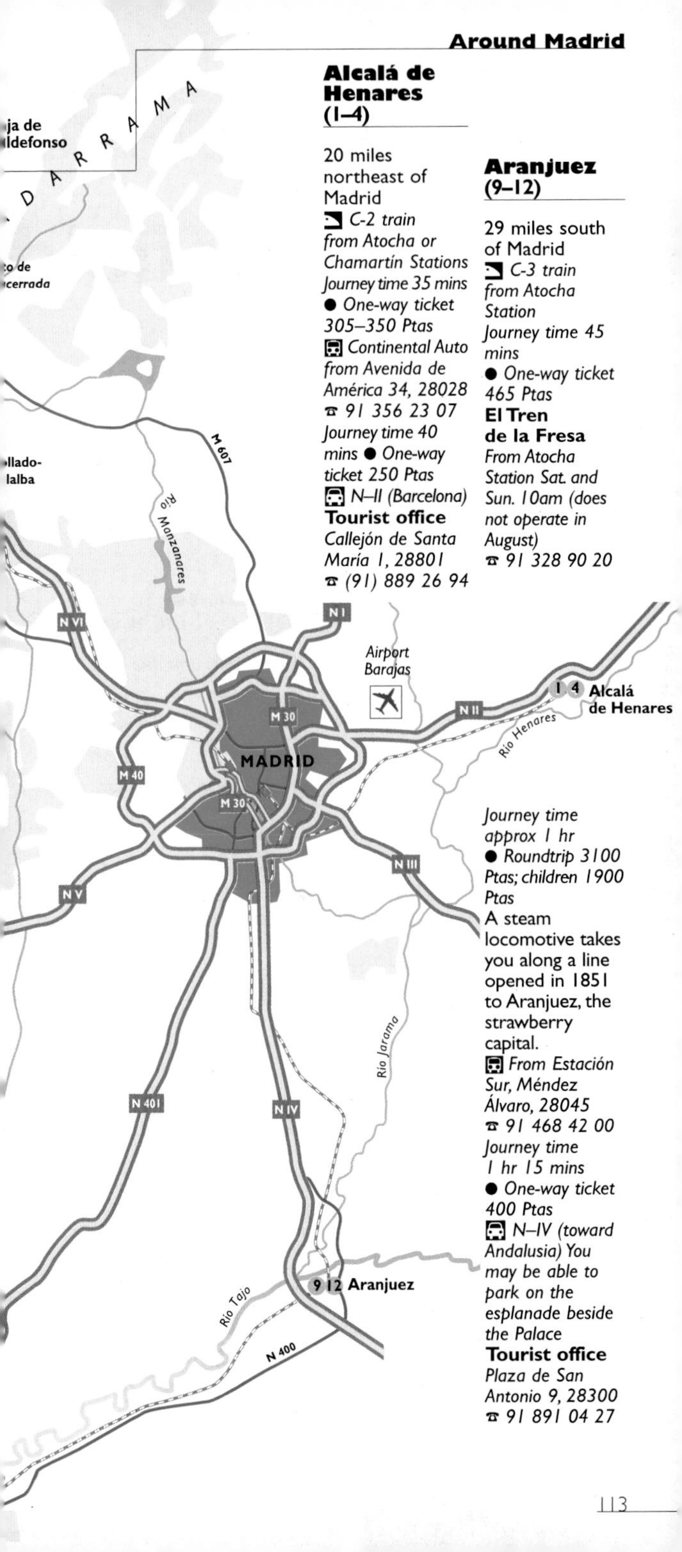

Alcalá de Henares (1–4)

20 miles northeast of Madrid

C-2 train from Atocha or Chamartín Stations Journey time 35 mins ● *One-way ticket 305–350 Ptas*

Continental Auto from Avenida de América 34, 28028 ☎ *91 356 23 07 Journey time 40 mins* ● *One-way ticket 250 Ptas*

N–II (Barcelona)

Tourist office *Callejón de Santa María 1, 28801* ☎ *(91) 889 26 94*

Aranjuez (9–12)

29 miles south of Madrid

C-3 train from Atocha Station Journey time 45 mins ● *One-way ticket 465 Ptas*

El Tren de la Fresa *From Atocha Station Sat. and Sun. 10am (does not operate in August)* ☎ *91 328 90 20 Journey time approx 1 hr* ● *Roundtrip 3100 Ptas; children 1900 Ptas*

A steam locomotive takes you along a line opened in 1851 to Aranjuez, the strawberry capital.

From Estación Sur, Méndez Álvaro, 28045 ☎ *91 468 42 00 Journey time 1 hr 15 mins* ● *One-way ticket 400 Ptas*

N–IV (toward Andalusia) You may be able to park on the esplanade beside the Palace

Tourist office *Plaza de San Antonio 9, 28300* ☎ *91 891 04 27*

In the area

Once an important Roman city, in the Middle Ages, Alcalá became an Arab market town rivaling that of Toledo ➥ 122. The old streets and 14th-century walls remain, as does the Castilian-style Plaza Mayor. The medieval and Renaissance nucleus has been declared a historic monument.

Further afield

Universidad Complutense (1)

Founded by Cardinal Cisneros in 1495, the Universidad Complutense (*Complutum* was the Roman name of the city) formed the cultural hub of the town. The university consisted of 'major' and 'minor' colleges, together with numerous convents and churches. Among the students were humanists, politicians and great theologians such as Quevedo, Francisco Suárez and Saint Ignatius Loyola. Miguel de Cervantes – the famous author of *Don Quixote* – was born here in 1547. In 1561 Philip II transferred the capital to Madrid, though the town kept its university status until 1836, when the Complutense was moved to Madrid, causing Alcalá to slide into decline.

Colegio de San Ildefonso (2)

Plaza de Santo Domingo, 28801 ☎ 91 885 40 00

daily 10am–6pm • free *☎ 91 882 13 54 15 • 300 Ptas*

Of the original building, only the Mudéjar amphitheater, with its fine coffered ceiling and plateresque rostrum, survives. The College façade is one of the purest examples of the plateresque style, so-called because its intricacy resembles worked silver (*platero* means silversmith). It was built in 1537 to a design by Rodrigo Gil de Hontañón, architect of the Cathedral of Segovia ➥ 120. Only two of the three great cloisters survive: the Baroque-style *Patio de Santo Tomás de Villanueva*, and the *Patio Trilingüe*, built in Italian Renaissance style.

Iglesia Magistral (3)

Plaza de los Santos Niños, 28801

***Mass** 9.15am, 12.15pm, 6pm, 8pm*

The Iglesia Magistral was erected at the beginning of the 16th century in a style inspired by the Cathedral of Toledo ➥ 122. It contains the tomb of the great Baroque sculptor Gregorio Fernández and an altarpiece by Felipe Vigarny, dating from the early 16th century.

Convento de San Bernardo (4)

Plaza de las Bernardas, 28801 ☎ 91 888 11 22

***Church** daily* *daily ☎ 91 882 13 54 15 • **Museum** 300 Ptas; **Church** free*

Founded in 1618, this was the work of Juan Gómez de Mora. Oval-shaped in plan, it contains six chapels, the principal one housing an altarpiece in the form of an architectural canopy. This church, the Archbishop's Palace and the Madre de Dios convent are all part of the same complex.

Not forgetting

■ **Teatro Cervantes** Cervantes, 28801 ☎ 91 882 24 97 *One of the oldest classical theaters in Spain.* ■ **Convento de San Diego** Beatas 7, 28801 ☎ 91 888 03 05 *The famous* garrapiñadas *(caramelized almonds) are prepared by the nuns.* ■ **La Hostería del Estudiante** Colegios 3, 28801 ☎ 91 888 03 30 *Castilian cuisine. On public holidays, taste the famous* migas con chocolate *(fried bread dabbed with chocolate) – perfect with morning coffee.*

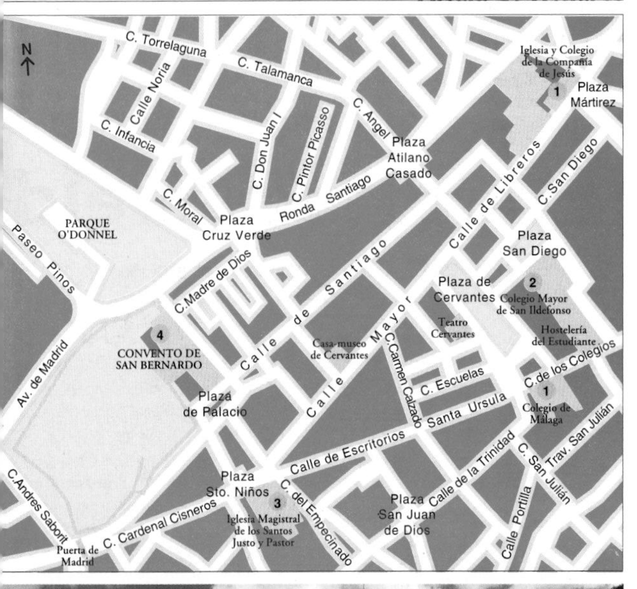

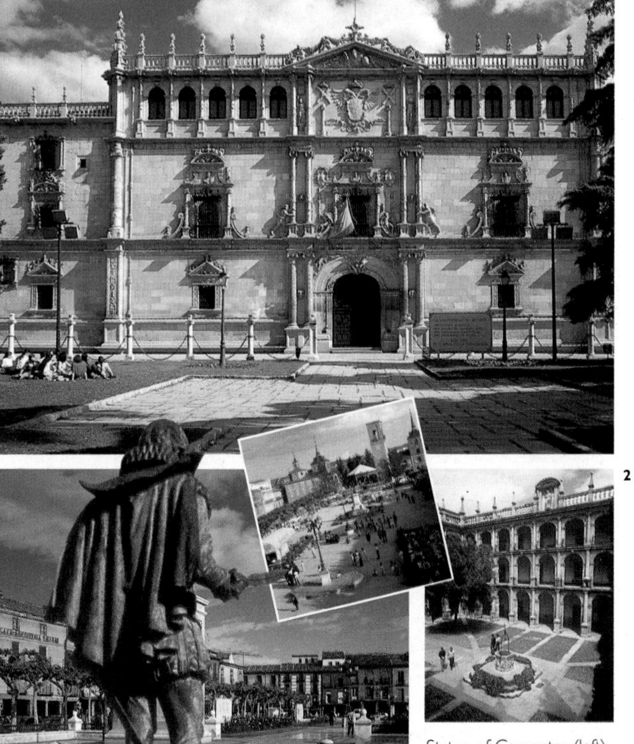

2

Statue of Cervantes (left) and a square named after him.

In the area

The town here grew up around the monastery and palace complex commissioned by Philip II and completed in 1584. Set in the gardens of the park is the Casita del Príncipe, a tiny neoclassical palace designed by Juan de Villanueva, architect of the Prado Museum ➥ 96.

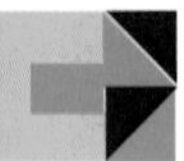

Further afield

Monasterio de San Lorenzo (5)

Paseo Juan de Borbón, 28200
☎ (91) 890 59 03

Summer: Tue.–Sun. 10am–7pm; winter / Tue.–Sun. 10am–6pm ● *850 Ptas; over-65s, students 350 Ptas; Wed. children free*

King Philip II had this monastery built to commemorate the Spanish victory over the French at the Battle of San Quintín in 1557. San Lorenzo was to serve also as a pantheon for the king's father, Charles I of Spain, and for future Spanish monarchs. In 1563 Philip II commissioned a design from Juan Bautista de Toledo, who had worked in Rome with Michelangelo. Work continued under Juan de Herrera, San Lorenzo's true creator, with the involvement of the king himself. The result was dubbed 'the eighth wonder of the world'. The structure is impressive and austere, reflecting the personality of the king, who was the supreme defender of Counter-Reformation ideas. The building forms an immense rectangle. Its long façade runs 680 feet, with four patios and represents the martyrdom of Saint Laurence (he was roasted to death on a gridiron). A Flemish-style pinnacle tower rises from each of its four corners. A statue of San Lorenzo and the Hapsburg coat of arms are the only ornamentation on its main face.

The library (6)

The library, clad in precious wood, is one of the highlights of the visit. The barrel-vaulted ceiling is decorated with allegorical figures representing the Seven Liberal Arts (Grammar, Rhetoric, Logic, Arithmetic, Music, Geometry and Astronomy). The bookshelves include fine reproductions of the first Castilian texts, a Mozarabic codex dating from the 10th century, the breviaries of the Catholic Monarchs and of Philip II, and numerous illuminated miniatures.

Basílica (7)

The basilica's 295-foot high cupola contains the Capilla Mayor (Great Chapel), which features a remarkable Renaissance altarpiece made of marble and porphyry. Note the sculptural groups, the work of Leone and Pompeyo Leoni, on either side of the presbytery, one representing the Emperor and his family at prayer, the other Philip II and his family at prayer.

Philip II's chambers (8)

These two simple rooms are surprisingly understated in comparison with the rest of the building. The bedroom has a balcony overlooking the Capilla Mayor, so that the king could hear Mass from his bed. The floor is covered with 16th-century Talavera tiles.

Not forgetting

■ **Fonda Genara** Plaza de San Lorenzo 2, 28200 ☎ 91 890 33 30 *Home cooking. Specialty:* puchero *(stew)* de Luisa. *Unusual décor.*

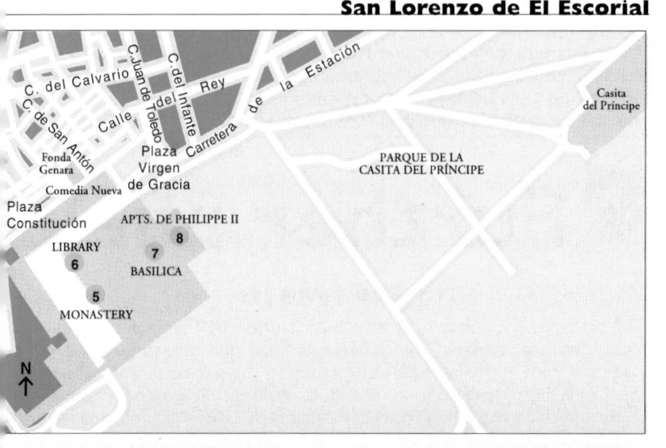
C. del Calvario
C.Juan de Toledo
C.del Infante
Calle del Rey
Carretera de la Estación
C. de San Antón
Fonda Genara
Plaza Virgen de Gracia
Comedia Nueva
Plaza Constitución
APTS. DE PHILIPPE II
8
LIBRARY
6
7
BASILICA
5
MONASTERY
N
Casita del Príncipe
PARQUE DE LA CASITA DEL PRÍNCIPE

5

In the area

A fine example of a royal town, now a historic monument. At the end of the 15th century the Catholic Monarchs made it their *Real Sitio* (royal site). In the 16th century, Philip II built a new palace here. Philip V made this the Court's summer residence at the start of the 18th century.

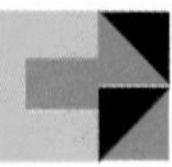

Further afield

The town (9)

The plans for the town were drawn up in 1747 by Ferdinand VI and Italian architect Bonavia. The streets were laid out in Baroque style, on a grid plan, with grand avenues converging on the palace. It was here that the Court witnessed some of the most momentous events in Spanish history, such as the *motín* (riot) of Aranjuez in 1808 – the conspiracy which paved the way for the Napoleonic invasion. The buildings are well preserved, and include a number of three- and four-storey houses dating from the 18th and 19th centuries with gardens and courtyards. The residences of the *oficios y caballeros* on Plaza de San Antonio, the palace of the Dukes of Medinaceli (now a restaurant), the hospital of San Carlos and the Convento de San Pascual are all worth seeing.

Palacio Real (10)
Avenida del Palacio Real ☎ 91 891 13 44

June–Sep.: Tue.–Sun. 10am–6.30pm; / Oct.–May: Tue.–Sun. 10am–5.30pm ● *500 Ptas; over-65s, students, children 250 Ptas, Wed. free*

The main body of the palace, in the fashionable Baroque style of the 18th century, was enlarged by the addition of two neoclassical wings, designed by Sabatini, which flank the Plaza Armería. ★ Do not miss the Porcelain Room.

Jardín de la Isla (11)
Behind the palace

Tue.–Sun. 8am–8.30pm ● *free*

A superb series of promenades modeled on Versailles. The paths and formal walks are punctuated by monumental fountains, arbors and magnificent trees, and cooled by the Tajo (Tagus) river.

Jardín del Príncipe (12)
Reina, toward la Casa del Labrador

Gardens *Tue.–Sun. 8am–8.30pm* ● *free* ***Casa del Labrador*** *10am–6.15pm* ● *425 Ptas; over-65s, students, children 225 Ptas* ***Casa de Los Marinos*** *10am–6.15pm* ● *325 Ptas, over-65s, students, children 225 Ptas*

A garden laid out for the young Charles IV (1788–1808). Planted with a rich variety of trees, the garden covers almost 400 acres and is the perfect setting for a stroll. The Empire-style Casa del Labrador was formerly a Bourbon hunting lodge, and is well worth visiting for its collection of clocks. The Casa de Marinos is now a boating museum where Court barges are displayed.

Not forgetting

■ **Casa Pablo** Almíbar 42, 28300 ☎ 91 891 14 51 *Specialties: pheasant, suckling pig, lamb, seafood.* ■ **La Rana Verde** Reina 1, 28300 ☎ 91 891 32 38 *The dining rooms and terraces are worth a visit, but for the view over the Tajo rather than for the food.* ■ **El Bodegón** Gobernador 62, 28300 ☎ 91 892 51 73 *Occupies the old brick wine cellars and stables of the Medinaceli palace. Suckling pig and lamb roasted over a wood fire.*

12
JARDÍN DEL PRÍNCIPE
Río Tajo
Carretera N.IV
Carretera N.IV
Río Tajo
Calle de la Reina
Calle de Alpajés
C.de las Moreras
Calle del Foso
C.de la Primavera
Calle Príncipe
Calle de Infantas
Calle del Rey
Calle de las Infantas
Calle de Capitán
Montesinos
Antonio
La Rana Verde
Calle
Casa Pablo
Jardín de Isabel II
El Bodegón
JARDÍN DE LA ISLA
11
Jardín del Parterre
9
Plaza de San Antonio
Calle San Antonio
Calle de Gómez
Calle de Gobernador
Calle del Castrillón
PALACIO REAL
10
Plaza de Parejas
Calle de Abastos
Calle del Almíbar
Calle de Stuart
Calle de Postas
Crt.de Toledo
Avenida de
C.de la Paz
Calle del
Calle de la Florida
Carretera de Andalucía

10

The Tajo river and fountains of Aranjuez cool the arid plains of Castile.

In the area

This historic town, now a world heritage site, is perched on a granite rock between the Eresma and Clamores rivers. Originally a Roman settlement, it became a major center of textile and livestock production during the Middle Ages.

Further afield

The aqueduct (13)

Plaza del Azoguejo

The aqueduct is Segovia's most famous monument, and the best preserved building of the Western Roman Empire. Bringing water from 8 miles away to the Plaza del Azoguejo, where it reaches a height of 92 feet, it dates from the 2nd century AD, and is made of granite blocks joined together without the aid of mortar.

Plaza de San Martín (14)

Keep *times vary* ***Church*** *Mass 11.30am, 12.30pm, 9pm*

Site of the Romanesque church of San Martín. The Lozoya tower is a splendid example of a 14th-century fortified residence. A fine group is formed by the Renaissance-style Bornes Palace, the house known as the '15th-century house' and the Library.

The Cathedral (15)

Plaza Mayor, 40006 ☎ 921 46 22 05

Museum and cloisters *daily 9.30am–7pm* ● *250 Ptas*

Begun in 1525, this is the last of the great Gothic cathedrals in Spain. Perched at the highest point of the town, the three naves above the altar rise to 108 feet. Between the cathedral and the Alcázar, do not miss one of the eighteen Romanesque churches of Segovia, San Esteban, with its elegant, tapering tower.

El Alcázar (16)

Plaza de la Reina Victoria Eugenia, 40003 ☎ 921 46 07 59

Spring–summer: daily 10am–7pm; autumn–winter: daily 10am–6pm
● *375 Ptas, children 175 Ptas*

In the 15th century Isabella the Catholic's father decided to erect a palace over a 12th-century tower. The Disney-style castle, all towers and turrets, now houses a military museum.

Iglesia de la Vera Cruz (17)

Carretera de Zamarramala ☎ 921 43 14 75

Apr.–Sep.: Tue.–Sat. 10.30am–1.30pm, 3.30–7pm / Oct.–Mar.: Tue.–Sun. 10.30am–1.30pm, 3.30–6pm ● *175 Ptas*

Built on a dodecagonal (twelve-sided) plan, this beautiful church belonging to the Knights Templar is well worth a visit. Its bell tower offers a breathtaking view over the town and the Alcázar.

Not forgetting

■ **Mesón Casa Cándido** Plaza del Azoguejo 5, 40001 ☎ 921 42 51 03
A renowned restaurant overlooking the aqueduct. Specialties include milk-fed lamb and pork.

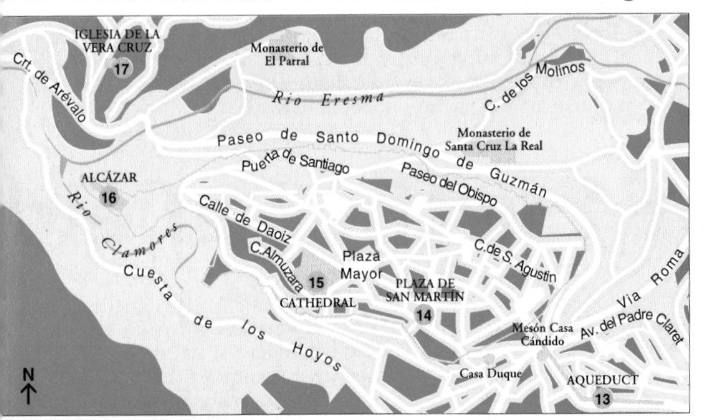

The 128 pillars and 163 arches of the Roman aqueduct carried water to Segovia up until 1988.

In the area

In 554 Toledo was the political and religious capital of Spain, and later became the seat of important councils. It was also a Moorish town. For some five centuries the three great cultures of the Iberian Peninsula – Muslim, Christian and Jewish – merged here.

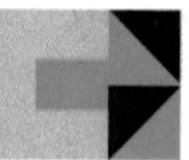

Further afield

The Old Town (18)

Renowned for its damascenes (intricate, water-like inlays on steel) ➡ 134, Toledo has preserved its maze of medieval streets. The medieval Alcázar and Great Mosque were incorporated into a castle and cathedral, but the 16th-century Puerta de Bisagra and 12th–14th century Puerta del Sol at the entrance to the town can still be seen, as can the San Martín and Alcántara bridges, and the Moorish baths.

The cathedral (19)
Arco de Palacio 2, 45001 ☎ 925 22 22 41

Oct 1–Apr. 30: Mon.–Sat. 10.30am–1pm, 3.30–6pm, Sun. 10.30am–1.30pm, 4–7pm / May 1–Sep. 30: Mon.–Sat. 10.30am–1pm, 3.30–7pm, Sun. 10.30am–1.30pm, 4–7pm ● 500 Ptas

The cathedral was begun in 1227 and completed in 1493. Its interior reveals various styles – note the Flamboyant Gothic high altar and the Renaissance choir and stalls. Worth seeing are the *Transparente* (screen) by Narciso Tomé, and the museum, which features works by El Greco and Van Dyck.

Santa María la Blanca (20)
Reyes Católicos 2, 45002 ☎ 925 22 72 57

Oct. 1–Apr. 30: daily 10am–1.45pm, 3.30–6.45pm / May 1–Sep. 30: daily 10am–1.45pm, 3.30–5.45pm ● 150 Ptas

This stunning five-aisled Almohad – style synagogue dating from the 12th century was transformed into a church in the 15th century. The original horseshoe arches and interlaced decoration have been retained. Very pretty small garden at the entrance.

Iglesia de Santo Tomé (21)
Plaza del Conde 1, 45002 ☎ 925 25 60 98

daily 10am–6.45pm ● 150 Ptas

A 14th-century church with a Mudéjar tower, and El Greco's *Burial of the Count of Orgaz* (1586), painted specifically for the church.

Mezquita del Cristo de la Luz (22)

If you can find the person with the keys...

A tiny mosque completed in 999, as testified by the Kufic inscription. The only entirely Moorish monument in the town, it was built in the Caliph style, with Visigothic columns and horseshoe arches.

Not forgetting

■ **Parador Nacional de Turismo Conde de Orgaz** Paseo los Cigarales, 45002 ☎ 925 22 18 50 *Splendid views over the town. Cuisine from La Mancha.* ■ **Casa Aurelio** Sinagoga 6, 45001 ☎ 925 22 20 97 *Castilian cuisine.* ■ **Asador Adolfo** Granada 5, 45001 ☎ 925 22 73 21 *Traditional cooking meets nouvelle cuisine.*

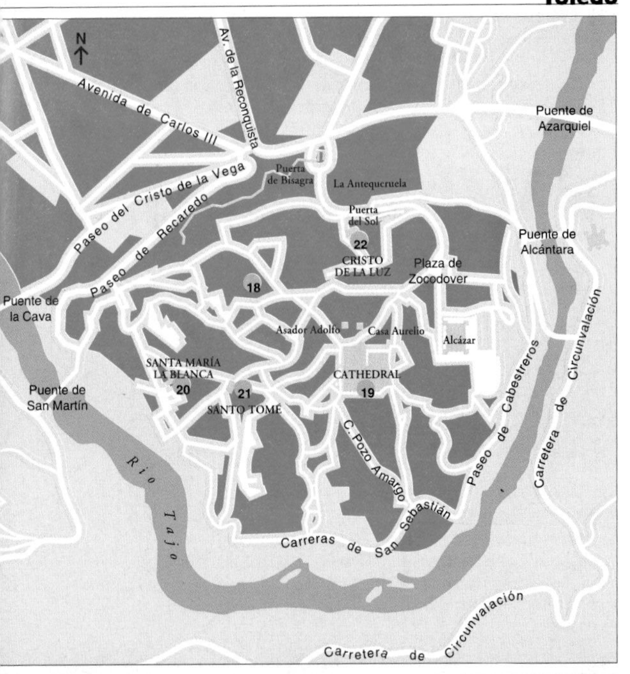
N
Avenida de Carlos III
Av. de la Reconquista
Paseo del Cristo de la Vega
Paseo de Recaredo
Puerta de Bisagra
La Antequeruela
Puerta del Sol
22
CRISTO DE LA LUZ
Plaza de Zocodover
Puente de Azarquiel
Puente de Alcántara
18
Puente de la Cava
Asador Adolfo
Casa Aurelio
Alcázar
SANTA MARÍA LA BLANCA
20
21
SANTO TOMÉ
CATHEDRAL
19
Puente de San Martín
C. Pozo Amargo
Paseo de Cabestreros
Carretera de Circunvalación
Río Tajo
Carreras de San Sebastián
Carretera de Circunvalación

18
20
18
18
19

Where to shop

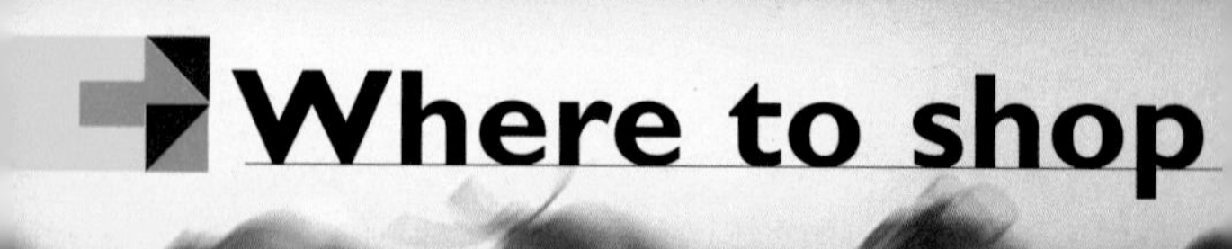

Where to shop
Look for luxury goods in the Salamanca distinct; jewelry in Calle Serrano and Gran Vía; fashion in Calle Almirante; traditional Spanish styles around the Puerta del Sol; department stores on Calle Serrano, Goya and Preciados.

Sales
Rebajas de temporada – seasonal sales – are held twice a year: January–February and July–August.

What to bring back

A torero's costume, a flamenco dress, castanets, a mantilla, a Spanish hairnet and a fan; a string of *Majorica* pearls and a piece of damascene work from Toledo; leather or a Real Madrid jersey; a fashionable handbag or shoes; olive oil, *jamón Serrano* and *turrón*.

THE INSIDER'S FAVORITES

INDEX BY TYPE

In the area

The main reason for visiting this part of the city is its wonderful architecture, but don't miss the stores in the center of Madrid which overflow with souvenirs. ■ Where to stay ➡ 18 ■ Where to eat ➡ 36 ➡ 38 ■ After dark ➡ 76 ➡ 78 ➡ 82 ■ What to see ➡ 92

Where to shop

El Caballo Cojo (1)

Segovia 7, 28005 ☎ 91 366 43 90

M *Sol, Ópera* ***Handicrafts, ceramics*** *Mon.–Fri. 10am–2pm, 5–8.30pm; Sat. 10am–2pm; closed August*

Behind a 19th-century shop front is a magnificent array of ceramics reproduced in period styles. Particularly impressive are the blown glass objects from Mallorca in their characteristic blue, writing desks, candelabra and a collection of holy-water basins priced between 1000 Ptas and 40,000 Ptas.

Monsy (2)

Plaza Mayor 20, 28012 ☎ 91 548 15 14

M *Sol* ***Souvenirs*** *Mon.–Sat. 9.30am–1.30pm, 4.30–8pm*

Lovers of kitsch will be spoilt for choice among this feast of bric-à-brac: bottles of Tío Pepe made in Jerez, bullfighters' costumes, castanets, El Cid's sword, Real Madrid merchandise ➡ 108, and damascene objects from Toledo ➡ 122.

Justo Algaba (3)

Paz 4, 28012 ☎ 91 523 35 95 ➠ 91 523 37 17

M *Sol* ***Bullfighters' costumes, flamenco-style dresses*** *Mon.–Fri. 10am–2pm, 5–8pm; Sat. 10am–2pm*

This tailor serves some of the biggest names in bullfighting ➡ 100. Behind the window protected from the sun's rays, you can buy stockings, a *montera* (bullfighter's hat) and pumps to transform yourself into the perfect *torero*. From the workshop you can order an authentic made-to-measure *traje campero* (the suit worn by bullfighters for out-of-town practise sessions) or a flamenco-style dress with all the proper accessories. Prices depend on the number of hours of work involved and the quality of the materials and embroidery.

Seseña (4)

Cruz 23, 28012 ☎ 91 531 68 40

M *Sol* ***Capes*** *Mon.–Fri. 10am–3pm, 4.30–8pm; Sat. 10am–2pm*

Picasso, Hemingway and Hillary Clinton are among the many who have been unable to resist Seseña's warm, dramatic Madrid-style capes. Seseña is now the only store specializing in this romantic garment. It is worth a visit just to admire the window display. Men's capes from 60,000 Ptas.

Not forgetting

■ **Casa Yustas (5)** Plaza Mayor 30, 28012 ☎ 91 366 58 34
Every kind of headgear from military caps to the famous Andalusian headdresses.
■ **El Riojano (6)** Mayor 10, 28003 ☎ 91 366 44 82
Living up to its reputation since 1855. Worth a visit as much for the décor as for the cakes.

■ Where to shop ➥ 144

2

4

6

6

2

In the area
Steeped in Spanish tradition, this is the place to buy Spanish costumes, feminine finery and traditional sweets. ■ After dark ➡ 76 ■ What to see ➡ 92 ➡ 94 ■ Where to shop ➡ 130

Casa Jiménez (7)

Preciados 42, 28013 ☎ 91 548 05 26

Callao, Santo Domingo **Shawls, mantillas** *Mon.–Sat. 10.30am–1.30pm, 5–8pm*

Manila shawls imported from the Philippines and mantillas of silken lace are the specialties of this store which claims to be 'the best-stocked and oldest in Spain'. For almost a century it has been selling sumptuous, hand-embroidered shawls in brilliant colors with oriental motifs. Originally worn to keep out the cold, in the 18th century they came to be regarded as fashion accessories. Now part of Spanish tradition, shawls are still very popular and are worn for special occasions. Machine-made shawls start at 5000 Ptas, top-of-the-range 40,000 Ptas.

Casa Mira (8)

Carrera de San Jerónimo 30, 28014☎ 91 429 67 96 ➡ 91 429 82 21

Sol, Sevilla **Turrón** *Mon.–Sat. 9.30am–2pm, 6.30–9pm, Sun. 10.30am–2.30pm, 5.30–9pm*

Turrón (Spanish nougat) and *mazapán* (marzipan) are top of every Spaniard's list of Christmas goodies. If you happen to be passing by during the festive season, don't be surprised to find an endless queue of *Madrileños* waiting their turn to buy the *turrón* and other treats made here since 1885. Try *turrones* from Segovia ➡ 120 or Alicante, flavored with nuts, coconut, fruit or chocolate, or guirlache, another type of nougat. About 4000 Ptas a kilo.

Casa de Diego (9)

Plaza Puerta del Sol 12, 28013 Madrid
☎ 91 522 66 43 ➡ 91 531 02 23

Sol **Umbrellas, fans** *Mon.–Sat. 9.45am–1.30pm, 4.30–8pm*
Mesonero Romanos 4, 28013 ☎ 91 521 02 23

'Tomorrow it will rain' is the motto of this old store in the Puerta del Sol ➡ 94. Since 1858 they have been selling umbrellas made in their own workshops, as well as walking sticks, sunshades, shawls, mantillas, combs and a huge range of fans, made from paper, mother-of-pearl or gold. Fans start at 350 Ptas, but expect to pay 50,000 Ptas for hand-painted ones with mother-of-pearl blades.

Not forgetting

■ **M. Gil (10)** Carrera de San Jerónimo 2, 28014 ☎ 91 521 25 49
Established 1880: mantillas, embroidered table linen from Lagartera (Toledo region ➡ 122), traditional hairnets, embroidered shawls and typical Madrileño costumes.
■ **Carpincho (11)** Preciados 33, 28013 ☎ 91 521 13 60
Range of high-quality ceramics from Seville, appointed agent for Majorica *pearls and Lladró porcelain.*
■ **Manuel Herrero (12)** Preciados 7–16, 28013 ☎ 91 521 29 90
Reasonably-priced leather fashions and shoes.
■ **La Violeta (13)** Plaza de Canalejas 6, 28014 ☎ 91 522 55 22
This store has been selling its famous sweets, colored, flavored and shaped like violets, since 1915.

Gran Vía
Callao
Plaza del Callao
C.de Jacometrezo
Calle Abada
C. Mesonero
Calle de Preciados
Calle del Carmen
Plaza del Carmen
Tetuán
Calle de la Montera
Calle Aduana
Calle de Alcalá
Calle de Sevilla
Sevilla
C.Cedaceros
C. de Arlabán
Plaza Canalejas
Jerónimo
V.de la Vega
Calle de Echegaray
C. del Príncipe
Calle de la Cruz
C. Victoria
C.Espoz y Mina
C.Carrera San
Puerta del Sol
Sol
C.del Arenal
Calle de
Mtro. Victoria
C.Misericordia
Plaza San Martín
C.Trujillos
C.Veneras
C.Priora Flora
Calle
Casa Mira
Turrones
Dulces
Mazapanes
Polvorones
Casa
Mira
Madrid
Calle de Preciados
8
9
10
11

Basic facts
Madrid's shopping scene is dominated by El Corte Inglés where you will find everything from fashions to food all under one roof. More appealing are the smaller shopping malls incorporating small boutiques set in bright, stylish surroundings with plenty of bars and cafés; just the thing

Where to shop

El Corte Inglés (14)

Preciados 1-2-3-4, 28013 ☎ 91 379 80 00 ➡ 91 521 56 57

M Sol ***Fashions, records, tapes and CDs, videos, books, toys*** *Mon.–Sat. 10am–9.30pm Raimundo Fernández Villaverde 79, 28003 ☎ 91 556 33 00; Princesa 42, 28008 ☎ 91 542 48 00; Goya 76, 28009 ☎ 91 577 71 71; Goya 87, 28001 ☎ 91 577 71 71; Serrano 47, 28001 ☎ 91 432 93 00*

At the turn of the century, El Corte Inglés was just a tailor's workshop on Calle Preciados, specializing in gentlemen's outfits with a distinctly 'English' cut. As the years went by, their range of products and services increased enormously and Corte Inglés stores multiplied. Now the chain offers such services as coffee shops and restaurants, beauty and hairdressing salons, tobacconists, travel agencies and supermarkets. At present, Madrid has no fewer than sixteen shopping malls and stores under the banner of El Corte Inglés, all strategically situated and offering complementary services: the branch at Goya 76 sells fashions, leather goods, jewelry, perfumes and sportswear; along the street at Goya 87, the range includes household goods, books, photographic

for those who prefer relaxed, leisurely shopping.

equipment, CDs and videos. The huge selection of goods and brands, and the efficiency and quality of its services ensure the continued success of El Corte Inglés. It is now the only store in Madrid that can truly be called a 'department store'.

Not forgetting

El Jardín de Serrano
(15) Goya 6–8, 28001
☎ 91 577 00 12
Winner of the European Design Prize in the shopping mall category. Elegant and well situated, with boutiques on two levels, a large café and a shady garden.

ABC Serrano (16) Serrano 61, 28004 ☎ 91 577 50 31
Recently opened conversion of the old ABC and Blanco y Negro newspaper offices. Four levels of stores in a bright, congenial setting. Wonderful neo-plateresque façade on the Paseo de la Castellana side.

Multicentro Serrano 88 (17) Serrano 88, 28006 ☎ 91 547 50 01
One of Madrid's very first shopping malls, containing fashion boutiques and gift stores, and a pleasant café.

17 16 14

In the area

Elegant stores and cafés, theaters and state-of-the-art movie theaters, the Gran Vía is a must for visitors. ■ Where to stay ➡ 18 ➡ 20 ■ After dark ➡ 72 ➡ 74 ■ What to see ➡ 94

Where to shop

Zara (18)

Gran Vía 32, 28013 ☎ 91 522 97 27 ➡ 91 532 95 31

Ⓜ *Callao* ***Men's and women's ready-to-wear*** ⏲ *Mon.–Sat. 10am–8.30pm* ▭ ◆ *Princesa 63, 28008 ☎ 91 543 24 15; Bravo Murillo 104, 28039 ☎ 91 533 10 50*

Ever since it opened, Zara has been a fashion phenomenon with dozens of branches all over Spain and in big cities around the world (including New York). The secret of their success is simple: up-to-date styles at unbeatable prices. All over Madrid, their shop windows display the latest trends in men's, women's and children's clothes, as well as shoes, handbags and other accessories.

Casa del Libro (19)

Gran Vía 29, 28013 ☎ 91 521 21 13 ➡ 91 522 77 58

Ⓜ *Gran Vía, Callao* **Books** ⏲ *Mon.–Sat. 9am–9pm* ▭ ◆ *Maestro Victoria 3, 28013 ☎ 91 521 48 98*

Books on every imaginable subject take up the five levels of this huge store. With a permanent stock of around 500,000 volumes, it is one of Europe's biggest bookstores. Despite its size it is still a friendly place and it is easy to while away a pleasant afternoon browsing through its shelves. Casa del Libro recently opened a large foreign language section.

Cortefiel (20)

Gran Vía 27-76, 28013 ☎ 91 522 00 93 ➡ 91 522 19 99

Ⓜ *Gran Vía, Callao* **Ready-to-wear** ▭ ⏲ *Mon.–Sat. 10am–8.30pm* ◆ *Aguileras 62, 28015 ☎ 91 543 04 05; Paseo de la Castellana 146, 28046 ☎ 91 458 29 30*

With various branches scattered around the city, this chain store has, since the early 1930s, sold reasonably-priced casual fashions in fairly classic styles. A little further along the Gran Vía (at no. 59), Springfield caters for younger, sports-minded customers.

Grassy (21)

Gran Vía 1, 28013 ☎ 91 532 10 07 ➡ 91 575 48 67

Ⓜ *Banco de España, Gran Vía* ***Jewelry*** ⏲ *Mon.–Fri. 9.30am–1.30pm, 4.30–8pm, Sat. 9.30am–3.30pm* ▭ ◆ *José Ortega y Gasset 17, 28006 ☎ 91 577 94 35*

One of Madrid's oldest and most prestigious jewelry stores, with the style and atmosphere of a bygone age.

Not forgetting

■ **Aldao (22)** Gran Vía 15, 28013 ☎ 91 522 11 56
A classic among Madrid jewellers.

■ **Madrid Rock (23)** Gran Vía 25, 28013 ☎ 91 523 26 52
Music store catering for every taste, with the accompaniment of very loud Spanish rock.

Calle del Desengaño
C.de Valverde
C.Fuencarral
Calle de la Reina
Gran Vía
C. del Clavel
Gran Vía
Gran Vía
C. Montera
Calle Caballero de Gracia
C.Jardines
Calle de Alcalá
C.Marqués de Cubas
Callao
18
19
7
20
23
9
22
12
8
21
19
6

19
ESPASA CALPE
CASA DEL LIBRO
19
PIAGET
+20°
BAUME & MERCIER
GRASSY

In the area

In the neighborhood west of the Gran Vía, traditional jewellers and ceramics stores stand side-by-side with modern fashion boutiques. All of them contribute to the buzz of this cosmopolitan thoroughfare.

■ Where to stay ➡ 20 ■ Where to eat ➡ 38 ■ After dark ➡ 80

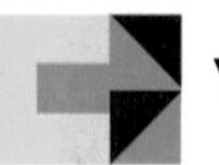

Where to shop

Antigua Casa Talavera (24)

Isabel la Católica 2, 28013 ☎ 91 547 34 17

M *Santo Domingo* **Ceramics** *Mon.–Fri. 10am–1.30pm, 5–8pm; Sat. 10am–1.30pm*

This turn-of-the-century store is an Aladdin's cave of traditional Spanish pottery, with reproductions of pieces dating from the 10th to the 18th century. These are manufactured in family-run workshops in Talavera (a little village in the Toledo region ➡ 122), Sevilla, Puente del Arzobispo, Granada and Manises. Baptismal fonts, candelabra, tiles (on which they will engrave a proverb of your choice), decorative plates and tureens are all sold here.

Hernández (25)

Gran Vía 56, 28013 ☎ 91 547 06 54

M *Santo Domingo, Callao* **Handicrafts, jewelry, fans** *Mon.–Sat. 10am–1.30pm, 4.30–8.30pm*

The window of this traditional store looks like any other in the neighborhood, but go in and you will discover a wonderful array of feminine finery: fans, *Majorica* pearls, costume jewelry and damascene (steel with inlaid gold) knick-knacks from Toledo ➡ 122.

Zaraúz (26)

Gran Vía 45, 28013 ☎ 91 547 17 36

M *Santo Domingo* **Men's and women's ready-to-wear** *Mon.–Sat. 10am–2pm, 5–8.30pm* *Goya 7–9, 28001 ☎ 91 435 49 48*

Locals love Zaraúz for the fine quality and discreet, elegant style of its suits and sportswear. Remarkable selection of neckties, prices up to 12,000 Ptas.

Regalos Ar (27)

Gran Vía 46, 28013 ☎ 91 522 68 69 ➡ 91 531 56 47

M *Callao* **Handicrafts, porcelain, jewelry** *Mon.–Sat. 10am–8pm*

A modern store whose window displays an endless variety of gifts and attractive souvenirs, all 'made in Spain'. These include stunning porcelain, including a famous collection of figurines by Lladró for whom Regalos Ar is an appointed agent. Equally outstanding are the *Majorica* pearls, glassware and craft items.

Not forgetting

■ **Camper (28)** Gran Vía 54, 28013 ☎ 91 547 52 23
An internationally-famous Spanish firm whose first priority is comfort. Offers a huge range of designer shoes and boots, from the classic to the trendy, with some very witty touches.

■ **Bravo Java (29)** Gran Vía 54, 28013 ☎ 91 522 22 00
Renowned for the range and quality of its shoes.

28

25

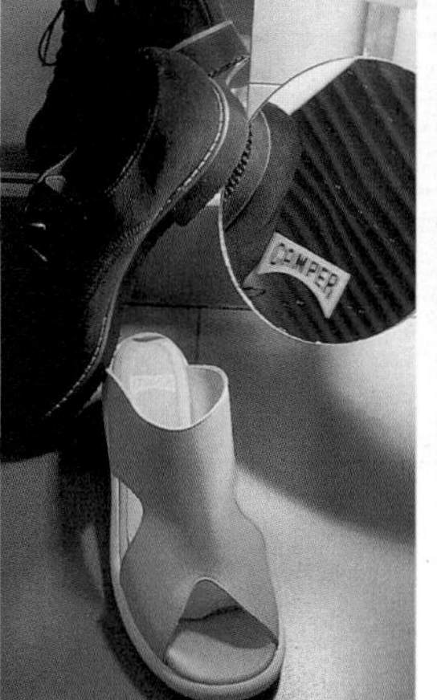

Majorica pearls, made on the island of Mallorca, are the nearest thing to real and cultured pearls. It's very hard to tell the difference.

In the area

Calle Almirante was the place to be in the heady days of 1980s fashion. It turned out to be a flash in the pan, but some talent still survives.

■ Where to stay ➥ 22 ■ Where to eat ➥ 44 ■ After dark ➥ 68 ➥ 76 ➥ 78 ➥ 84 ■ What to see ➥ 104

Where to shop

Ararat (30)

Almirante 10-11, 28004 ☎ 91 531 81 56 ➠ 91 532 10 47

Colón, Banco de España ***Women's ready-to-wear*** *Mon.–Sat. 11pm–2pm, 5–8.30pm*

Although the neighborhood's golden age is over, Ararat continues to be on the pulse with its designer boutiques, including Vértigo, VMR, Rosas Rojas and A Menos Cuarto. Evening and town wear.

Piamonte (31)

Piamonte 16, 28004 ☎ 91 522 45 80 ➠ 91 521 82 25

Colón, Banco de España ***Accessories, jewelry*** *Mon.–Sat. 10.30am–2pm, 5–8.30pm* *Marqués del Monasterio 5, 28004 ☎ 91 308 48 62*

Since the 1980s, this store has gained a strong reputation and a large clientele. Inside, accessories for every occasion are displayed in simple, attractive surroundings: belts, purses, gloves and a small but interesting collection of reasonably-priced jewelry. From Piamonte's own workshops you can order top-quality bags in leather, canvas or other materials, in the color of your choice. Orders take ten days. Around 15000 Ptas.

Joaquín Berao (32)

Conde de Xiquena 13, 28004 ☎ 91 310 16 20

Colón, Banco de España ***Jewelry*** *Mon.–Sat. 10.30am–2pm, 5–8.30pm* *Conde de Aranda 7, 28001 ☎ (91) 576 73 50*

In the mid-Eighties, Joaquín Berao left his experimental studio and set up this little jewelry store to sell his own creations. Since then, he has extended his collections of men's and women's jewelry and his fame has spread beyond the borders of Spain. His most renowned creation is the *raspa* (fishbone) a flexible necklet shaped like a fishbone. Specializing in silver jewelry, Joaquín Berao also makes pieces in painted or gilded bronze. The cheapest items are affordable: necklaces between 9000 Ptas and 80000 Ptas.

Not forgetting

■ **Patrimonio Comunal Olivarero (33)** Meija Lequerica 1, 28004 ☎ 91 308 0505 *All the olive oils sold here are from renowned producers.*

■ **Vime (34)** Augusto Figueroa 18, 28004 ☎ 91 532 0240 *There are more than a dozen shoe stores concentrated in Calle Augusto Figueroa and the surrounding streets. Ends of lines or models used for fashion exhibitions are offered at bargain prices. This is one of Madrid's oldest stores, selling men's and women's shoes.*

■ **María José Navarro (35)** Conde de Xiquena 9, 28004 ☎ 91 523 47 98 *Off-the-peg women's city wear with an international reputation for quality and elegance.*

■ **Almirante 23 (36)** Almirante 23, 28004 ☎ 91 308 12 02 *For the collector: postcards, cameras, tin boxes, bottles, spectacles, pictures, puzzles, lead soldiers and many more curiosities.*

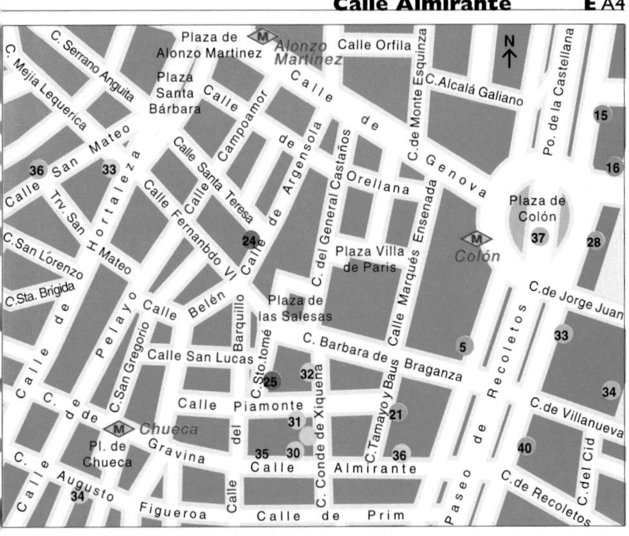
Plaza de Alonzo Martinez
Alonzo Martínez
Calle Orfila
N
C. Serrano Anguita
C. Mejía Lequerica
Plaza Santa Bárbara
Calle de Campoamor
Calle de Argensola
Calle de Genova
C.Alcalá Galiano
C.de Monte Esquinza
Po. de la Castellana
Calle San Mateo
Trv. San Mateo
Calle Hortaleza
Calle Santa Teresa
Calle Fernanbdo VI
Calle de Orellana
C. del General Castaños
Plaza de Colón
Colón
C.San Lorenzo
C.Sta. Brígida
Plaza Villa de Paris
Calle Marqués Ensenada
C.de Jorge Juan
Calle de Pelayo
Calle Belén
Calle Barquillo
Plaza de las Salesas
C. Barbara de Braganza
Paseo de Recoletos
Calle San Lucas
C.San Gregorio
C.Sto.tomé
Calle Piamonte
C.Tamayo y Baus
C.de Villanueva
Chueca
Pl. de Chueca
Calle de Gravina
C. Conde de Xiquena
Calle Almirante
C.del Cid
C.de Recoletos
Calle de Augusto Figueroa
Calle del Barquillo
Calle de Prim
15
16
36
33
24
37
28
5
33
25
32
21
34
31
35
30
36
40
34

Aceite de Oliva
Virgen Extra
(C.E) - ESP. 012
R.S. N.º 16.0157/TO
Vitóliva
Envasado por:
Patrimonio Comunal Olivarero
Prim, 12 - 28004 Madrid
en su planta de Mora (Toledo)
ACIDEZ MAX.
0,4°
CONTENIDO
0,75L e

31

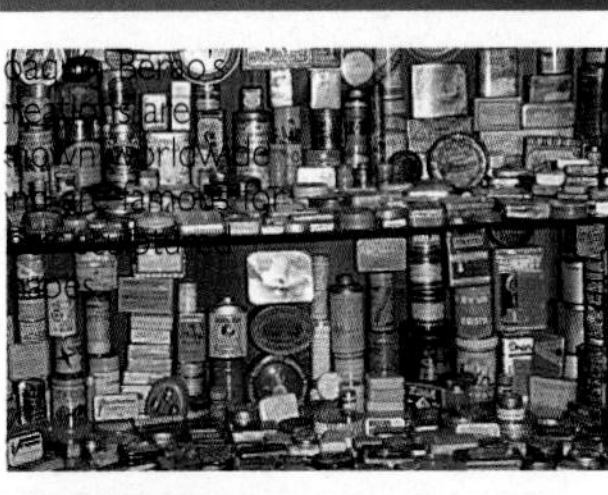

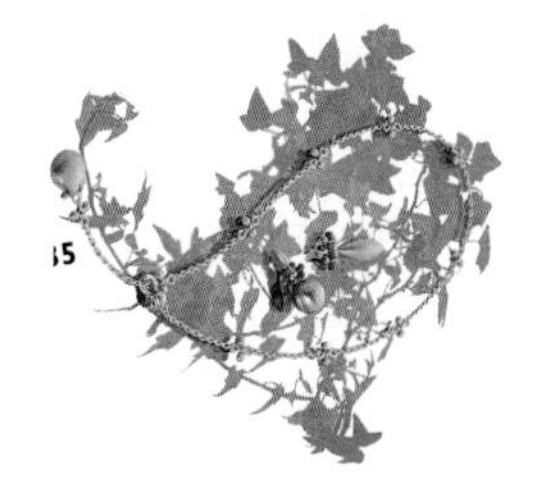

35

33

32

36

In the area

Some of Madrid's most stylish boutiques are in the neighborhood east of Paseo de Recoletos, behind the Biblioteca Nacional. ■ Where to stay ➡ 22 ■ Where to eat ➡ 42 ➡ 44 ➡ 46 ■ After dark ➡ 78 ➡ 84 ■ What to see ➡ 96 ➡ 104 ■ Where to shop ➡ 130 ➡ 144

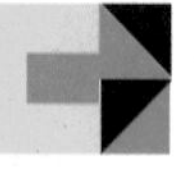

Where to shop

Ispahan (37)

Serrano 5, 28001 ☎ 91 575 20 12 ➠ 91 577 76 41

M *Retiro* ***Carpets*** *Mon.–Sat. 10am–2pm, 4.30–8.30pm*

This carpet store is worth a detour both for its stock and for the building, which underwent major renovations in order to provide space for an antiques center, designers and galleries. Ispahan has now taken over the entire space to display tapestries and Persian, Turkish, Chinese, Tibetan and Caucasian carpets, as well as reproductions of 15th- and 16th-century Spanish cartoons.

Farrutx (38)

Serrano 7, 28001 ☎ 91 576 94 93 ➠ 91 576 34 08

M *Serrano, Retiro* ***Shoes, handbags*** *Mon.–Sat. 10am–2pm, 5–8pm*

This highly prestigious Spanish shoe manufacturer, famed for its original, elegant style, is a leader in its field for quality and design.

Adolfo Domínguez (39)

Serrano 18, 28001 ☎ 91 576 70 53

M *Serrano Rubén Dario* ***Ready-to-wear for men and women*** *Mon.–Sat. 10am–2pm, 5–8pm* *Serrano 96 ☎ 91 576 80 51*

Simple lines, comfort and sophistication, harmonious colors and natural fabrics characterize the clothes created by this designer who became famous in the 1980s for his motto 'pleats are beautiful'. Adolfo Domínguez has since gained international renown and his beautiful sinuous creations appear in boutiques around the world.

Loewe (40)

Serrano 26, 28001 ☎ 91 577 60 56

M *Serrano* ***Accessories, ready-to-wear*** *Mon.–Sat. 9.30am–2pm, 4.30–8.30pm* *Gran Via 8, 23013 ☎ 91 522 68 15*

Loewe specializes in leather, carefully selecting and treating the raw material to produce genuine works of art. As well as leather clothes, there are interesting silk scarves and neckties. Everything here is 'deluxe' – including the prices.

Not forgetting

■ **La Pajarita (41)** Villanueva 14, 28001 ☎ 91 435 74 54
Madrid's other famous traditional candy store ➡ 128. Candy in sixteen different flavors.

■ **Roberto Verino (42)** Claudio Coello 27, 28001 ☎ 91 577 73 81
Talented designer of women's ready-to-wear fashions who emerged in the 1980s.

■ **El Callejón de Jorge Juan (43)** Jorge Juan 14, 28001
Little cul-de-sac with charming boutiques, away from the hustle and bustle of the city. In 1994, the city fathers awarded the tiny street a special prize for its contribution to the environment.

150 ANIVERSARIO
150 ANIVERSARIO
150 ANIVERSARIO
150 ANIVERSARIO
LOEWE
Madrid 1846

40

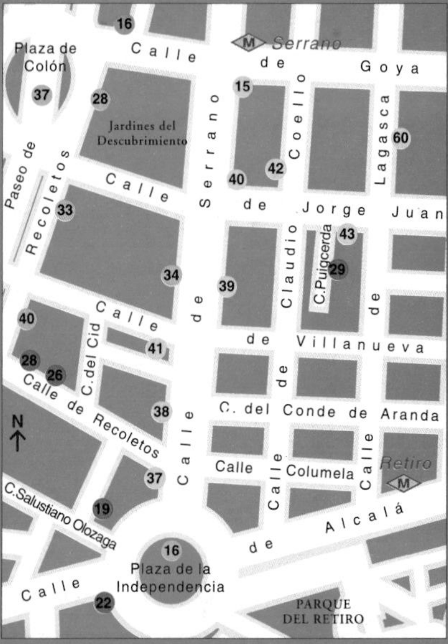
Plaza de Colón
Calle de Goya
Serrano
Jardines del Descubrimiento
Paseo de Recoletos
Calle de Serrano
Claudio Coello
Lagasca
Calle de Jorge Juan
C.Puigcerda
Calle de Villanueva
C. del Cid
Calle de Recoletos
C. del Conde de Aranda
Calle Columela
Retiro
C.Salustiano Olozaga
Plaza de la Independencia
Calle de Alcalá
PARQUE DEL RETIRO
N
16 15 28 37 60 33 40 42 43 29 34 39 41 26 38 37 19 22

ROBERTO VERINO

42

42

38

In the area

Salamanca is the place to go for luxury goods and modern Spanish and international fashion. Its style complements the neighborhood's majestic architecture. ■ Where to stay ➥ 22 ➥ 24 ■ Where to eat ➥ 44 ➥ 46 ➥ 50 ■ After dark ➥ 72 ➥ 78 ■ What to see ➥ 104

Where to shop

Artespaña (44)

Hermosilla 14, 28001 ☎ 91 435 02 21 ➠ 91 575 34 55

Ⓜ *Serrano* ***Handicrafts*** 🕒 *Mon.–Sat. 10.15am–2pm, 5–8.30pm* ▭

In this magnificent store, the national handicrafts organization offers a selection of furniture, accessories, fabrics and decorative items from Spain's finest craftspeople. Vases, tapestries and household linen are among the things that you can admire or buy here.

Del Pino (45)

Serrano 48, 28001 ☎ 91 435 26 70 ➠ 91 431 86 42

Ⓜ *Serrano* ***Jewelry*** 🕒 *Mon.–Sat. 10am–2pm, 5–8.30pm* ▭

A vast but well-chosen range of jewelry, in the latest shapes, colors and materials. The treasures displayed on the shelves and in the windows are hard to resist.

Elena Benarroch (46)

José Ortega y Gasset 14, 28006 ☎ 91 435 51 44 ➠ 91 431 49 60

Ⓜ *Núñez de Balboa* ***Furs*** 🕒 *Mon.–Sat. 10am–2pm, 4.30–8pm* ▭

After devoting seventeen years to revolutionizing fur design, Elena Benarroch turned her attentions to her firm's vast shop window, which she intended to be 'a place where people stop rather than simply pass by'. She achieved her objective. A spectacular Murano glass chandelier illuminates a space dedicated to sophisticated design. Luxury items carrying the best international labels are tastefully displayed. The selection extends from mink coats to sable rugs, through handmade Santa María Novella soaps, cashmere coats from Loro Plana, Philip Treacy hats, and shoes and bags from Bottega Veneta. Our advice: take time to soak up the atmosphere.

El Caballo (47)

Lagasca 55, 28001 ☎ 91 576 40 37 ➠ 91 578 08 80

Ⓜ *Serrano* ***Saddlery and riding habits*** 🕒 *Mon.–Fri. 10am–2pm, 5–8.30pm; Sat. 10.15am–2pm, 5–8pm* ▭

Bags, suitcases, belts, boots, walking shoes, saddles, riding accessories – the store offers an endless selection of leather goods of the highest quality, and a huge array of articles and clothes whose shape and motifs are inspired by Andalusian style. Everything on sale is manufactured in Seville, where the first El Caballo workshop was founded in 1892.

Not forgetting

■ **Santa (48)** Serrano 56, 28001 ☎ 91 576 86 46
Luxurious Madrid chocolate manufacturer. A feast for the eyes as well as the taste buds.

■ **¡ Oh ! Qué Luna (49)** Ayala 32, 28001 ☎ 91 431 37 25 *Nightwear for all the family. A lovely, original selection of lingerie and a new line in household linen..*

Where to shop ➡ 130 ➡ 144

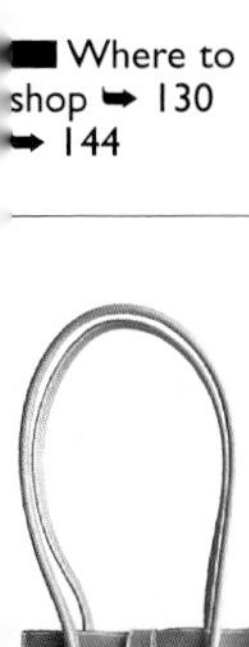

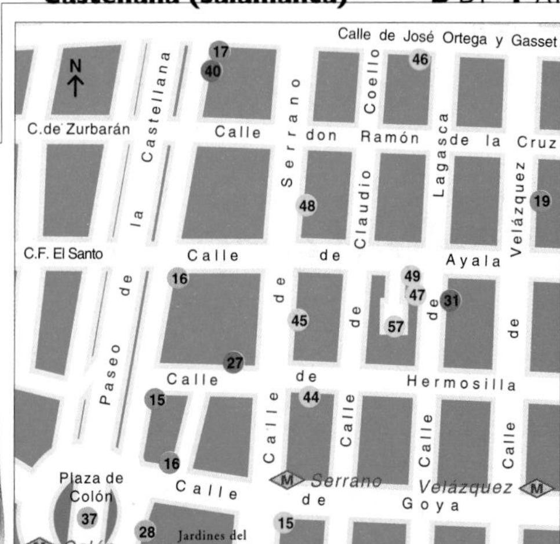

47

46

Elena Benarroch's ventures demonstrate an intelligent and courageous creative talent.

In the area

This is the most modern part of Madrid, where you will find lots of lively, practical shopping complexes. ■ Where to stay ➥ 30 ➥ 32 ■ Where to eat ➥ 58 ■ After dark ➥ 68 ➥ 72 ➥ 74 ■ What to see ➥ 108

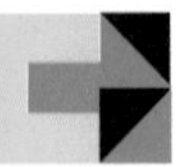

Where to shop

Musgo (50)

Paseo de La Habana 34, 28036 ☎ / ➠ 91 562 86 24

M *Santiago, Bernabéu* ***Gifts*** ◷ *Mon.–Sat. 10.15am–2.15pm, 5–8.30pm* ▭ ◈ *Hermosilla 34, 28001 ☎ 91 431 55 10 ; Serrano 18, 28001 ☎ 91 575 33 50*

What used to be a little gift store has become, twenty years later, a mighty chain with outlets all around the city. The shop windows are stunning at Christmas, when Musgo uses every trick in the book to attract customers. This store specializes in clothes, leather accessories, costume jewelry, watches, ornaments and practical household goods, including small items of furniture. There is also a recently-opened department selling children's and babies' clothes.

Massimo Dutti (51)

Paseo de La Habana 40, 28036 ☎ 91 563 93 22

M *Santiago, Bernabéu* ***Men's and women's ready-to-wear*** ◷ *Mon.–Sat. 10am–8.30pm* ▭ ◈ *Velázquez 46, 28001 ☎ 91 431 77 90*

In the early 1980s a young entrepreneur revolutionized menswear stores by offering vast numbers of shirts in different styles but at the same price. It was a complete success and the numerous stores in the chain now offer even greater variety while sticking to the same principle. Today, Massimo Dutti dresses men from head to toe in quality garments at reasonable prices. Women, too, can now buy practical, comfortable clothes here for every occasion.

Coronel Tapiocca (52)

Paseo de La Habana 52, 28036 ☎ 91 562 64 68 ➠ 91 563 37 40

M *Santiago, Bernabéu, Concha Espina* ***Fashions, sportswear and outdoor gear*** ◷ *Mon.–Sat. 10am–2pm, 5–8.30pm* ▭ ◈ *Serrano 81, 28006 ☎ 91 563 22 21; Genova 23, 28004 ☎ 91 308 29 08*

Clothing and accessories for intrepid adventurers and urban explorers; all-purpose boots, flasks, mountaineers' hats, rucksacks, compasses, leather and linen bomber jackets, pocket flashlights and sweaters. Coronel Tapioca also stocks comfortable and inexpensive casual styles to wear around town.

Not forgetting

■ **Moda Shopping (53)** Avenida General Perón 40, 28020 ☎ 91 581 15 25 *Large shopping mall with more than seventy stores under one glass roof.*

■ **Todo Real Madrid (54)** La Esquina del Bernabéu, Avenida Concha Espina 1, 28036 ☎ 91 458 69 25 *On the top floor of this shopping mall, a boutique exclusively devoted to the wares of Real Madrid football club ➥ 108.*

■ **Antonio Parriego (55)** La Esquina del Bernabéu, 28036 ☎ 91 344 17 06 *One of the five Parriego boutiques in Madrid. Fine quality leather shoes and accessories at reasonable prices.*

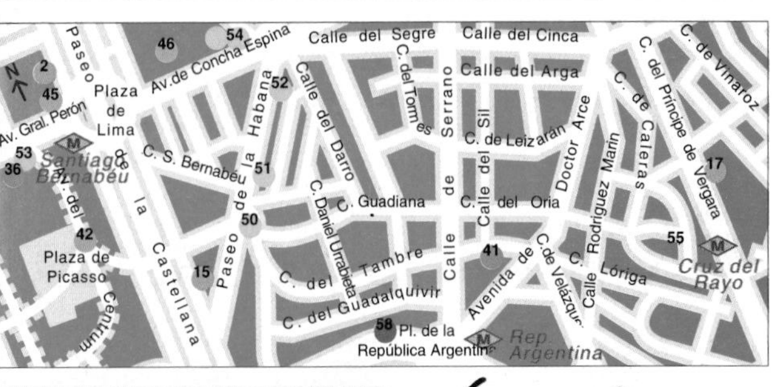

54

MODA SHOPPING
CENTRO COMERCIAL
TU GUIA

53

52

A mingling of main roads and quiet streets around Santiago Bernabéu, the quarter dedicated to the round ball. The developments of the stadium date from 1992, the year when Spain hosted the World Cup.

Basic facts

Set aside at least a morning to mingle with the market crowds. Here, you will capture the authentic, or *castizo* atmosphere of the city. The Rastro, most famous of the flea markets, occupies what used to be the *barrios bajos* (working-class neighborhood). The markets specializing in

Where to shop

El Rastro (56)

Ribera de Curtidores and surroundings, 28005

M *Tirso de Molina, La Latina* ***Flea market*** *Sun. and public holidays from 9am*

In the 16th century, makeshift stalls crowded this neighborhood's tanneries and abattoirs. The abattoirs have now gone, but the Rastro has become a Sunday institution. The market is a fascinating insight into Madrid life for the curious visitor and has become something of a ritual for the locals. Stop and take a look at some of the objects on offer. The stalls and stores with their idiosyncratic displays are irresistible: bric-à-brac, some antiques, handicrafts, clothes, plants, animals, books, furniture, household utensils... almost anything you can imagine could turn up here. You may be lucky enough to unearth some treasure, or you may find some curiosity you simply can't resist. Courteous bartering is acceptable in the street, but it's not so welcome in the stores. While strolling along the Ribera, the nearby river bank, don't forget to look in at some of the antique galleries: Nuevas Galerías (no. 12), Galerías Ribera (no. 15), Galerías Piquer (no. 29).

Mercado de la Paz (57)

Ayala 28, 28001 ☎ 91 435 07 43

M *Serrano* ***Food*** *Mon.–Sat. 9–3pm, 5–8.30pm*

In this remarkably well-organized food market selling some exceptional quality produce, you can choose a tasty souvenir from among Spain's finest and best-known gourmet delights: serrano or jabugo ham, chorizo, *lomo*, rustic cheeses, olives, fresh vegetables and fruits, or just feast your eyes and senses on the riches of this prosperous agricultural land.

56

58

food and second-hand books are also worth a detour. An opportunity to pick up a bargain, or waste a few pesetas.

Cuesta de Moyano (58)

Cuesta de Claudio Moyano, 28014

Atocha ***Second-hand books*** *nearly all the stalls are open during the week; on Sundays you have to get there between about 9.30am and 2pm*

The pretty wooden stalls along the Cuesta de Moyano have recently been renovated. Shaded by the awnings and the tall trees of the botanical gardens ➡ 98, you may find rare, second-hand books, as well as new ones at bargain prices. The book market marks the beginning of one the Madrileños' favorite walks, leading to Parque del Retiro ➡ 98.

Not forgetting

Mercado de Sellos y Monedas (59) Plaza Mayor, 28012
Sun., public holidays mornings
Stamp and coin market where collectors, dealers and curious onlookers gather under the arcades of Plaza Mayor ➡ 92.

Centro de Anticuarios de Lagasca (60) Lagasca 36, 28001
Antique dealers are scattered all over the Salamanca neighborhood. Some of the best ones, but also the most expensive, operate from this center.

56

56

56

Finding your way

Location of the city

Latitude N. 40° 24' - Longitude W. 3° 42'
Madrid is at the heart of the Iberian Peninsula, 400 miles from Barcelona and 350 miles from Seville. At 2120 feet above sea level, it is also Europe's highest capital.

City layout

Madrid is divided into 21 *Distritos Municipales*, numbered from the center outward: 01 (Centro), 02 (Arguanzela), 03 (Retiro) etc. Prefixed by the figure 280, the number determines the city code. Beware: this is not the same as a zip code (also prefixed by 280).

7 Maps

Mini street glossary

Avenida: avenue
Calle: street
Callejón: alley, cul-de-sac
Camino: way
Carretera: road
Costanilla: sloping alley
Cuesta: sloping street
Glorieta: traffic circle
Pasaje: passage
Paseo: boulevard
Plaza: square
Puerta: gate
Ronda: ring road
Travesía: way, passage

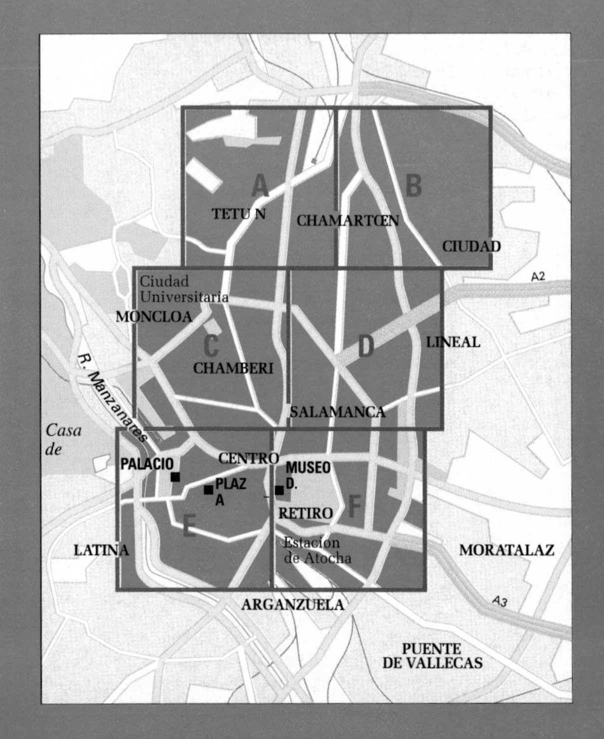

Street index

Each street name is followed by a bold letter indicating which map to refer to, and a grid reference.

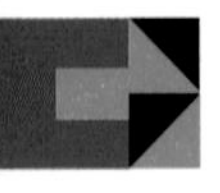

Index

A

B

C

Abbreviations

Av. = Avenida	*Glr.* = Glorieta	*Pl.* = Plaza
C. = Calle	*M.* = Metro	*Po.* = Paseo

Subway map

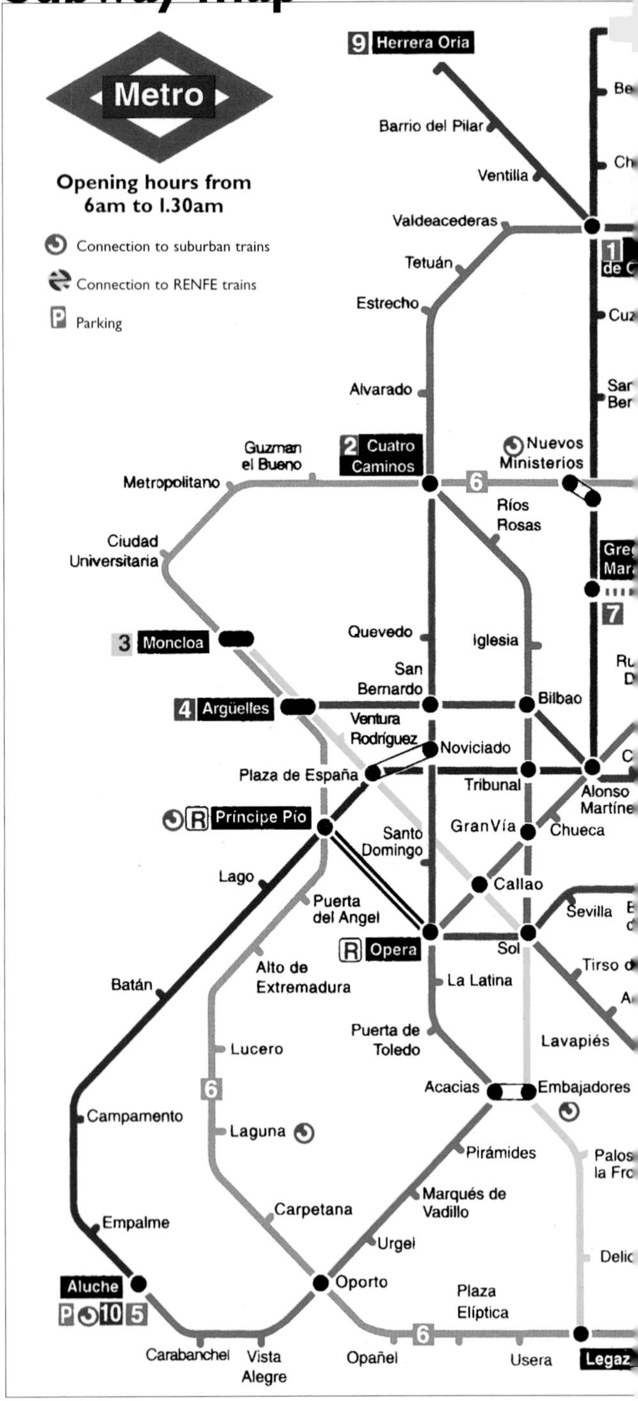

Metro

Opening hours from 6am to 1.30am

- Connection to suburban trains
- Connection to RENFE trains
- Parking

9 Herrera Oria
Barrio del Pilar
Ventilla
Valdeacederas
Tetuán
Estrecho
Alvarado
2 Cuatro Caminos
Guzman el Bueno
Metropolitano
Ciudad Universitaria
Nuevos Ministerios
6
Ríos Rosas
3 Moncloa
Quevedo
Iglesia
San Bernardo
4 Argüelles
Bilbao
Ventura Rodríguez
Noviciado
Plaza de España
Tribunal
Alonso Martínez
Príncipe Pío
Santo Domingo
Gran Vía
Chueca
Lago
Callao
Puerta del Angel
Sevilla
Opera
Sol
Alto de Extremadura
La Latina
Batán
Lucero
Puerta de Toledo
Lavapiés
Acacias
Embajadores
6
Campamento
Laguna
Pirámides
Marqués de Vadillo
Carpetana
Empalme
Urgel
Aluche
Oporto
Plaza Elíptica
10 5
6
Carabanchel
Vista Alegre
Opañel
Usera
7

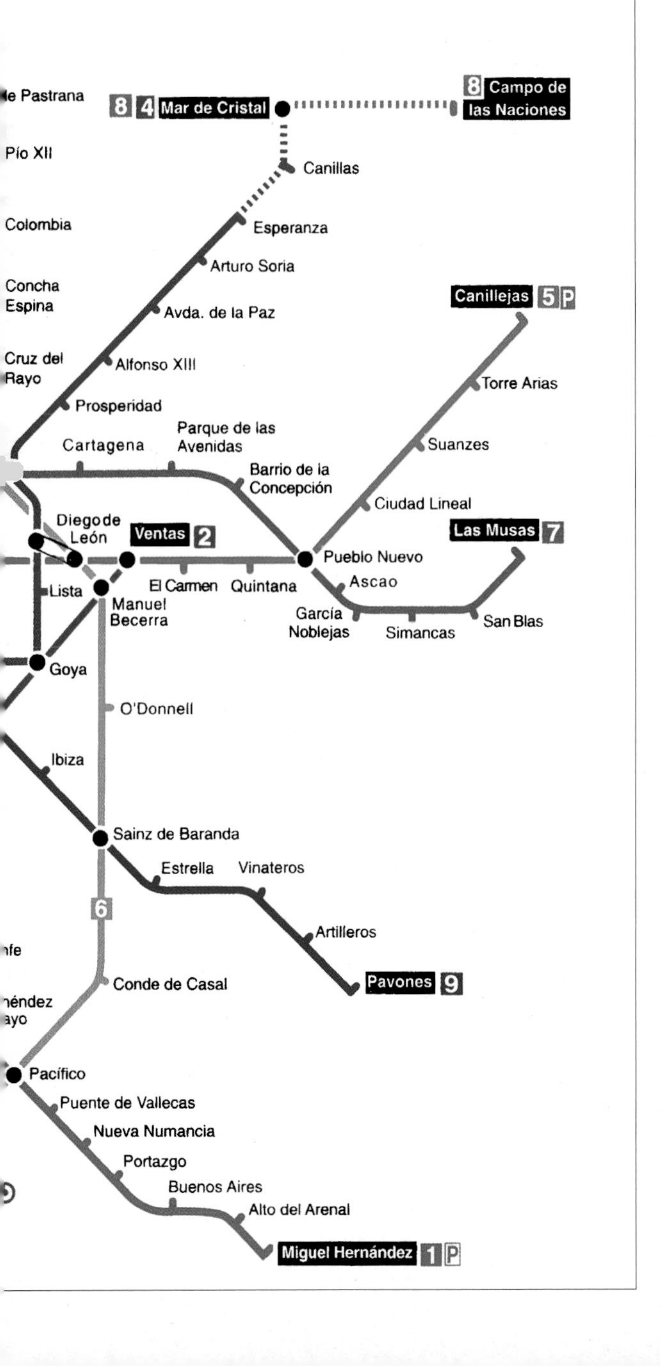

le Pastrana
8 4 Mar de Cristal
8 Campo de las Naciones
Pío XII
Canillas
Colombia
Esperanza
Arturo Soria
Concha Espina
Avda. de la Paz
Canillejas 5 P
Cruz del Rayo
Alfonso XIII
Torre Arias
Prosperidad
Parque de las Avenidas
Cartagena
Suanzes
Barrio de la Concepción
Ciudad Lineal
Diego de León
Ventas 2
Las Musas 7
Pueblo Nuevo
Lista
El Carmen
Quintana
Ascao
Manuel Becerra
García Noblejas
Simancas
San Blas
Goya
O'Donnell
Ibiza
Sainz de Baranda
Estrella
Vinateros
6
Artilleros
Conde de Casal
Pavones 9
Pacífico
Puente de Vallecas
Nueva Numancia
Portazgo
Buenos Aires
Alto del Arenal
Miguel Hernández 1 P

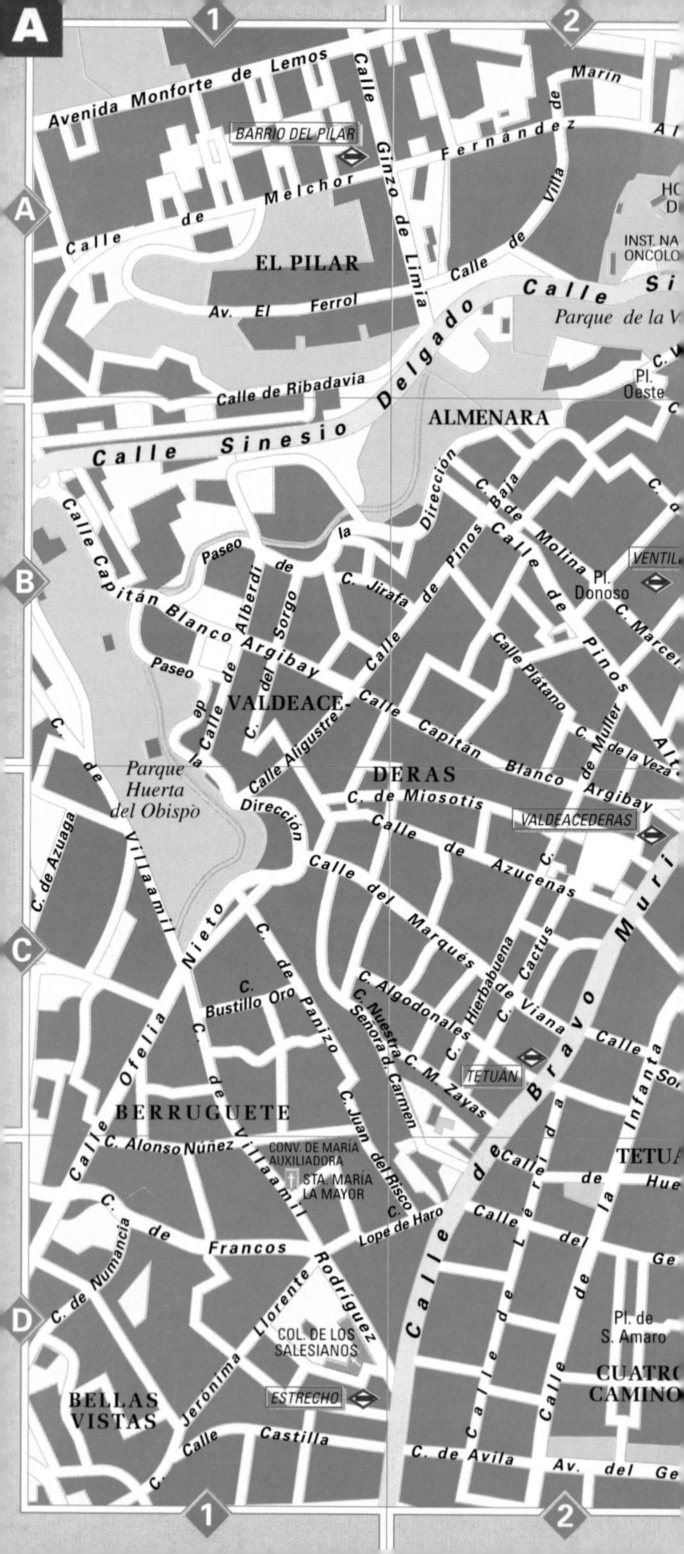
A
1
2
A
B
C
D
Avenida Monforte de Lemos
Calle Ginzo de Limia
BARRIO DEL PILAR
Calle de Melchor Fernández
Marín
Calle de Villa
EL PILAR
Av. El Ferrol
Calle Sinesio Delgado
Parque de la V
INST. NA ONCOLO
Pl. Oeste
Calle de Ribadavia
ALMENARA
Paseo de la Dirección
C. Baja
Calle de Molina
Calle de Pinos
VENTIL
Pl. Donoso
C. Jirafa
Calle de Pinos
C. Marcel
Calle Capitán Blanco Argibay
Calle Alberdi
C. del Sorgo
Calle Plátano
Paseo de la Dirección
VALDEACE-DERAS
Calle Aligustre
Calle Capitán Blanco Argibay
C. de Muller
C. de la Veza
Parque Huerta del Obispo
C. de Miosotis
VALDEACEDERAS
C. de Azuaga
C. de Villaamil
Calle de Azucenas
Calle del Marqués de Viana
Calle de Bravo Murillo
Nieto
C. de Panizo
C. Cactus
C. Hierbabuena
C. Bustillo Oro
C. Algodonales
C. Nuestra Señora d. Carmen
C. M. Zayas
TETUÁN
Calle Ofelia
C. de Villaamil
C. Juan del Risco
BERRUGUETE
C. Alonso Núñez
CONV. DE MARÍA AUXILIADORA
STA. MARÍA LA MAYOR
Calle de Lérida
Calle de la Infanta
TETUA
Calle de Hue
C. de Francos
C. Lope de Haro
Calle del Ge
C. de Numancia
Calle de
Rodríguez
Llorente
Pl. de S. Amaro
COL. DE LOS SALESIANOS
Calle de
CUATRO CAMINO
BELLAS VISTAS
Jerónima
ESTRECHO
Calle Castilla
C. de Avila
Av. del Ge
1
2

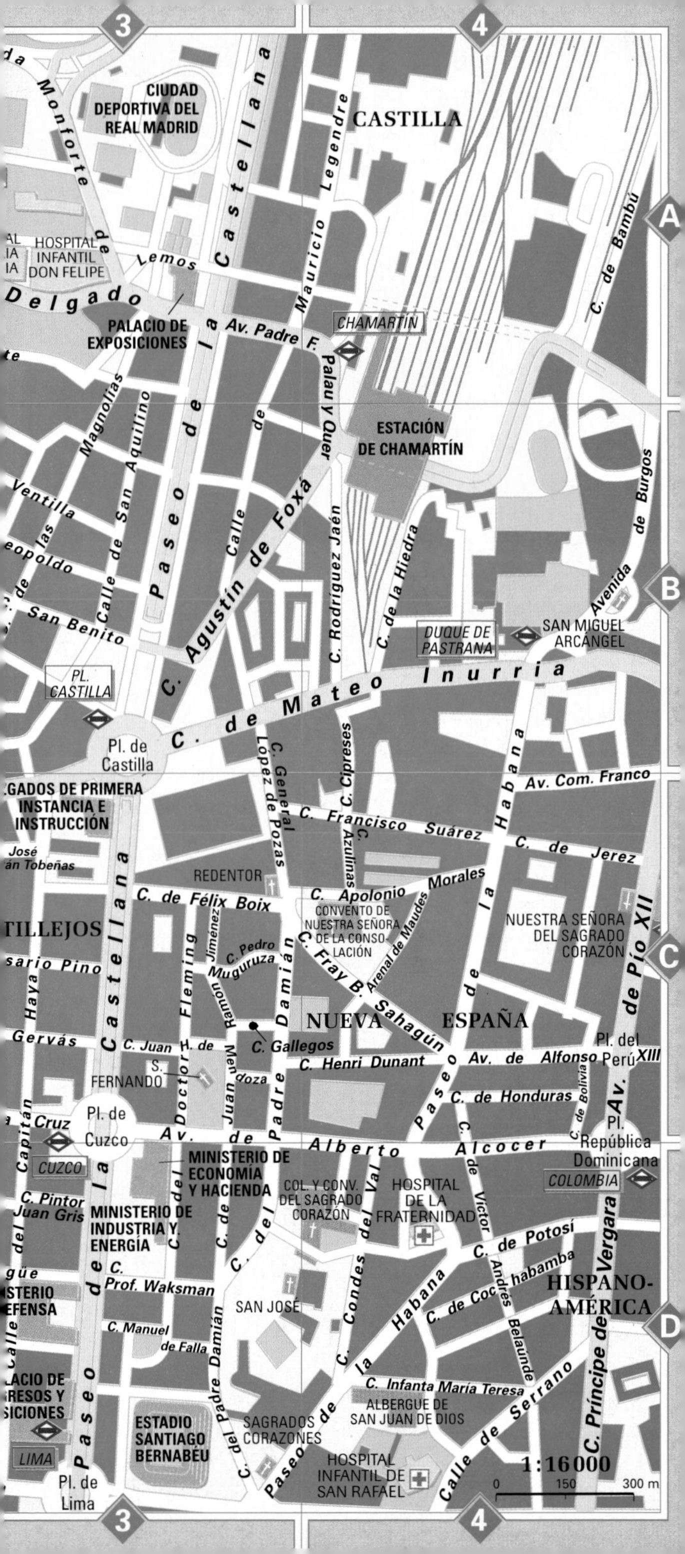

3
4
CIUDAD DEPORTIVA DEL REAL MADRID
CASTILLA
HOSPITAL INFANTIL DON FELIPE
PALACIO DE EXPOSICIONES
CHAMARTÍN
ESTACIÓN DE CHAMARTÍN
DUQUE DE PASTRANA
SAN MIGUEL ARCÁNGEL
PL. CASTILLA
Pl. de Castilla
REDENTOR
CONVENTO DE NUESTRA SEÑORA DE LA CONSOLACIÓN
NUESTRA SEÑORA DEL SAGRADO CORAZÓN
NUEVA ESPAÑA
S. FERNANDO
Pl. de Cuzco
CUZCO
Pl. del Perú
Pl. República Dominicana
COLOMBIA
MINISTERIO DE ECONOMÍA Y HACIENDA
MINISTERIO DE INDUSTRIA Y ENERGÍA
COL. Y CONV. DEL SAGRADO CORAZÓN
HOSPITAL DE LA FRATERNIDAD
SAN JOSÉ
HISPANOAMÉRICA
ALBERGUE DE SAN JUAN DE DIOS
ESTADIO SANTIAGO BERNABÉU
SAGRADOS CORAZONES
HOSPITAL INFANTIL DE SAN RAFAEL
LIMA
Pl. de Lima
1:16000
0
150
300 m
A
B
C
D
Paseo de la Castellana
Av. Padre F. Palau y Quer
C. Agustín de Foxá
C. de Mateo Inurria
C. de Bambú
Avenida de Burgos
C. Rodríguez Jaén
C. de la Hiedra
Mauricio Legendre
Monforte de Lemos
Calle de San Aquilino
Magnolias
Av. Com. Franco
C. Francisco Suárez
C. de Jerez
C. General López de Pozas
C. Cipreses
C. Azulinas
C. Apolonio Morales
C. de Félix Boix
C. Pedro Muguruza
C. Fray B. Sahagún
Arenal de Maudes
Paseo de la Habana
Av. de Pío XII
Av. de Alfonso XIII
C. Gallegos
C. Henri Dunant
C. de Honduras
C. de Bolivia
Av. de Alberto Alcocer
C. de Víctor Andrés Belaúnde
C. de Potosí
C. de Cochabamba
C. Príncipe de Vergara
Calle de Serrano
C. Infanta María Teresa
C. Condes del Val
C. del Padre Damián
C. Prof. Waksman
C. Manuel de Falla
C. Pintor Juan Gris
C. Juan H. de Mendoza
Doctor Fleming
Jiménez
Ramón
Capitán Haya
Sarrio Pino
Gervás
Cruz
TILLEJOS
Ventilla
San Benito

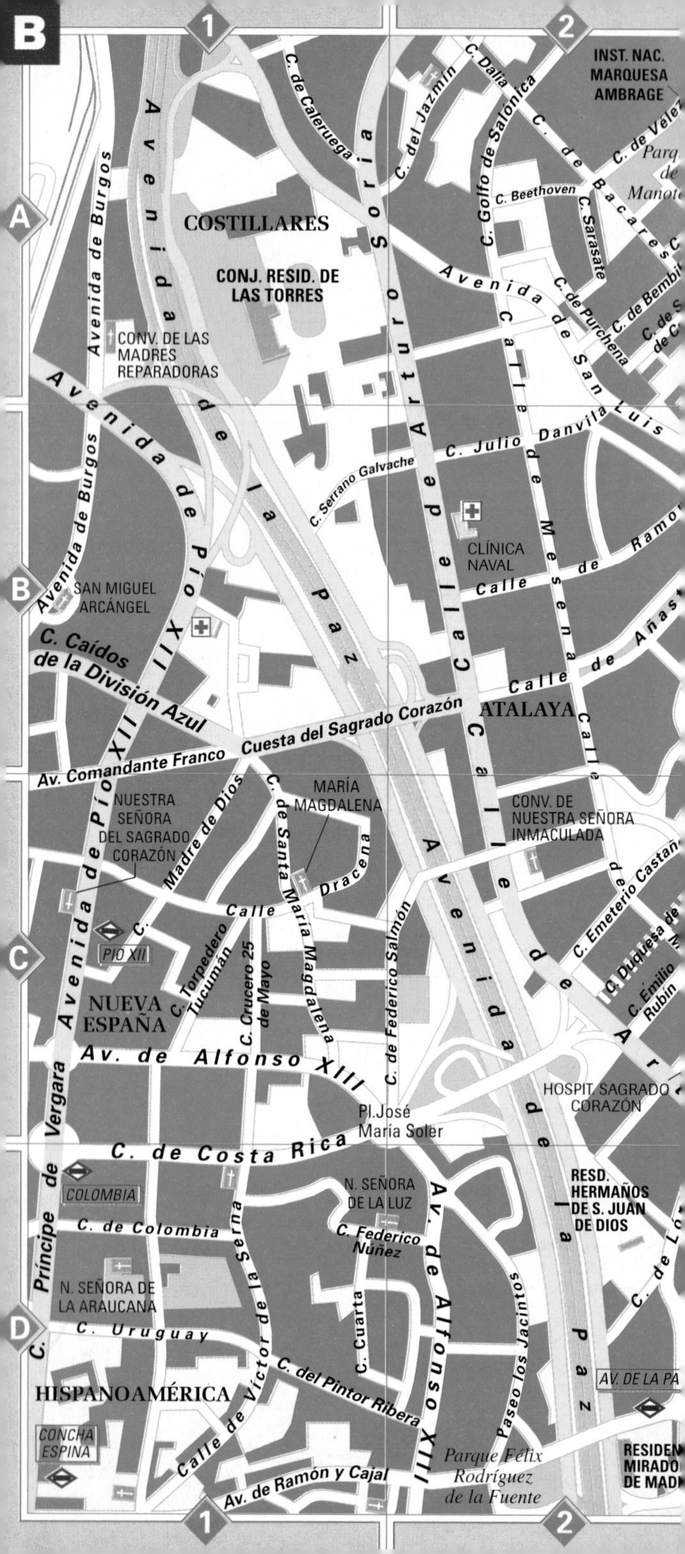

B
1
2
A
B
C
D
COSTILLARES
CONJ. RESID. DE LAS TORRES
CONV. DE LAS MADRES REPARADORAS
INST. NAC. MARQUESA AMBRAGE
Parque de Manoteras
Avenida de Burgos
Avenida de la Paz
Avenida de Pío XII
C. de Caleruega
C. del Jazmín
C. Dalia
C. Golfo de Salónica
C. Beethoven
C. Sarasate
C. de Bacares
C. de Vélez
C. de Purchena
C. de Bembibre
Avenida de San Luis
Calle de Arturo Soria
C. Julio Danvila
C. Serrano Galvache
CLÍNICA NAVAL
Calle de Mesena
Calle de Ramón
SAN MIGUEL ARCÁNGEL
C. Caídos de la División Azul
Calle de Añastro
ATALAYA
Cuesta del Sagrado Corazón
Av. Comandante Franco
NUESTRA SEÑORA DEL SAGRADO CORAZÓN
C. Madre de Dios
C. de Santa María Magdalena
MARÍA MAGDALENA
Calle Dracena
CONV. DE NUESTRA SEÑORA INMACULADA
C. Emeterio Castaños
C. Duquesa de
C. Emilio Rubín
Avenida de Pío XII
PIO XII
C. Torpedero Tucumán
C. Crucero 25 de Mayo
C. de Federico Salmón
NUEVA ESPAÑA
Av. de Alfonso XIII
HOSPIT. SAGRADO CORAZÓN
Pl. José María Soler
C. de Costa Rica
C. Príncipe de Vergara
COLOMBIA
N. SEÑORA DE LA LUZ
RESD. HERMAÑOS DE S. JUAN DE DIOS
C. de Colombia
C. Federico Núñez
Av. de Alfonso XIII
N. SEÑORA DE LA ARAUCANA
C. de Lo
C. Uruguay
Calle de Víctor de la Serna
C. Cuarta
Paseo los Jacintos
C. del Pintor Ribera
AV. DE LA PA
HISPANOAMÉRICA
CONCHA ESPINA
Parque Félix Rodríguez de la Fuente
RESIDEN MIRADO DE MAD
Av. de Ramón y Cajal

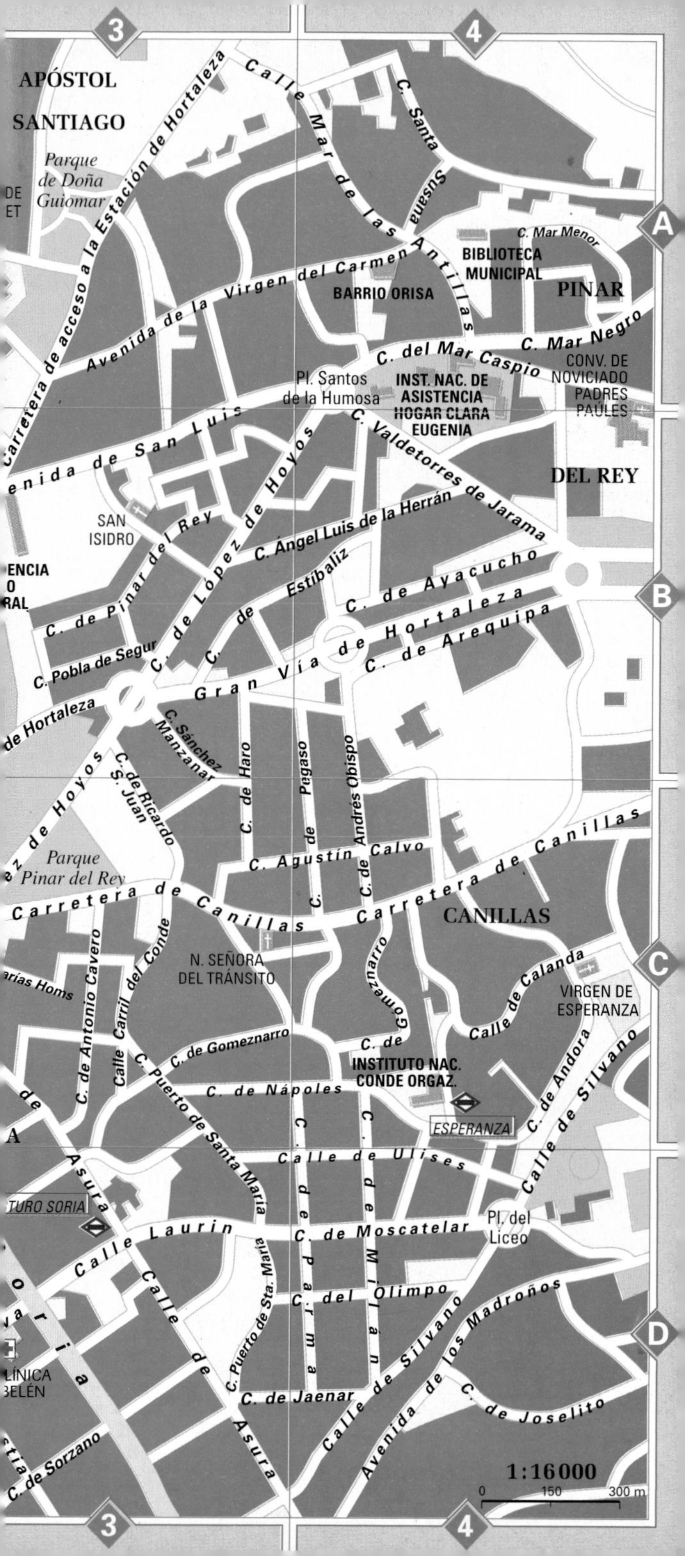
3
4
A
B
C
D
APÓSTOL SANTIAGO
Parque de Doña Guiomar
Calle Mar de las Antillas
C. Santa Susana
Carretera de acceso a la Estación de Hortaleza
Avenida de la Virgen del Carmen
C. Mar Menor
BIBLIOTECA MUNICIPAL
BARRIO ORISA
PINAR
C. Mar Negro
C. del Mar Caspio
CONV. DE NOVICIADO PADRES PAÚLES
Pl. Santos de la Humosa
INST. NAC. DE ASISTENCIA HOGAR CLARA EUGENIA
Avenida de San Luis
C. Valdetorres de Jarama
DEL REY
SAN ISIDRO
C. Ángel Luis de la Herrán
C. de López de Hoyos
C. de Pinar del Rey
C. de Estíbaliz
C. de Ayacucho
Gran Vía de Hortaleza
C. de Arequipa
C. Pobla de Segur
C. Sánchez Manzanar
C. de Ricardo S. Juan
C. de Haro
C. de Pegaso
C. de Andrés Obispo
C. Agustín Calvo
Parque Pinar del Rey
Carretera de Canillas
CANILLAS
N. SEÑORA DEL TRÁNSITO
C. de Antonio Cavero
Calle Carril del Conde
C. de Gomeznarro
Calle de Calanda
VIRGEN DE ESPERANZA
INSTITUTO NAC. CONDE ORGAZ.
ESPERANZA
C. de Andora
Calle de Silvano
C. Puerto de Santa María
C. de Nápoles
C. de Parma
C. de Millán
Calle de Ulises
Calle de Asura
Pl. del Liceo
Calle Laurin
C. de Moscatelar
C. del Olimpo
C. Puerto de Sta. María
Avenida de los Madroños
C. de Jaenar
C. de Joselito
C. de Sorzano
1:16000
0
150
300 m

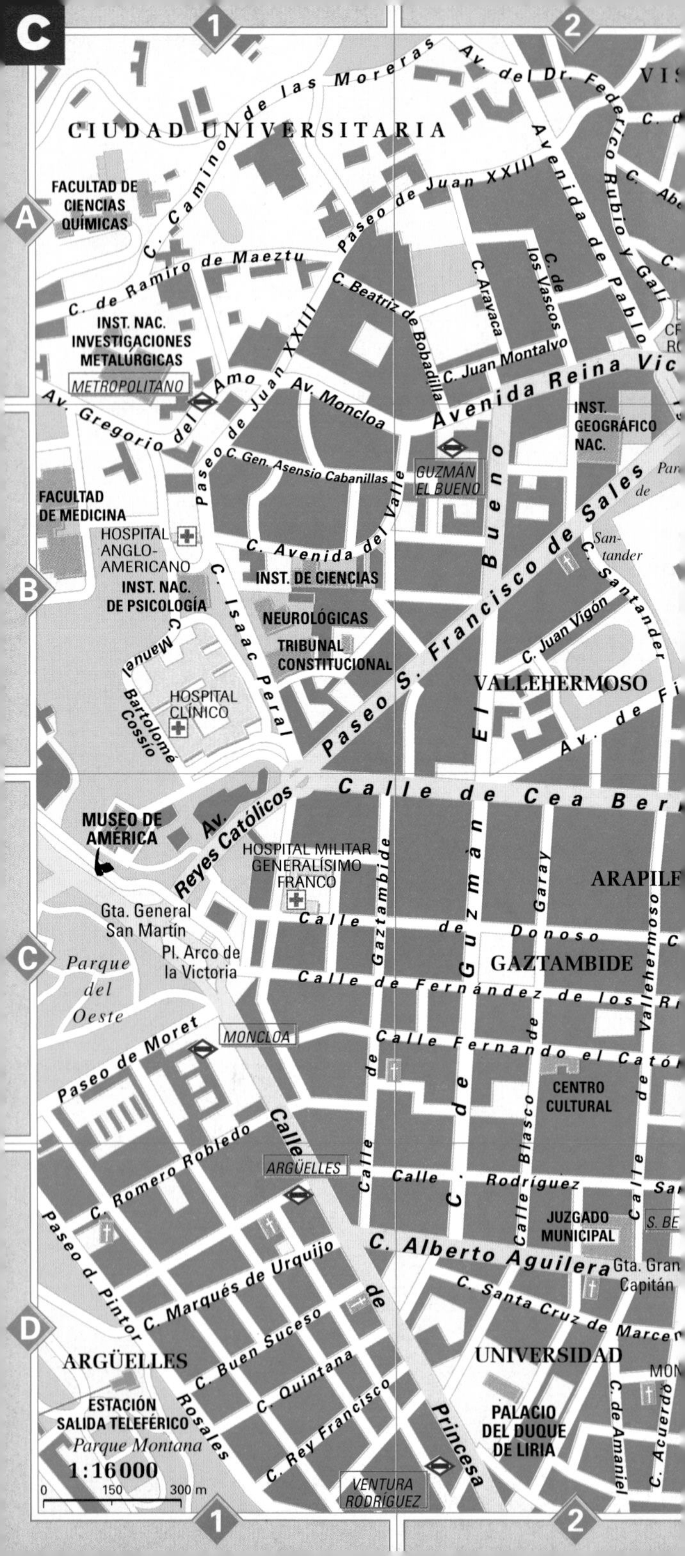
C
CIUDAD UNIVERSITARIA
FACULTAD DE CIENCIAS QUÍMICAS
INST. NAC. INVESTIGACIONES METALÚRGICAS
METROPOLITANO
FACULTAD DE MEDICINA
HOSPITAL ANGLO-AMERICANO
INST. NAC. DE PSICOLOGÍA
HOSPITAL CLÍNICO
INST. DE CIENCIAS NEUROLÓGICAS
TRIBUNAL CONSTITUCIONAL
GUZMÁN EL BUENO
INST. GEOGRÁFICO NAC.
VALLEHERMOSO
MUSEO DE AMÉRICA
HOSPITAL MILITAR GENERALÍSIMO FRANCO
ARAPILES
GAZTAMBIDE
Gta. General San Martín
Pl. Arco de la Victoria
Parque del Oeste
MONCLOA
CENTRO CULTURAL
ARGÜELLES
JUZGADO MUNICIPAL
Gta. Gran Capitán
UNIVERSIDAD
ARGÜELLES
ESTACIÓN SALIDA TELEFÉRICO
Parque Montana
PALACIO DEL DUQUE DE LIRIA
VENTURA RODRÍGUEZ
1:16000
0 150 300 m
C. Camino de las Moreras
Av. del Dr. Federico Rubio y Galí
Avenida de Pablo
Paseo de Juan XXIII
C. de Ramiro de Maeztu
C. Beatriz de Bobadilla
C. Aravaca
C. de los Vascos
C. Juan Montalvo
Avenida Reina Victoria
Av. Gregorio del Amo
Av. Moncloa
C. Gen. Asensio Cabanillas
C. Avenida del Valle
C. Isaac Peral
C. Manuel Bartolomé Cossío
Paseo S. Francisco de Sales
El Bueno
C. Santander
C. Juan Vigón
Av. de Filipinas
Calle de Cea Bermúdez
Av. Reyes Católicos
Calle de Gaztambide
C. de Guzmán el Bueno
Calle de Donoso
Calle de Fernández de los Ríos
Calle Fernando el Católico
Calle de Vallehermoso
Calle Blasco de Garay
Paseo de Moret
Calle de Princesa
C. Romero Robledo
Calle Rodríguez San Pedro
C. Alberto Aguilera
C. Santa Cruz de Marcenado
Paseo d. Pintor Rosales
C. Marqués de Urquijo
C. Buen Suceso
C. Quintana
C. Rey Francisco
C. de Amaniel
C. Acuerdo
S. BE
MON

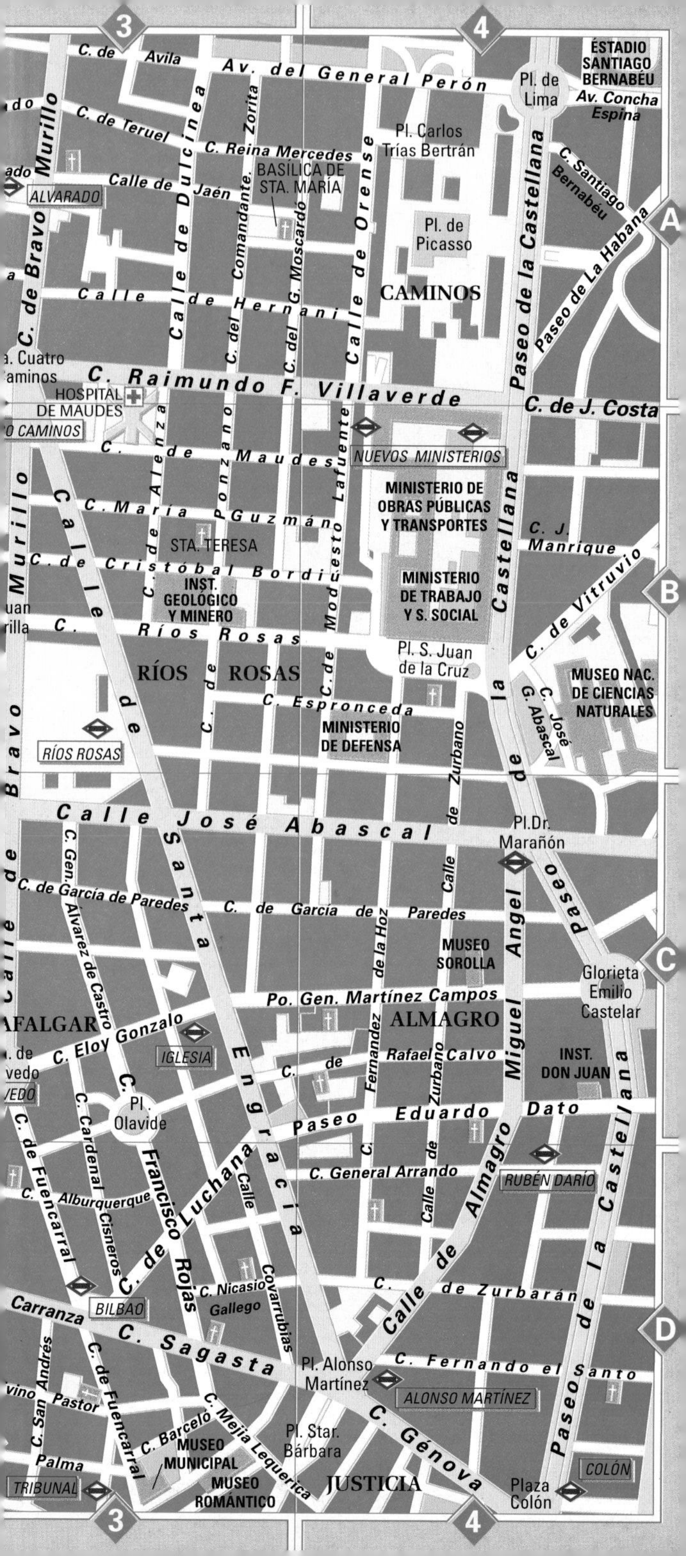
3
4
A
B
C
D
C. de Avila
Av. del General Perón
Pl. de Lima
ESTADIO SANTIAGO BERNABÉU
Av. Concha Espina
C. de Teruel
C. Reina Mercedes
Pl. Carlos Trías Bertrán
Murillo
Calle de Jaén
BASÍLICA DE STA. MARÍA
C. Santiago Bernabéu
ALVARADO
Pl. de Picasso
Paseo de La Habana
C. de Bravo Murillo
Calle de Dulcinea
C. del Comandante Zorita
C. del G. Moscardó
Calle de Orense
Paseo de la Castellana
CAMINOS
Calle de Hernani
C. Raimundo F. Villaverde
C. de J. Costa
HOSPITAL DE MAUDES
C. de Maudes
NUEVOS MINISTERIOS
MINISTERIO DE OBRAS PÚBLICAS Y TRANSPORTES
C. María de Guzmán
C. de Alenza
C. Ponzano
C. de Modesto Lafuente
STA. TERESA
C. J. Manrique
C. de Cristóbal Bordiú
INST. GEOLÓGICO Y MINERO
MINISTERIO DE TRABAJO Y S. SOCIAL
C. de Vitruvio
C. Ríos Rosas
Pl. S. Juan de la Cruz
MUSEO NAC. DE CIENCIAS NATURALES
RÍOS ROSAS
C. Espronceda
C. José G. Abascal
MINISTERIO DE DEFENSA
RÍOS ROSAS
Calle de Santa Engracia
Calle de Zurbano
Calle José Abascal
Pl.Dr. Marañón
C. Gen. Álvarez de Castro
C. de García de Paredes
C. de García de Paredes
C. de Fernández de la Hoz
MUSEO SOROLLA
Miguel Ángel
Paseo
Glorieta Emilio Castelar
Po. Gen. Martínez Campos
ALMAGRO
C. Eloy Gonzalo
IGLESIA
C. de Rafael Calvo
INST. DON JUAN
Pl. Olavide
Paseo Eduardo Dato
C. Cardenal Cisneros
C. de Fuencarral
C. Francisco Rojas
C. General Arrando
RUBÉN DARÍO
C. Alburquerque
C. de Luchana
Calle de Almagro
Paseo de la Castellana
C. de Zurbarán
C. Nicasio Gallego
Covarrubias
Carranza
BILBAO
C. Sagasta
Pl. Alonso Martínez
C. Fernando el Santo
ALONSO MARTÍNEZ
C. San Andrés
Pastor
C. de Fuencarral
C. Barceló
C. Mejía Lequerica
Pl. Star. Bárbara
C. Génova
MUSEO MUNICIPAL
Palma
MUSEO ROMÁNTICO
JUSTICIA
Plaza Colón
COLÓN
TRIBUNAL

D
ESTADIO SANTIAGO BERNABÉU
SAGRADOS CORAZONES
HOSPITAL INFANTIL DE SAN RAFAEL
CONCHA ESPINA
Avenida de Concha Espina
Pl. Sagrados Corazones
Av. de Ramón y
Paseo de La Habana
C. del Segre
C. del Cinca
Parque Berlín
CIUDAD JARDÍN
INST. DE ESTUDIOS ISLÁMICOS
C. del Darro
Calle de Serrano
Calle del Sil
C. del Genil
C. de Pradillo
CENTRO CULTURAL N. SALMERÓN
Pl. Sta. Gema
C. del Tambre
C. Nervión
Av. del Doctor Arce
C. Emilio Campión
AUDITORIO NAC. DE MUSICA
C. de Suero
Calle de Vergara
Calle de Mantuano
Calle de Marcenado
Calle de Joaquín Costa
Pl. de la República Argentina
EL VISO
Pl. Sagrado Corazón de Jesús
PROSPERIDAD
de Quiñones
C. de Vitruvio
REP. ARGENTINA
Velázquez
C. de Gabriel Lobo
CRUZ DEL RAYO
Calle de López de Hoyos
C. J. Bautis
SANAT. S. FRANCISCO DE ASÍS
C. Particular
C. Pablo Aranda
Calle Príncipe
C. de Canillas
C. de Quintiliano
C. de Cartagena
MINISTERIO TRANSPORTE
ARCHIVO HISTÓRICO NACIONAL
Castellón de la Plana
Calle de
Glorieta López de Hoyos
MUSEO NAC. DE CIENCIAS NATURALES
C. S. Fernando de Jarama
TORR BLAN
Pl. Carlos María Castro
C. Pedro de Valdivia
Calle del Pinar
AV. DE AMÉRICA
Avenida
Calle María de Molina
Calle de López de Hoyos
MUSEO LÁZARO GALDIANO
Castelló
C. de Coslada
C. Agustín
C. de Méji
Calle del General Oráa
Glorieta Emilio Castelar
DIEGO DE LEÓN
Calle Diego de León
del Gral. Pardiñas
C. Alonso
Calle de Francisco
MUSEO DE ARTE ABSTRACTO
MUSEO DE ARTE INFANTIL
Lagasca
NÚÑEZ DE BALBOA
C. de Maldonado
HOSP. DE LA PRINCESA
Calle de Juan Bravo
Calle Príncipe de Vergara
CASTELLANA
Paseo de la Castellana
C. Marqués de Villamejor
Claudio Coello
Calle de Padilla
BIBLIOT PÚBL
Calle de José Ortega y Gasset
Pl. Marqués de Salamanca
Conde de Peñalver
de Alcántara
TRIBUNAL DE MENORES
Calle de Don Ramón de la Cruz
LIS
Calle de Ayala
TENENCIA DE ALCALDÍA
Calle del General Pardiñas
Calle de Hermosilla
SERRANO
VELÁZQUEZ
GOYA
1
2
A
B
C
D

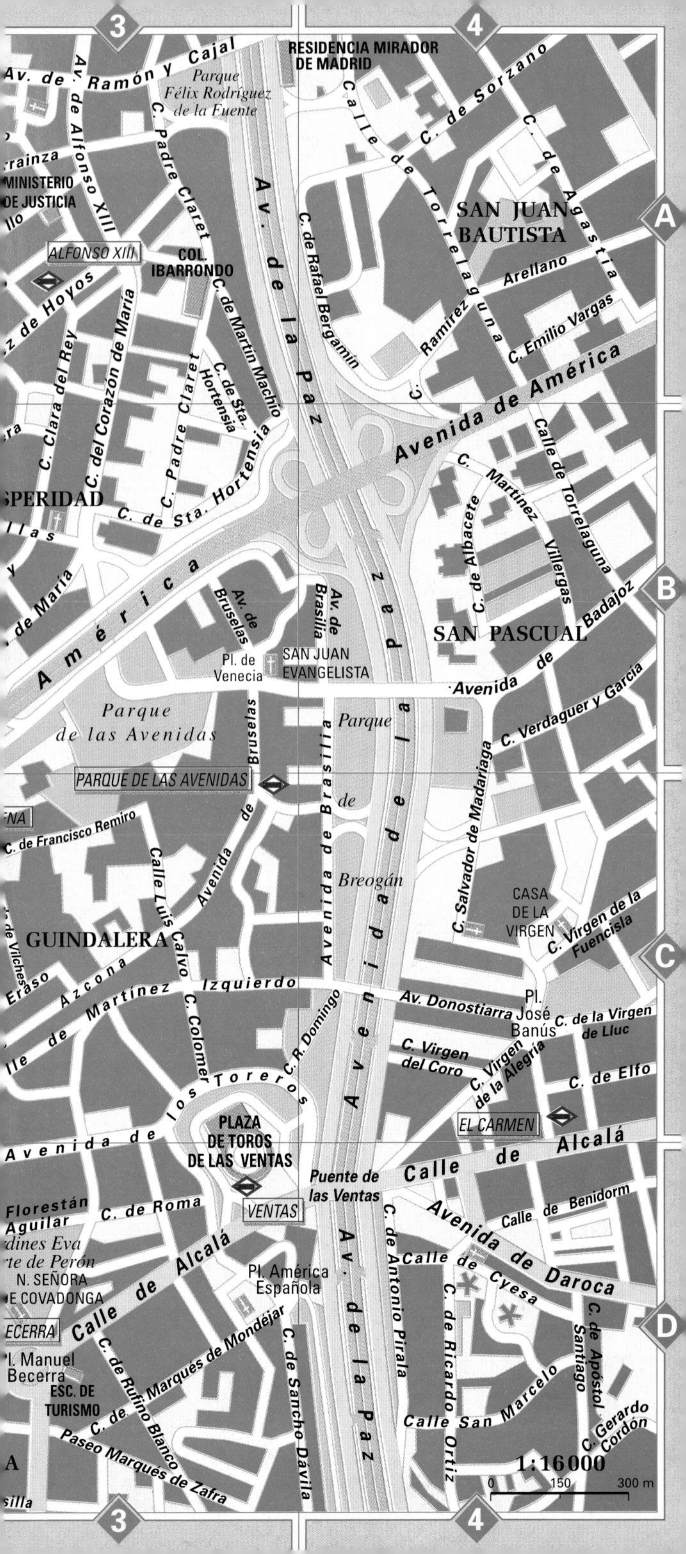

3
4
A
B
C
D
RESIDENCIA MIRADOR DE MADRID
Av. de Ramón y Cajal
Parque Félix Rodríguez de la Fuente
Av. de Alfonso XIII
C. Padre Claret
MINISTERIO DE JUSTICIA
ALFONSO XIII
COL. IBARRONDO
C. de Martín Machío
Av. de la Paz
C. de Rafael Bergamín
Calle de Torrelaguna
C. de Sorzano
C. de Agastia
SAN JUAN BAUTISTA
Arellano
Ramírez
C. Emilio Vargas
Avenida de América
C. Clara del Rey
C. del Corazón de María
C. de Sta. Hortensia
C. Padre Claret
C. de Sta. Hortensia
C. Martínez Villergas
Calle de Torrelaguna
C. de Albacete
Av. de Bruselas
Av. de Brasilia
SAN PASCUAL
Avenida de Badajoz
Pl. de Venecia
SAN JUAN EVANGELISTA
Parque de las Avenidas
Parque de Breogán
C. Verdaguer y García
C. Salvador de Madariaga
PARQUE DE LAS AVENIDAS
C. de Francisco Remiro
Calle Luis Calvo
Avenida de Bruselas
Avenida de Brasilia
Avenida de la Paz
CASA DE LA VIRGEN
C. Virgen de la Fuencisla
GUINDALERA
Azcona
Calle de Martínez Izquierdo
C. Colomer
C. R. Domingo
Av. Donostiarra
Pl. José Banús
C. de la Virgen de Lluc
C. Virgen del Coro
C. Virgen de la Alegría
C. de Elfo
Avenida de los Toreros
EL CARMEN
PLAZA DE TOROS DE LAS VENTAS
Puente de las Ventas
Calle de Alcalá
VENTAS
Calle de Benidorm
Avenida de Daroca
C. de Roma
Florestán Aguilar
Calle de Alcalá
Pl. América Española
C. de Antonio Pirala
Calle de Cyesa
N. SEÑORA DE COVADONGA
C. de Ricardo Ortiz
C. de Apóstol Santiago
Pl. Manuel Becerra
ESC. DE TURISMO
C. de Rufino Blanco
C. de Marqués de Mondéjar
C. de Sancho Dávila
Av. de la Paz
Calle San Marcelo
C. Gerardo Cordón
Paseo Marqués de Zafra
1:16000
0
150
300 m

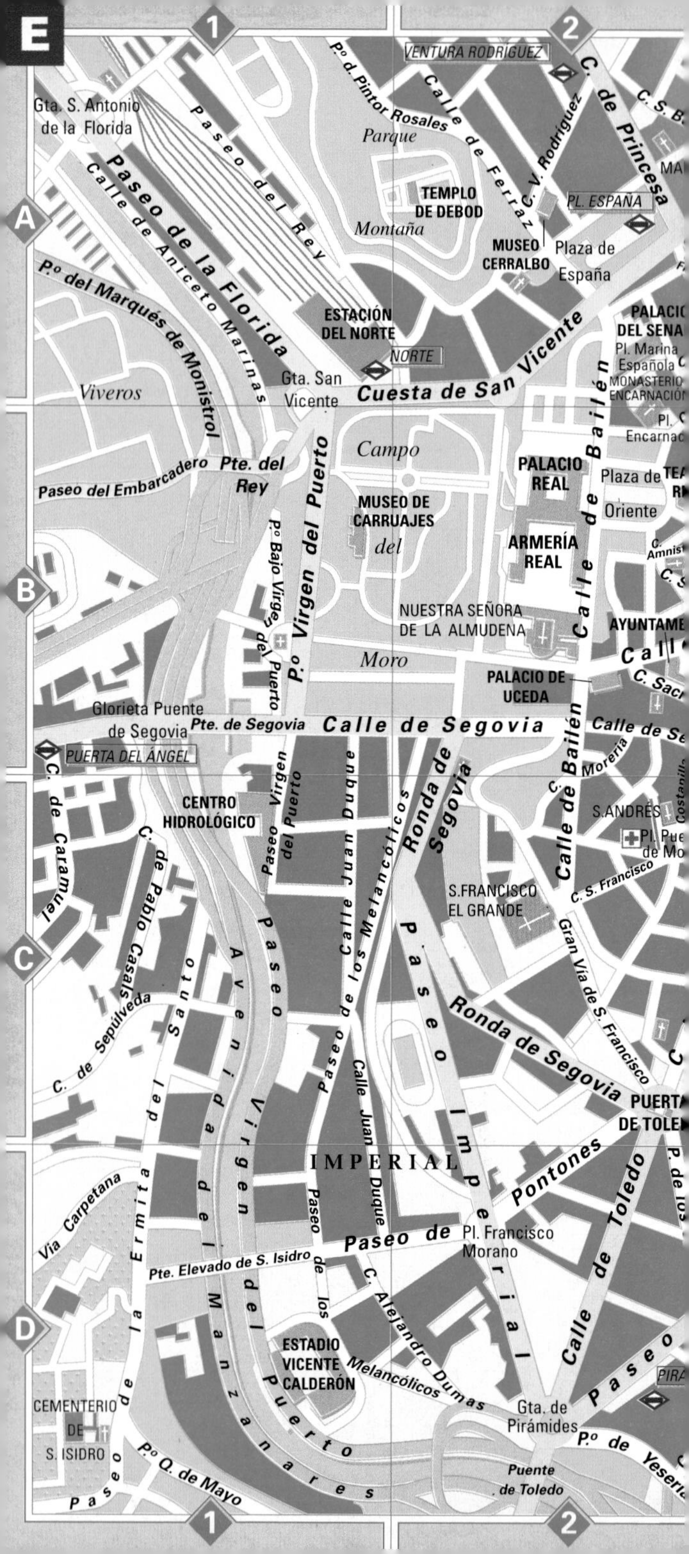

E
1
2
A
B
C
D
VENTURA RODRÍGUEZ
Pº d. Pintor Rosales
Calle de Ferraz
C. V. Rodríguez
C. de Princesa
Gta. S. Antonio de la Florida
Paseo del Rey
Parque
TEMPLO DE DEBOD
Montaña
PL. ESPAÑA
MUSEO CERRALBO
Plaza de España
Paseo de la Florida
Calle de Aniceto Marinas
Pº del Marqués de Monistrol
ESTACIÓN DEL NORTE
NORTE
Gta. San Vicente
Cuesta de San Vicente
Viveros
Pl. Marina Española
Campo
Paseo del Embarcadero
Pte. del Rey
Pº Bajo Virgen del Puerto
Pº Virgen del Puerto
MUSEO DE CARRUAJES
del
PALACIO REAL
Calle de Bailén
Plaza de Oriente
ARMERÍA REAL
NUESTRA SEÑORA DE LA ALMUDENA
Moro
PALACIO DE UCEDA
Glorieta Puente de Segovia
Pte. de Segovia
Calle de Segovia
PUERTA DEL ÁNGEL
C. de Caramuel
CENTRO HIDROLÓGICO
Paseo Virgen del Puerto
Calle Juan Duque
Paseo de los Melancólicos
Ronda de Segovia
Morería
S.ANDRÉS
C. S. Francisco
S.FRANCISCO EL GRANDE
C. de Pablo Casals
C. de Sepúlveda
Paseo de la Ermita del Santo
Avenida del Manzanares
Paseo Virgen del Puerto
Paseo Imperial
Gran Vía de S. Francisco
Ronda de Segovia
IMPERIAL
Paseo de Pontones
Calle de Toledo
Vía Carpetana
Pte. Elevado de S. Isidro
Pl. Francisco Morano
C. Alejandro Dumas
Paseo de los Melancólicos
ESTADIO VICENTE CALDERÓN
Gta. de Pirámides
CEMENTERIO DE S. ISIDRO
Pº Q. de Mayo
Puente de Toledo

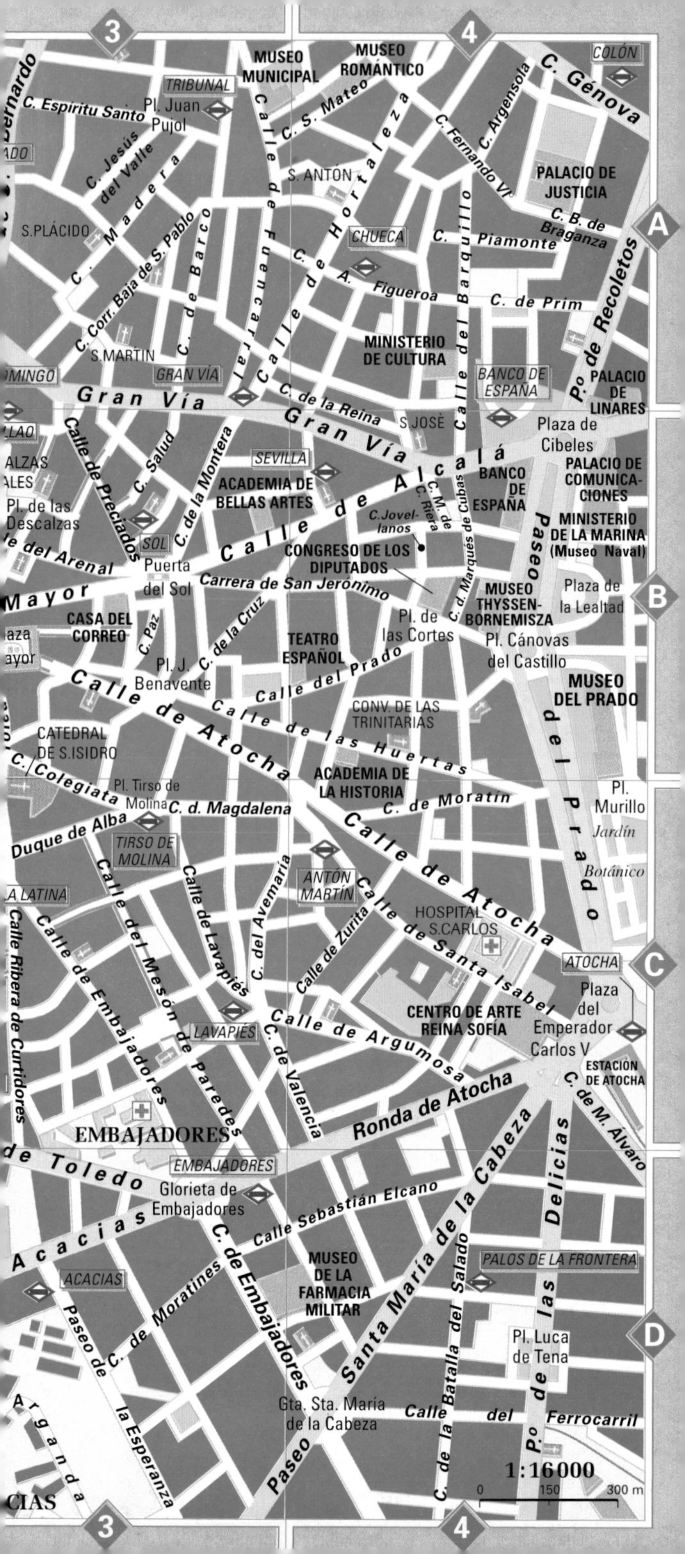
3
4
COLÓN
MUSEO MUNICIPAL
MUSEO ROMÁNTICO
TRIBUNAL
C. Génova
C. Espiritu Santo
Pl. Juan Pujol
C. S. Mateo
C. Argensola
C. Fernando VI
C. Jesús del Valle
S. ANTÓN
PALACIO DE JUSTICIA
C. Madera
Calle de Fuencarral
Calle de Hortaleza
Calle del Barquillo
S.PLÁCIDO
CHUECA
C. Piamonte
C. B. de Braganza
A
C. Corr. Baja de S. Pablo
C. de Barco
C. A. Figueroa
C. de Prim
Pº de Recoletos
S.MARTÍN
MINISTERIO DE CULTURA
GRAN VÍA
BANCO DE ESPAÑA
PALACIO DE LINARES
Gran Vía
C. de la Reina
S.JOSÉ
Plaza de Cibeles
Calle de Preciados
C. Salud
C. de la Montera
SEVILLA
Calle de Alcalá
BANCO DE ESPAÑA
PALACIO DE COMUNICACIONES
ACADEMIA DE BELLAS ARTES
C. M. de C. Riera
Pl. de las Descalzas
C.Jovellanos
C. d. Marqués de Cubas
MINISTERIO DE LA MARINA (Museo Naval)
SOL
CONGRESO DE LOS DIPUTADOS
Paseo del Prado
C. del Arenal
Puerta del Sol
Carrera de San Jerónimo
MUSEO THYSSEN-BORNEMISZA
Plaza de la Lealtad
B
Mayor
CASA DEL CORREO
C. Paz
C. de la Cruz
TEATRO ESPAÑOL
Pl. de las Cortes
Pl. Cánovas del Castillo
Pl. J. Benavente
Calle del Prado
MUSEO DEL PRADO
Calle de Atocha
Calle de las Huertas
CONV. DE LAS TRINITARIAS
CATEDRAL DE S.ISIDRO
C./Colegiata
Pl. Tirso de Molina
ACADEMIA DE LA HISTORIA
C. d. Magdalena
C. de Moratín
Pl. Murillo
Jardín Botánico
Duque de Alba
TIRSO DE MOLINA
ANTÓN MARTÍN
LA LATINA
Calle de Lavapiés
C. del Avemaría
Calle de Zurita
Calle de Santa Isabel
HOSPITAL S.CARLOS
ATOCHA
C
Calle Ribera de Curtidores
Calle de Embajadores
Calle del Mesón de Paredes
LAVAPIÉS
Calle de Argumosa
CENTRO DE ARTE REINA SOFÍA
Plaza del Emperador Carlos V
ESTACIÓN DE ATOCHA
C. de Valencia
Ronda de Atocha
C. de M. Álvaro
EMBAJADORES
de Toledo
EMBAJADORES
Glorieta de Embajadores
Calle Sebastián Elcano
Paseo Santa María de la Cabeza
Pº de las Delicias
Acacias
C. de Embajadores
MUSEO DE LA FARMACIA MILITAR
PALOS DE LA FRONTERA
ACACIAS
C. de Moratines
C. de la Batalla del Salado
D
Pl. Luca de Tena
Paseo de la Esperanza
Gta. Sta. María de la Cabeza
Calle del Ferrocarril
Arganda
1:16000
0
150
300 m
CIAS
3
4

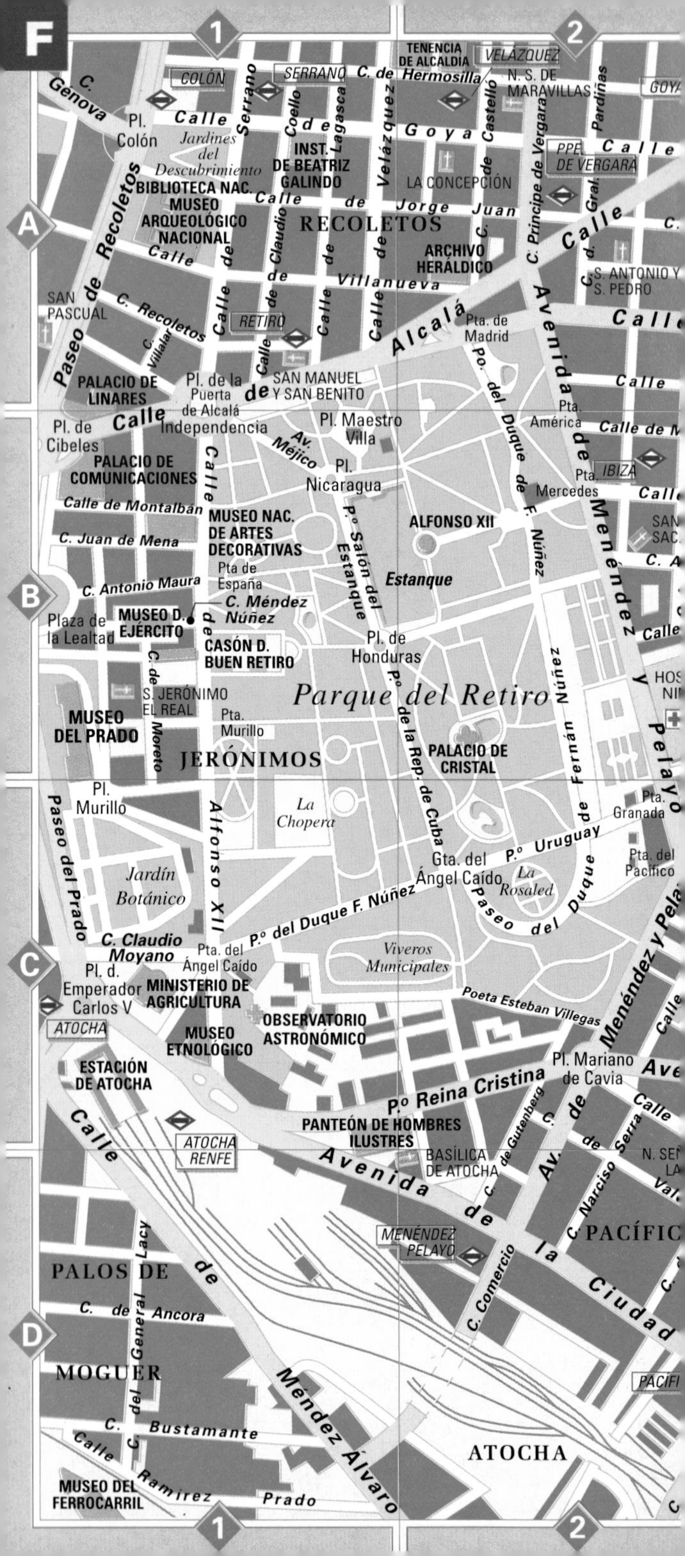

F
Paseo de Recoletos
Pl. Colón
Jardines del Descubrimiento
BIBLIOTECA NAC.
MUSEO ARQUEOLÓGICO NACIONAL
RECOLETOS
ARCHIVO HERÁLDICO
INST. DE BEATRIZ GALINDO
LA CONCEPCIÓN
TENENCIA DE ALCALDÍA
N. S. DE MARAVILLAS
S. ANTONIO Y S. PEDRO
SAN PASCUAL
PALACIO DE LINARES
Pl. de la Puerta de Alcalá
SAN MANUEL Y SAN BENITO
Calle de Alcalá
Pl. de Cibeles
PALACIO DE COMUNICACIONES
MUSEO NAC. DE ARTES DECORATIVAS
MUSEO D. EJÉRCITO
CASÓN D. BUEN RETIRO
MUSEO DEL PRADO
S. JERÓNIMO EL REAL
JERÓNIMOS
Parque del Retiro
ALFONSO XII
Estanque
PALACIO DE CRISTAL
La Chopera
Jardín Botánico
La Rosaled
Viveros Municipales
MINISTERIO DE AGRICULTURA
MUSEO ETNOLÓGICO
OBSERVATORIO ASTRONÓMICO
ESTACIÓN DE ATOCHA
PANTEÓN DE HOMBRES ILUSTRES
BASÍLICA DE ATOCHA
PALOS DE MOGUER
PACÍFIC
ATOCHA
MUSEO DEL FERROCARRIL
COLÓN
SERRANO
VELÁZQUEZ
GOYA
PPE. DE VERGARA
RETIRO
IBIZA
ATOCHA RENFE
MENÉNDEZ PELAYO
Avenida de Menéndez y Pelayo
Avenida de la Ciudad
Calle de Méndez Álvaro
Paseo del Prado

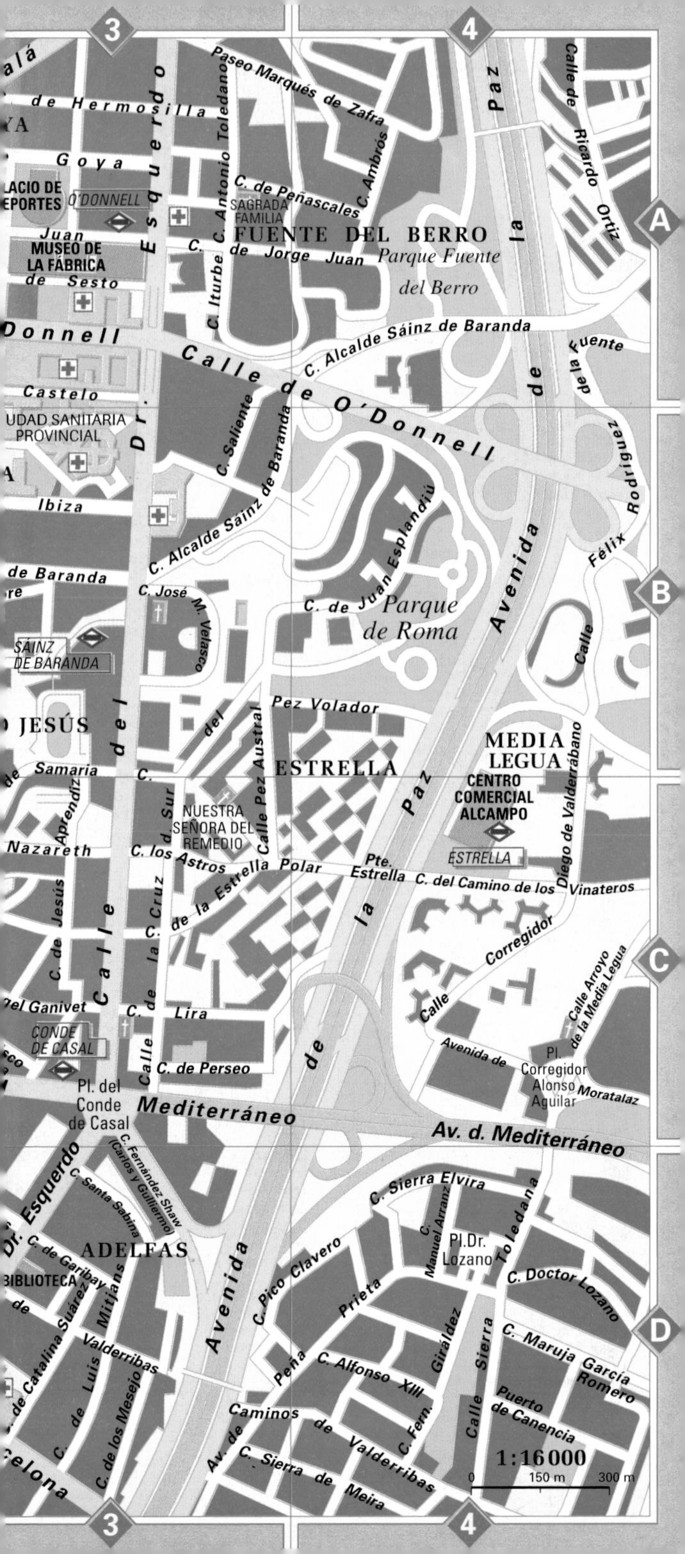

3
4
de Hermosilla
Goya
LACIO DE
EPORTES
O'DONNELL
Juan
MUSEO DE
LA FÁBRICA
de Sesto
Donnell
Castelo
UDAD SANITARIA
PROVINCIAL
Ibiza
de Baranda
SÁINZ
DE BARANDA
JESÚS
Samaria
Nazareth
C. de Jesús
Aprendiz
el Ganivet
CONDE
DE CASAL
Pl. del
Conde
de Casal
Paseo Marqués de Zafra
C. Antonio Toledano
C. de Peñascales
C. Ambrós
SAGRADA
FAMILIA
FUENTE DEL BERRO
Parque Fuente
del Berro
C. de Jorge Juan
C. Iturbe
Dr. Esquerdo
Calle de O'Donnell
C. Alcalde Sáinz de Baranda
C. Saliente
C. Alcalde Sainz de Baranda
C. de Juan Esplandiú
Parque
de Roma
C. José M. Velasco
Pez Volador
ESTRELLA
Calle Pez Austral
C. del Sur
NUESTRA
SEÑORA DEL
REMEDIO
C. los Astros
C. de la Estrella Polar
Pte.
Estrella
C. de la Cruz del Sur
C. Lira
Calle de la
C. de Perseo
Mediterráneo
Calle del Dr. Esquerdo
Calle de Ricardo Ortiz
Avenida de la Paz
C. de la Fuente
Calle Félix Rodríguez de la Fuente
MEDIA
LEGUA
CENTRO
COMERCIAL
ALCAMPO
ESTRELLA
Diego de Valderrábano
C. del Camino de los Vinateros
Calle Corregidor
Calle Arroyo
de la Media Legua
Avenida de Moratalaz
Pl.
Corregidor
Alonso
Aguilar
Av. d. Mediterráneo
Dr. Esquerdo
C. Santa Sabina
C. Fernández Shaw
(Carlos y Guillermo)
ADELFAS
C. de Garibay
BIBLIOTECA
C. de Catalina Suárez
C. de Luis Mitjans
Valderribas
C. de los Mesejo
celona
C. Sierra Elvira
C. Manuel Arranz
Pl. Dr.
Lozano
Toledana
C. Doctor Lozano
C. Pico Clavero
Peña Prieta
C. Alfonso XIII
C. Fern. Giráldez
Calle Sierra
C. Maruja García Romero
Puerto
de Canencia
Caminos de Valderribas
Av. de
C. Sierra de Meira
1:16000
0
150 m
300 m
A
B
C
D

General index

See pages 6–15 for practical information about getting there, getting around, and getting by.

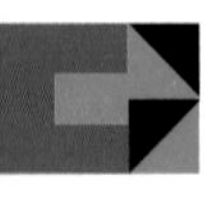

Index

M

N

O

P

R

S

T

U

V

W

Z

We would like to thank the *Spanish Tourist Office* (OET), *Javier Calbet* of Acento Editorial, and all the organizations listed in the guide for their cooperation.

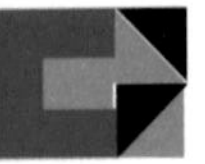

Picture Credits

1 *and cover illustration Donald Grant*
6 *Vincent de Lapomarède*
8 *Kristof Chemineau (Airport map), Vincent de Lapomarède*
9 *Hotel Sofitel*
10 *RENFE (station exteriors, parking lot and trains), OET (station interior)*
12 *Vincent de Lapomarède (subway and bus), Gallimard-Éric Guillemot (subway tickets)*
14 *Gallimard-Éric Guillemot (money and newspapers)*
15 *Gallimard-Éric Guillemot (phonecards)*
16 *Vimagen Fotografos S.L.*
19 *1 Ritz, 2 Palace, 4 Tryp Reina Victoria*
21 *7 Arosa, 8 Gaudí, 9 Imaginaria, 10 Tryp Ambassador*
23 *13 NH Santo Mauro, 14 NH Embajada, 15 Tryp Fenix, 16 NH Sanvy*
25 *17 Villa Magna, 18 Wellington*
27 *22 Guy Saint Clair, 24 Vimagen Fotografos S.L., 25 NH Parque de las Avenidas, 27 NH Príncipe de Vergara*
29 *29 Vincent de Lapomarède, 30 Fernando Gordillo, 32 Style Escultor*
31 *34 Meliá Castilla, 37 Lola Heras, 39 Cuzco (doorman), 39 Vincent de Lapomarède (drawings)*
33 *41 La Residencia de El Viso, 42 Aristos*
34 *Pedro Larumbe-Juan A. Sancho*
37 *1 Casa Lucio, 2 Caroline Cuny, 4 De la Riva*
39 *5 Botín, 7 La Esquina del Real, 10 La Bola, 11 Cornucopia*
41 *12 Viridiana, 14 Errota -Zar, 16 Goya, 17 La Vaca Verónica*
43 *18 San Carlo, 19 Nicolás, 20 La Gamella*
45 *24 Ciao Madrid, 26 Al Mounia, 28 Pelotari*
47 *29 El Amparo, 30 La Paloma, 31 Teatriz, 32 La Trainera, 33 El Fogón*
49 *35 Gargantuel, 36 Castello 9, 37 El Pescador*
51 *39 Pedro Larumbe-Juan A. Sancho, 40 Berceo*
53 *43 El Bodegón, 44 Belagua, 45 Fdo. Sacristan*
55 *47 Las Batuecas, 49 Ana Fernandez*
57 *50 O'Pazo, 51 Goizeko Kabi, 55 Alboran*
59 *57 Casa Benigna, 58 La Atalaya*
61 *59 El Comité, 60 La Tahona, 62 El Cenachero*
63 *64 Casa d'a Troya, 65 La Misión, 66 Nicomedes*
65 *69 Aldaba, 70 (exterior) and 72 Vincent de Lapomarède, 70 Cabo Mayor (interior), 71 Vimagen Fotografos S.L.*
66 *Joy*
69 *3 Vincent de Lapomarède, 4 Cafe de Oriente, 5 El Espejo*
71 *7 Handicap, 8 and badge Caroline Cuny, 9 Cerveceria Alemana, 10 La Daniela, 11 Las Cumbres, platter of tapas, Hotel Villa Magna*
73 *12 Cock, 13 Julio Moya, 16 Castellana 8*
75 *17 Auditorio Nacional de Música, 18 Fondation Juan March*
77 *19 Teatro de Bellas Artes, 21 Caroline Cuny, 22 Teatro Español, 23 Chicho (auditorium), 23 Vincent de Lapomarède (exterior), 23 Alberto Corazón (poster)*
79 *25 Teatro de la Zarzuela, 27 and 28 Vincent de Lapomarède*
81 *29 Gallimard-Éric Guillemot (plate), 29 Corral de la Morería (dancers), 30 Vincent de Lapomarède, castanets Hotel Villa Magna*
83 *34 Gallimard-Éric Guillemot, 35 Florida Park, 36 Vincent de Lapomarède, 37 Scala Melía*
85 *39 Joy, 41 Dusko Despotovic, 43 Palacio de Gaviria*
86 *OET*
89 *OET*
91 *1 (door) and 3 Caroline Cuny, 1 (façade, dining room) and 2 OET*
93 *OET*
95 *9 (Baroque door) and 12 Caroline Cuny, 9 OET (Metropolis building)*
97 *13 Museo del Prado, 14 Museo Thyssen-Bornemisza, 19 Museo del Ejército*
99 *20 (building), 21 (lake) and 22 OET, 20 Centro Cultural Reina Sofia (interior), 21 (Palacio de Cristal) and 23 Caroline Cuny*
101 *26 Javier Calbet (façade), 26 OET (bullring), 26 J. M. Navia (torero and picador)*
103 *28 Museo de América, 30 OET, 32 Caroline Cuny*
105 *33 OET, 34 Archivo Fotográfico Museo Arqueológico Nacional, 35 Museo Municipal, 37 Vincent de Lapomarède*
107 *plaques, 40 and 41 (panoramic view) Caroline Cuny, 41 Vincent de Lapomarède (sculpture)*
109 *42 and 43 OET, 44 Caroline Cuny, 45 Palacio de Congresos*
110 *OET*
112 *OET*
115 *OET*
117 *OET*
121 *OET*
123 *OET*
124 *Gallimard-Javier Calbet*
127 *2 Monsy, 4 Seseña, 6 Javier Sanz*
129 *7 Casa Jiménez, 8 and 10 Gallimard-Éric Guillemot, 9 and 11 Vincent de Lapomarède, 13 J. Jorge*
131 *14 El Corte Inglés, 16 Pedro Larumbe (façade), 16 (flags), 16 (street) and 17 Caroline Cuny*
133 *19 Casa del Libro, 21 Grassy*
135 *24 Antigua Casa Talavera, 25 Hernández, 28 Gallimard-Javier Calbet*
137 *31 Piamonte, 32 Joaquín Berao, 33 Patrimonio Comunal Olivarero, 36 Almirante 23*
139 *38 Farrutx, 40 Lœwe, 42 Roberto Verino*
141 *46 ABB Fotografos, 47 El Caballo, 48 Santa*
143 *52 Coronel Tapioca, 53 Moda Shopping, 54 Estudio San Simon*
145 *56 (bags), 56 (birds), 57 and 58 Caroline Cuny, 56 Vincent de Lapomarède (umbrella and bric-à-brac)*
146 *Alfonso Vargas García*